# Ultimate Node.js for Cross-Platform App Development

## Learn to Build Robust, Scalable, and Performant Server-Side JavaScript Applications with Node.js

**Ramesh Kumar**

www.orangeava.com

**First published:** February 2024
**Published by:** Orange Education Pvt Ltd, AVA™
**Address:** 9, Daryaganj, Delhi, 110002

**ISBN:** 978-81-96815-15-8
www.orangeava.com

# Dedicated To

My beloved parents:

Late Shri Jai Prakash Narayan
Late Shanti Devi

and

My wife Arti, my son Aayansh, and my daughter Anaisha

# About the Author

**Ramesh Kumar** is currently working as an Engineering Manager at Moback Technologies India Pvt Ltd. He possesses over 13+ years of experience in Full-Stack Development based on ASP.NET, .NET Core, and popular JavaScript frameworks like Angular/NodeJS. His responsibilities include managing a team of 15 engineers, and assisting the team prioritize items and deliver products to stakeholders.

In addition, Ramesh contributes to development activities, such as developing features, code reviews, and resolving technical blockers. worked on building web applications using Microsoft Technologies like C#, Asp.net Core, GIT, and SQL Server. He has experience in front-end technologies like jQuery, Angular, and React.

In a recent project, Ramesh worked on NodeJS backend development. He has hands-on experience in DevOps tools such as TFS, Git, Azure DevOps, and Webpack.

His work can be found on GitHub under the username "rameshksh." He is highly self-motivated and eager to try newer technologies and use them to build next-generation software.

Ramesh has extensive experience working on Agile-based projects and delivering them on time with the highest quality product and has also worked on different cloud platforms like Azure and GCP.

# About the Technical Reviewers

**Bhargav Bachina** is a distinguished figure in the IT industry, boasting a remarkable 12-year journey marked by innovation and leadership in software architecture. His career is a testament to his profound expertise across technological stacks, from front-end and back-end development to the complexities of cloud computing. Bhargav's proficiency in Java, JavaScript, Python, and Node.js has made him a versatile and adept navigator in the world of software development.

As a visionary software architect, Bhargav is renowned for his skill in architecting and implementing comprehensive end-to-end solutions. His commitment to excellence and a deep-seated passion for technology have been instrumental in developing cutting-edge web and mobile platforms. His approach, consistently driven by a quest for excellence, has not only led to the success of numerous projects but also established him as a thought leader in the field.

In his current role as the CTO of a startup in the educational domain, Bhargav is on the brink of launching an innovative project, adding yet another milestone to his illustrious career. Furthermore, his contributions as a fractional CTO have made him a sought-after guide and mentor in the startup community. His insights and guidance are highly valued by emerging startups that connect with him on LinkedIn for his expertise.

Beyond his technical and leadership roles, Bhargav is a prolific writer. His journey as a writer began five years ago on Medium, where he has penned over 700 articles. These writings have reached an audience of over 8 million globally, resonating deeply within the tech community. His articles have been pivotal in guiding and enlightening many, earning him a significant following of 22k on Medium. His influence extends to LinkedIn, where his contributions are frequently lauded for their impact.

Bhargav's commitment to sharing knowledge is further evidenced by his active presence on GitHub. With around 431 repositories, he has become a resource for many in the tech community, evidenced by the regular stars and forks his repositories receive. Bhargav Bachina's journey is more than a career narrative; it's a source of inspiration and a roadmap for aspiring IT professionals worldwide.

To learn more about Bhargav, please visit the following sites:

- **Medium**: https://medium.com/@bhargavbachina
- **GitHub**: https://github.com/bbachi
- **YouTube**: https://www.youtube.com/@bachinalabs

**Vikas Kad** is a highly skilled professional boasting a decade of hands-on experience in the dynamic realm of technology. Specializing as a full-stack JavaScript developer, he has cultivated expertise in crafting comprehensive solutions across various domains. His proficiency extends to working on both mono and microservices, showcasing a versatile approach to software development.

Within the intricate landscape of technology, Vikas has made notable contributions in domains such as CAD, E-commerce, AIOPS, and blockchain. His technical acumen is not confined to a specific niche, allowing him to adapt and excel in diverse environments.

Over the course of his 10-year journey, Vikas has demonstrated a passion for creating robust and scalable applications. Whether delving into the intricacies of CAD systems, navigating the complexities of E-commerce platforms, leveraging AIOPS for intelligent operations, or exploring the revolutionary world of blockchain, Vikas has consistently delivered innovative solutions.

This wealth of experience has positioned him as a valuable asset in the tech industry, embodying a commitment to staying at the forefront of advancements. Vikas Kad's journey reflects a dedication to excellence in full-stack JavaScript development and a profound understanding of various domains, making him a sought-after professional in the ever-evolving tech landscape.

# Acknowledgements

THANK YOU!

First of all, praise and thanks to almighty God for his blessings during my journey towards writing this book and successful completion of work. I would like to express my deep and sincere gratitude to Orange AVA for offering me to write a book based on the Node.js technology stack. It was a great privilege and honor to work with such a great publication and their incredible support for writing this book.

I sincerely thank my wife and entire family for their cooperation and patience during the overall journey. Without them, I couldn't have focused entirely on presenting my idea.

I am extremely grateful to my parents for their love, prayers, care, and sacrifices in educating me to such an extent that today I have become an author.

Special thanks to Sonali and Priyanka for providing their constant feedback and encouragement on completing my work. I express special thanks to Bhargav Bachina for the technical review of my work.

Finally, I would like to thank all the people who directly or indirectly supported me during this challenging time and helped to overcome all the obstacles and finish my work.

# Preface

This book covers many aspects of web development using Node.js. This book also introduces the important concepts of Node.js which can be used to build real-time web applications.

This book takes a practical approach for web developers who want to learn Node.js from scratch and develop a good understanding of how to develop real-time web applications using Node.js.

This book is divided into 15 chapters. We will cover most of the Node.js basic concepts and some advanced concepts that are used for developing backend applications.

In **Chapter 1**, we will learn a few terms and concepts that are crucial to understanding Node.js. Some of the key concepts will include non-blocking events, event loops, asynchronous execution, JavaScript runtime environment, REPL, NPM, and so on. This introduction chapter will help in getting started with Nodejs and involve activities like installation, running cli commands, running the first Nodejs program.

In **Chapter 2**, we will dive deeper and learn about the core built-in modules and underlying features that are responsible for making Node.js a great technology. We will cover some of the core concepts, including Event Loop, Asynchronous programming, Event, and callbacks.

In **Chapter 3**, we will learn about Express and cover topics like Introduction to Express core concepts, along with installation on local systems. We will also learn how to create our first backend server using express.js which supports routes and middlewares.

In **Chapter 4**, we're going to take a closer look at the fundamentals of RESTful services and focus on creating some of the backend RESTful APIs and handling different routes. We will learn about request validations and response transformation, which is an important part of building APIs using Node.js.

In **Chapter 5**, we will learn about the NoSQL database that we can use for a variety of requirements in our application. This chapter will focus on exploring more MongoDB and cover basic things about how to install and use MongoDB as a backend database and perform some basic CRUD operations using Mongo-cli.

In **Chapter 6**, we will try to hook Node.js with our backend database, i.e., MongoDB, and perform some of the CRUD operations to save and retrieve data from the database using REST APIs. This chapter deals mostly with storing in databases and performing data manipulation using Mongoose.

In **Chapter 7**, we will learn about template engines that we used to build and hook frontend web pages and how to add dynamic content using special syntax. We will explore EJS template engines and create some dynamic content for testing purposes.

In **Chapter 8**, we will learn about middleware and different types of commonly used middleware inside any real Node.js application. We will also learn how to create custom middleware and use it in our application.

In **Chapter 9**, we will learn how to secure our application using some popular authentication techniques, such as form validation, tokens, and cookies. We will also review topics like role-based Authorizations based on permissions.

In **Chapter 10**, we will be introducing socket.io for building real-time applications like chatbots. We will cover the theory of socket programming and use socket.io for creating simple chat applications to test communication between client and server.

In **Chapter 11**, we will learn how to handle errors and persisting logs which can be used for further debugging. This chapter will cover some of the techniques for error handling and logging them.

In **Chapter 12**, we will focus on understanding how to write test cases and perform unit tests using Mocha and chai tools.

In **Chapter 13**, we will learn how to debug any Node. js-related issues in local and production. Here we will explore some of the widely used tools like REPL, Node Inspector, and so on.

In **Chapter 14**, we will discuss topics on performing build and deploying your node application to a server. We will cover how to create and publish our package to the NPM repository so that the module can be used by another team or developer.

In **Chapter 15**, we will give a walk-through about some of the advanced topics that are not in the scope of this book, such as building highly distributed systems, leveraging messaging systems like Kafka, Multi-Threaded Systems, and so on. tandards Recommendations (PSR) to serve data for your Nuxt app.

# Downloading the code bundles and colored images

Please follow the links or scan the QR codes to download the
**Code Bundles and Images** of the book:

https://github.com/ava-orange-education/Ultimate-Node.js-for-Cross-Platform-App-Development

The code bundles and Images of the book are also hosted on
*https://rebrand.ly/ef14f9*

In case there's an update to the code, it will be updated on the existing
GitHub repository.

# Errata

We take immense pride in our work at **Orange Education Pvt Ltd,** and follow best practices to ensure the accuracy of our content to provide an indulging reading experience to our subscribers. Our readers are our mirrors, and we use their inputs to reflect and improve upon human errors, if any, that may have occurred during the publishing processes involved. To let us maintain the quality and help us reach out to any readers who might be having difficulties due to any unforeseen errors, please write to us at :

**errata@orangeava.com**

Your support, suggestions, and feedback are highly appreciated.

# DID YOU KNOW

Did you know that Orange Education Pvt Ltd offers eBook versions of every book published, with PDF and ePub files available? You can upgrade to the eBook version at **www.orangeava.com** and as a print book customer, you are entitled to a discount on the eBook copy. Get in touch with us at: **info@orangeava.com** for more details.

At **www.orangeava.com**, you can also read a collection of free technical articles, sign up for a range of free newsletters, and receive exclusive discounts and offers on AVA™ Books and eBooks.

# PIRACY

If you come across any illegal copies of our works in any form on the internet, we would be grateful if you would provide us with the location address or website name. Please contact us at **info@orangeava.com** with a link to the material.

# ARE YOU INTERESTED IN AUTHORING WITH US?

If there is a topic that you have expertise in, and you are interested in either writing or contributing to a book, please write to us at **business@orangeava.com**. We are on a journey to help developers and tech professionals to gain insights on the present technological advancements and innovations happening across the globe and build a community that believes Knowledge is best acquired by sharing and learning with others. Please reach out to us to learn what our audience demands and how you can be part of this educational reform. We also welcome ideas from tech experts and help them build learning and development content for their domains.

# REVIEWS

Please leave a review. Once you have read and used this book, why not leave a review on the site that you purchased it from? Potential readers can then see and use your unbiased opinion to make purchase decisions. We at Orange Education would love to know what you think about our products, and our authors can learn from your feedback. Thank you!

For more information about Orange Education, please visit **www.orangeava.com**.

# Table of Contents

# CHAPTER 1

# Getting Started with Node.js

## Introduction

This chapter will help in get started with Node.js, involving activities such as installation, running CLI commands, and creating our first Node.js applications. In this chapter, we will also briefly review some of the topics covered across further chapters of this book.

## Structure

In this chapter, the following topics will be covered:

- History of Node.js
- Defining Node.js
- Some Important Uses of Node.js
- Installing and Setting Up a Local Environment
- Understanding Some of the Core Concepts of Node.js
- Node.js Console REPL
- NPM and **package.json**
- Creating our First Applications

## History of Node.js

Today, JavaScript is one of the world's most popular programming languages. Node.js was created by Ryan Dahl back in 2009 and was initially supported only on Linux and MacOS. Its early development and maintenance were sponsored by Joyent.

In 2010, NPM, a package manager, was introduced, which makes it very easy for developers to publish and share the source code of Node.js. In late 2014, because of internal conflict over Joyent governance, a group of techies who were also contributors to the original node project forked Node into something called IO.js for rapid development and to make the latest features available. In early 2015, the Node.js foundation was announced with key members such as IBM, Intel, Microsoft, PayPal, and many more.

The first official release of Node.js after its merger with IO.js was versioned as 4.x. The new Node.js foundation has taken the entire framework to new heights by releasing new versions with the latest features as well as fixing several issues related to security and performance, which have become a key for the adoption of Node.js into mainstream enterprise web application development.

Unlike other programming languages such as JAVA and .NET, PHP Node is also a platform. This means you have full control over your app logic and the environment within which it must operate. You can effectively write your app code using JavaScript or TypeScript and utilize amazing server stack support.

# Defining Node.js

As per official documentation from the Node.js website:

*Node.js is an open-source and cross-platform JavaScript runtime environment. It is a popular tool for almost any kind of project!*

Let's break this definition down into three important parts, as follows:

First, Node.js is an **open-source** framework, which means the source code for Node.js is publicly available for sharing, modification, and improvements.

Second, Node.js is **cross-platform**, which means we can run any application developed using Node.js on any platform such as Mac, Windows, and Linux.

Finally, Node.js is a **JavaScript runtime environment**, which means it provides all required infrastructure and support to execute application code using the V8 JavaScript engine outside the browser environment.

Some other definitions are as follows. The following definition is taken from https://www.toptal.com:

Node.js is composed of Google's V8 JavaScript engine, the libUV platform abstraction layer, and a core library that is written in JavaScript. Additionally,

Node.js is based on the open web stack (HTML, CSS, and JS) and operates over the standard port 80.

As per flaviocopes (https://flaviocopes.com/nodejs/):

Node.js is open source and cross-platform, and since its introduction in 2009, it has become hugely popular and now plays a significant role in the web development scene. If GitHub stars are one popularity indication factor, having 100k+ stars means being very popular.

# Features of Node.js

Some of the core features of Node.js are as follows:

- **Asynchronous**

  The core of Node.js lies in the fact that its APIs are mostly based on asynchronous nature where Node.js doesn't wait for processing requests; it keeps on moving to the next one using the Event loop technique. It works on events, and when processing is done, it will get a response back to the caller of the service.

- **Event Driven**

  Node provides a module called `Event` that has an `EventEmitter` class, which gives us the power to implement event-driven programming. An event handler is a user-defined function that is called when an event is triggered. The main loop listens for event triggers and calls the appropriate event handler.

  An `EventEmitter` has several methods, including `emit()`, which is used to trigger the event. `emit()` has two arguments: the first is the name of the event, and the second argument is used to pass the data. The `on()` method is used to listen for and execute published events.

- **No Buffering**

  In Node.js, there is no buffering of data because of its asynchronous nature, and users always receive data more easily as they don't have to keep waiting for the entire operation to complete. This all happens when we use callback functions, which help to keep processing data until everything is done completely.

- **Single-Threaded Architecture**

  Node.js architecture is based on a **single-threaded event loop model** architecture that can handle multiple client requests at the same time.

The main event loop is executed by a single thread, but in the background, most of the time-consuming I/O work is done using separate threads. Due to this, all operations performed by Node.js are asynchronous (non-blocking design) to accommodate event loops. The event loop allows node.js to perform all non-blocking operations seamlessly.

- **Highly Scalable**

  Node.js backend applications are highly scalable and can handle millions of requests using a single thread asynchronously and can use child processes to partition applications horizontally to handle all requests.

- **Fast Execution**

  Node.js can execute code much faster by using the V8 engine, which compiles JavaScript code into machine code and helps to reduce the overall time taken to handle multiple requests in Node.js applications.

- **Cross-Platform**

  The main advantage of Node.js is running applications across multiple platforms like Windows, Mac, Linux, and more. Since it's a very lightweight framework, it helps to build and deploy easily on server-based processor architecture.

# Reasons for Node.js Popularity

While we have explored some of the key features that have made Node.js one of the popular frameworks across enterprises, it's not only driving the development community towards Node.js. Let's discuss some more general benefits of using Node.js to build enterprise applications:

- **Single JavaScript language**

  Node.js is a technology with which you can build end-to-end JavaScript applications. Learn one language, and you can develop both the frontend and backend for your apps.

- **Widely Adoption of Node.js**

  Several major companies, such as LinkedIn, Netflix, and PayPal, have all migrated from other back-end technologies to Node.js.

- **Full-stack Development Demand**

  Full-stack development is one of the most sought-after skill sets by companies right now. If you're a front-end developer, learning Node.js will help you become a full-stack developer easily.

- **Huge Community Support**

  There is a huge community support for Node.js, and you will always get help on any issues or concerns related to development.

Apart from this, the following are some of the key features that also made Node.js so popular:

- Building real-time apps like chat
- Real-time gaming applications
- Apps that require lots of asynchronous I/O operations
- Scalable web applications like e-commerce
- Serverless web apps using Azure function, AWS Lambda, or Google Cloud functions
- Lightweight mobile friendly RESTful APIs
- Power of running entire application on a single thread

There are many frameworks that are open source and can be used to develop applications on top of core Node.js, such as:

- Express.js
- Meteor.js
- Koa.js
- Sails.js
- Next.js
- Hapi.js

Node.js cannot be used in case of the following facts:

- Performance bottlenecks with heavy computation tasks
- **Callback** hell issue
- Immature tooling and dependency management
- Unstable APIs developed by third parties
- Applications using high CPU usage

# Node.js versus Browser JavaScript

The following table displays the difference between JavaScript and Node.js:

| | JavaScript | Node.js |
|---|---|---|
| 1 | JavaScript is a popular programming language mostly used for client-side scripting | Node.js is a JavaScript runtime environment, which is used to run on the server |
| 2 | JavaScript can run only on browser | Node.js runs outside the browser on backend servers like Linux/windows/mac |
| 3 | Mostly used for performing client-side scripting | Node.js helps to write backend server-side applications |
| 4 | JavaScript is used for DOM manipulation in HTML | Node.js is not used for doing DOM manipulations |
| 5 | JavaScript can run on any browser, which has support for running JavaScript engines | JavaScript code can only be run using the V8 engine available inside Node.js |
| 6 | Mostly used for developing frontend libraries | Node.js is primarily used for creating backend servers like RESTFul API |
| 7 | Used for building network-centric apps | Node.js applications are highly distributed and run on multiple servers |

*Table 1.1*: *Difference between Node.js and Browser JavaScript*

# Installing Node.js

There are various ways by which we can install Node.js on our local system. The easiest way to install is by downloading it from the official website of Node.js.

Perform the following steps to download and install Node.js on the **Windows** system:

1.  Go to the official website: https://nodejs.dev/download/

2.  Download for 64-bit Windows setup file `node-v20.10.0-x64.msi`

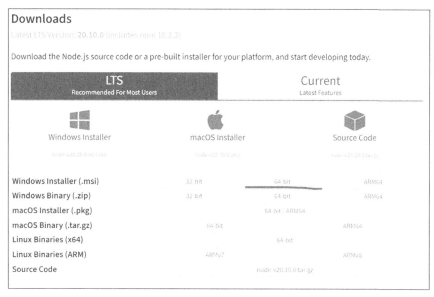

**Figure 1.1**: *Downloading Node.js setup file*

3. Run the setup by double-clicking the downloaded file from the setup files and follow these steps:

   a. Click Install and wait for it to finish setup.

   b. Once the setup is completed, open **cmd** or Terminal and type **node --version** to verify the successfully installed node version.

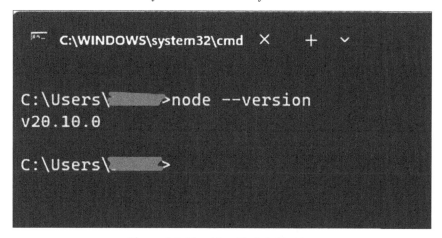

**Figure 1.2**: *Checking Node.js Version*

**Here are the following steps to install Node.js on a Mac system:**

1. Download the macOS installer from the official website:

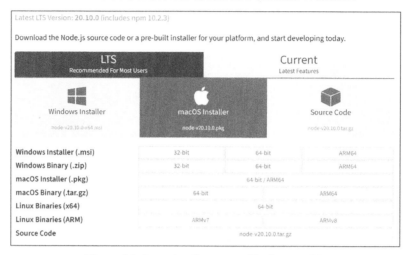

***Figure 1.3***: *Downloading setup file for macOS*

2. Running Node.js Installer:

```
Introduction -> Licence -> Select Destination -> Agree
Installation Type -> Install -> Authenticate with your Mac cred
-> Summary
```

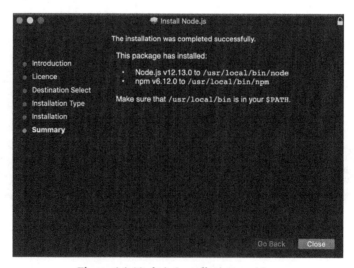

***Figure 1.4***: *Node.js Installation on Mac*

3.  Verify Node.js Installation:

    ```
    $ node -v node -v // The command tells what version of Node.js is
    installed currently.
    ```

4.  Update NPM version:

    ```
    $ sudo npm install npm --global // Update the npm cli client
    ```

**Now let's install Node.js on Linux/Unix.**

We can install any software on a Linux machine by using the APT package repository. Before installing any software, we need to update the System's Package repository.

5.  Update System's Package:

    ```
    $ sudo apt update
    ```

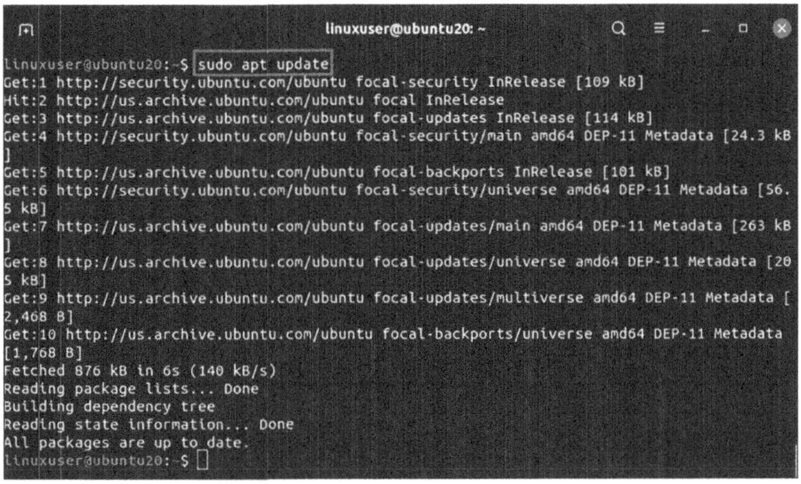

**Figure 1.5**: *Software update on Linux*

6.  Download and install Node.js:

    ```
    $ sudo apt install nodejs -y
    ```

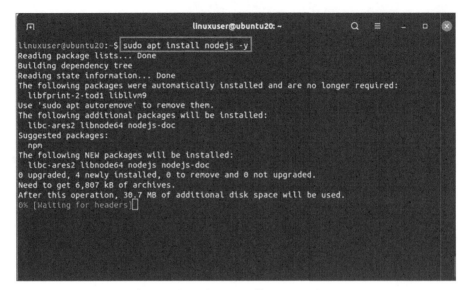

*Figure 1.6*: *Node.js Installation on Linux*

7.  Installing NPM:

```
$ sudo apt install npm -y
```

*Figure 1.7*: *NPM Installation on Linux*

8.  Checking installed versions:

```
$ nodejs -version
```

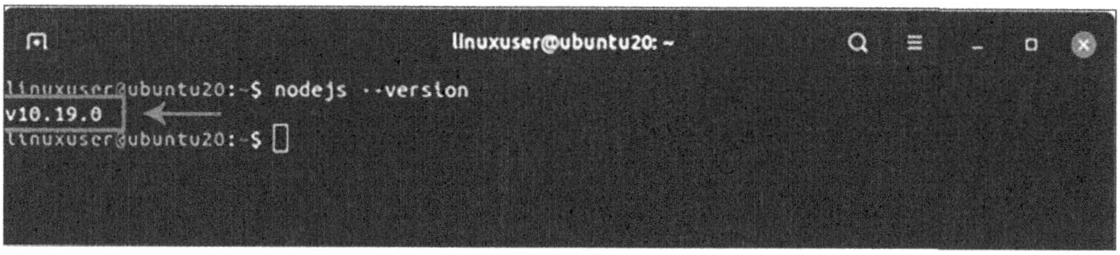

*Figure 1.8*: *Checking Node.js Installation on Linux*

# Installing NVM on Windows

We can install NVM through the following link:

https://learn.microsoft.com/en-us/windows/dev-environment/javascript/nodejs-on-windows

The following steps will be used to install NVM on Windows:

1.  We need to download the latest package from https://github.com/coreybutler/nvm-windows/releases

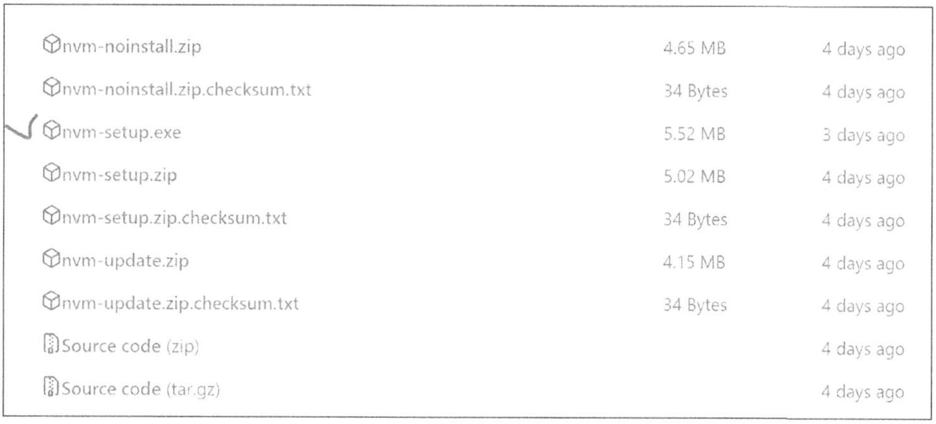

*Figure 1.9*: *Downloading NVM package*

2. Running installation from downloaded exe file:

**Figure 1.10**: *Starting NVM installation process*

3. Setting the installation path, keep the default:

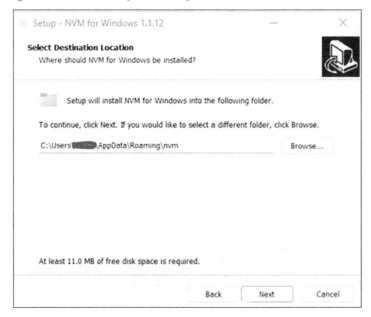

**Figure 1.11**: *Setting up installation path*

4.  Click Install to start the installation process:

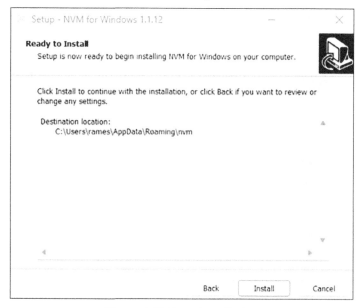

**Figure 1.12**: *Start installation*

5.  Accept the pop-up to `Node xxx is already installed. Do you want to NVM control this version`:

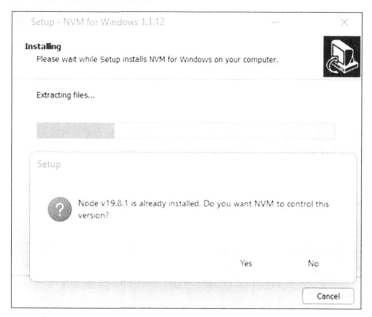

**Figure 1.13**: *Allow NVM to control existing Node.js version*

6. **Finish** setup.

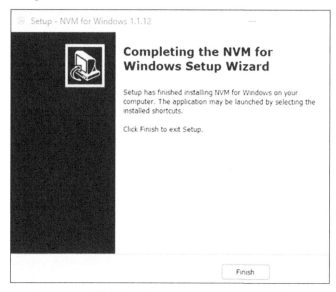

**Figure 1.14**: *Click Finish to complete NVM installation*

# Verifying NVM Installation

Let's perform the following step to verify NVM installation on our local system:

1. Open CMD and type **nvm** command:

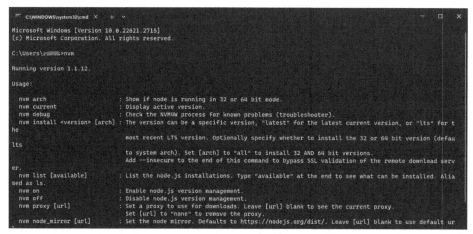

**Figure 1.15**: *Open CMD to verify installation*

2. To check the list of Node.js installation on Windows, type `nvm list`:

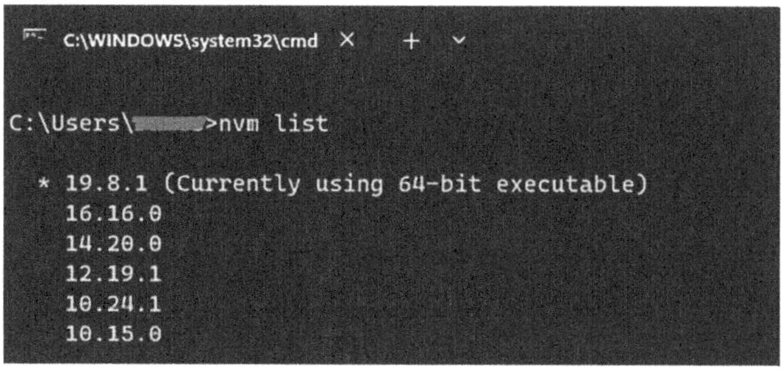

*Figure 1.16*: *Get the list of all Node.js versions*

3. To switch Node.js versions, type `nvm use 14.20.0`:

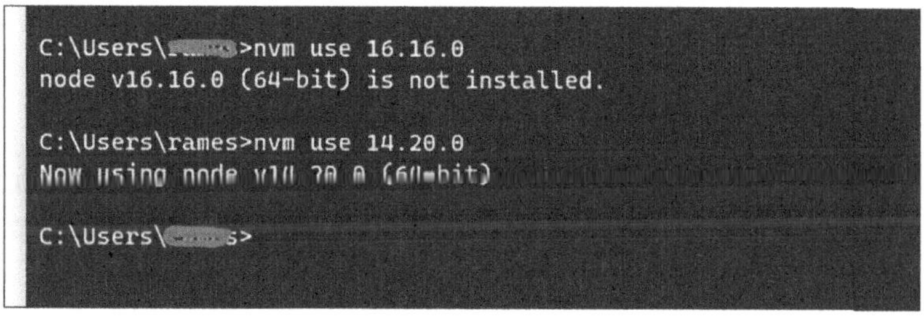

*Figure 1.17*: *Switching to different Node.js versions*

# Some Core Concepts of Node.js

Let us understand some core concepts of Node.js.

## V8 Engine

Node.js implements Google's incredibly powerful JavaScript engine, also known as Chrome V8.

**What exactly do we mean by JavaScript engine?**

A JavaScript engine is responsible for compiling and executing JavaScript code and managing resources and memory allocation written in C++. The V8 engine is already being used in our Chrome browser. V8 can be made to run as a standalone program or be embedded into any C++ program, thus enabling a JavaScript-based scripting interface, all the while delivering incredible performance and flexibility. This also allows you to expand and introduce your own flavor of JavaScript as needed in a specific scenario. Since V8 is a virtual machine, which means that it abstracts the underlying hardware from the actual JavaScript code by simulating a universal environment for the execution environment. You can use V8 and consequently not just on Windows, Mac, and Linux almost seamlessly. This is great since it enables developers to deploy their apps virtually into any kind of execution environment without worrying too much about the underlying hardware.

JavaScript, coupled with the performance benefits of C++ programming, can make a difference. Now as far as Node.js goes, V8 is implemented along with an abstraction layer called *libuv*, which enables Node.js to perform seamless input and output operations across a gamut of operating systems in a non-blocking way. Along with *libuv*, node.js also comes with a built-in core library that provides a host of useful methods that developers can use to write programs, such as web servers and network apps.

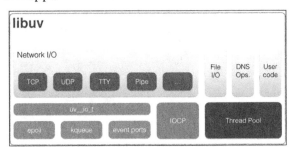

**Figure 1.18**: *V8 engine core layers*

# Blocking versus Non-blocking Operations

Let's try and understand what this really means, and why it makes Node.js different from other server technologies, such as Java, PHP, and more.

**Blocking** operations happen when the execution of JavaScript code inside the Node.js process has to wait until all the code executes synchronously and the control moves to execute the next statement.

For example, when we read a File System using the fs NPM package:

```
const fs = require("fs");
const data = fs.readFileSync("/file.md"); // blocks here until file
is read
console.log(data);
```

In the preceding code, **fs.readFileSync()** will block the execution of any additional JavaScript unless the entire file data is read completely and the output is shown in the console.

**Non-blocking** operations are asynchronous in nature and don't wait for the operation to complete; they continue to execute the next line of statements. Once the operation is successful, the code inside the error first callback function **(err, data)** is executed:

```
const fs = require("fs");
fs.readFile("/file.md", (err, data) => {
    if (err) throw err;
    console.log(data);
});
```

In the preceding example, the file content is read asynchronously. After operation is completed, the callback function **(err, data)** is executed to either throw an error or log data into the console.

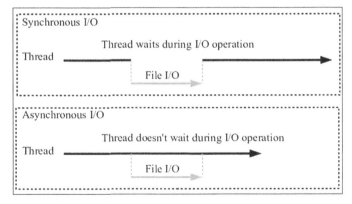

**Figure 1.19**: *Synchronous vs. Asynchronous I/O*

# Event Loop

Node.js is a single-threaded, event-driven framework that can execute asynchronous, non-blocking code. It is efficient regarding memory, thanks to these features. Although JavaScript is single-threaded, Node.js can conduct non-blocking I/O operations because of the event loop. This is accomplished by delegating tasks to the operating system whenever it is practical.

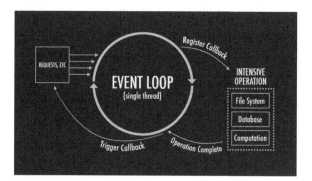

**Figure 1.20**: *Synchronous vs. Asynchronous I/O*

The **Event Loop** has one simple job - to monitor the Call Stack, the Callback Queue, and the Microtask queue. If the Call Stack is empty, the Event Loop will take the first event from the microtask queue and then from the callback queue and will push it to the Call Stack, which effectively runs it. Such an iteration is called a **tick** in the Event Loop.

As JavaScript is single-threaded, which means two statements in JavaScript cannot be executed in parallel. Execution happens line by line, which means each JavaScript statement is synchronous and blocking in nature. However, there is a way to run your code asynchronously or in parallel. If you use the `setTimeout()` function, your code executes after a specified time (in milliseconds).

Let's understand this with the following example:

```
console.log("Start");

setTimeout(function callbackFunc(){
    console.log("Settimeout called after 5 seconds");

    // now sum will be called"
    sum();
},5000);

fetch("http://example.com/").then(function outPutFunc(){
    console.log("Call back from example api");
});

function sum(x, y){
```

```
        return x +y;
    }


    //.....................
    //....................


    console.log("end");
```

**setTimeout** takes a callback function as the first parameter and a time in milliseconds as the second parameter. After the execution of the preceding statement in the browser console, it will print:

```
Start
End
Call back from example api
Settimeout called after 5 seconds
Now sum will be called
```

**Note:** Your asynchronous code runs after all the synchronous code is done executing.

Following are the key steps that happen while running the preceding application:

1. JS engine executes the first line and prints **Start** in the console.
2. The Second line sees the **setTimeout()**, a function named **callbackFunc**, and the JS engine pushes the **callbackFunc** function to the callback queue.
3. Subsequently, the pointer will directly jump to line seven, and there it will see the promise. The JS engine pushes the **outputFunc()** function to the microtask queue.
4. Then, it will execute other lines of code, and finally at the end of the program, it will print **End**.

After the main thread ends execution, the event loop will first check the microtask queue and then call back the queue. In our case, it takes the **callbackFunc()** function from the microtask queue and pushes it into the call stack. Then, it will pick the **outputFunc()** function from the callback queue and pushes it into the call stack.

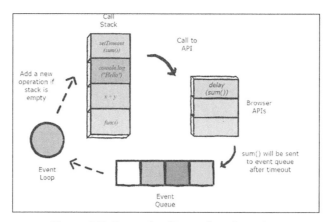

**Figure 1.21**: *Example of Event loop in action*

# Callback functions

JavaScript is synchronous by default, which means code will be executed in a sequential fashion. For example, the following code will be executed line by line and the final output will be logged to the console:

```
const a = 1;
const b = 2;
const c = a * b;
console.log(c);
doSomething();
```

As per the official definition from the Node.js website
https://nodejs.dev/en/learn/javascript-asynchronous-programming-and-callbacks

*A callback is a simple function that's passed as a value to another function and will only be executed when the event happens. We can do this because JavaScript has first-class functions, which can be assigned to variables and passed around to other functions (called **higher-order functions**)*

```
setTimeout(() => {
    // runs after 2 seconds
}, 2000);
```

Above the `setTimeout` function, there is a classic example that accepts the first argument as a callback function, and the second parameter is time in milliseconds after which the callback function will be executed.

Callback functions are a great way of handling asynchronous function calls, but with every callback, it adds a level of nesting and results in **callback hell** when there are lots of callbacks happening within the same code:

```
window.addEventListener('load', () => {
    document.getElementById('button').addEventListener('click',
    () => {
        setTimeout(() => {
            fetch("http://example.com/").then(function cbF() {
                items.forEach(item => {
                    // more code
                });
            });
        }, 2000);
    });
});
```

This example shows so many callback functions are invoked within 10 lines of code; it becomes very messy to handle this kind of situation of callback hell.

# Defining Callback Hell in Node.js

Callback functions are used for the lazy execution of a function until another function has executed and returned data. However, in some cases, we may need to nest multiple callbacks within callbacks. This nested nature of callbacks can stretch horizontally and become unreadable and confusing if you have many interdependent consecutive asynchronous requests. This nesting of callbacks within callbacks is called **callback hell** and is sometimes also referred to **pyramid of doom**.

In the following code, we have called multiple `setTimeout()`, which accept a callback function. In this case, every time a setTimeout callback function is executed, it triggers a new `setTimeout()` function in return:

```
function callbackhellexample() {
    // first setTimeout function
    setTimeout(() => {
        console.log(10)
        // second setTimeout function
        setTimeout(() => {
            console.log(20)
            // third setTimeout function
            setTimeout(() => {
                console.log(30)

            }, 500)
        }, 2000)
    }, 1000)
};
```

Once the innermost **setTimeout** function completes execution, then only the callback function returns execution to the outside upper callback function.

## Ways to Avoid Callback hell

The following are some of the ways to avoid callback hell issues in Node.js:

## Promise

A Promise is a JavaScript object that represents the eventual success or failure of an asynchronous operation and its final output. In other words, a Promise is an object to which you attach callback functions instead of passing directly into a function.

Following is an example of how we can create a promise, and based on the operation status, either resolve is called if successful, or reject in case of failure:

```
var displayGreeting = (name) => alert('Welcome ' + name);
```

```
var processUserInput = () => {
    return new Promise((resolve, reject) => {
        var name = prompt("please enter name");
        if (name) {
            resolve(name)
        }

        reject(false);
    });
}


processUserInput().then(res => displayGreeting(res));
```

A promise is a proxy for a value that isn't necessarily known at the time the promise is created. This enables the handler to be associated with the final success value or failure reason of the asynchronous action. This allows asynchronous methods to return values like synchronous methods. Instead of returning a final value immediately, an asynchronous method returns a promise to return the value later.

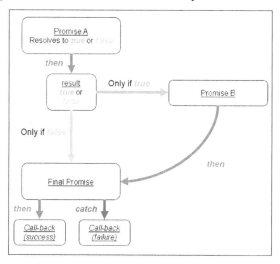

**Figure 1.22**: *Example of Promise execution*

A promise can have one of the following states:

- **Pending**: This is the initial state of promise, which is neither completed nor rejected.

- **Completed**: This means when the operation was completed successfully.
- **Failed**: This means the operation failed.

A promise has the following two key components:

- **resolve**

  The resolve callback function is executed when there is a successful execution of some operation and we want to return the result.

- **reject**

  The reject callback function is called and an error is returned after the operation fails due to some unexpected failure condition.

Let's try to understand with a simple example.

Here we define the function **getMulNum()** to calculate the multiplication of two integers a and b. In the function, we use the promise constructor **new Promise()** to create a new promise.

The multiplication of a and b is calculated. The callback is triggered if the sum is less than or equal to 50. Otherwise, a callback reject is called. The new promise is passed to the **myPromise** variable, which is then returned.

```
function getMulNum(a, b) {
    const myPromise = new Promise((resolve, reject) => {
        const mul = a * b;

        if (mul <= 50) {
            resolve("Successful result")
        } else {
            reject(new Error('Result must be less than 50'))
        }
    })

    return myPromise
}
```

# Async and Await

JavaScript execution happens by default in a synchronous nature. This means that every line of code gets executed from top to bottom without waiting for any results.

However, there are a lot of areas in our program that comprise asynchronous code, and one of the key ways to handle them is by using the *Async/Await* functionality, which we get as support in the language.

**Async**: The async function allows you to write code based on promises as if they were synchronous, making sure they don't interrupt the thread of execution. It works asynchronously on the event loop, and asynchronous functions always return a value. It guarantees that the promise will return, and if it doesn't, JavaScript will automatically wrap it into a promise that resolves by value.

```
const getUserData = async () => {
    var data = {firstname: 'john', lastname: 'Doe' };
    return data;
}


getUserData().then(data => console.log(`${data.lastname}
${data.lastname}`));
```

**Await**: The await function is used to wait for a promise to resolve or reject. This can only be used inside an async block. Using this keyword, you can make your code wait until the promise returns a result. It just makes the async block wait.

The `await` keyword tells the JavaScript engine to stop executing the current function until the promise is resolved and returns the value of the promise. You can think of it as an infinite loop that checks to see if the promise has been resolved and, if so, returns the value of the resolved promise.

The `await` keyword only works inside asynchronous functions (coroutines, as explained earlier). The problem with asynchronous functions is that they return promises instead of values. This means that every time you need to execute an async function, you must wait for it if you want to get the return value.

In *Figure* 1.23, Task 1 caller is invoked and waits for a response to come after the completion of the task. In the meantime, we can observe that the Task 2 caller is also invoked, and similar to Task 1, it also waits for a response.

Once Task 1 is completed, the response is returned, and after this, Task 2 returns the response.

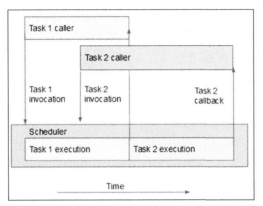

**Figure 1.23**: *Example of Async/Await execution*

Let's take another look at the **mathOpreationAsync** example. However, we use the sleep function instead of **setTimeout()**, so that we can later use await to implement **mathOpreationAsync**. The sleep function returns a promise resolved to ms milliseconds and works using **setTimeout**:

```
function sleep(ms) {
    return new Promise((resolve) => setTimeout(resolve, ms));
}


async function mathOpreationAsync(x, y) {
    // this code waits here for 500 milliseconds
    await sleep(500);
    // done waiting. let's calculate and return the value
    return x+y;
}


// mathOpreationAsync is an async function, which means it returns
a Promise.
mathOpreationAsync(5, 7).then((result) => {
    console.log("The result of the addition is:", result);
})
```

# Choosing the Appropriate Approach

You have the following options for doing asynchronous processing in JavaScript:

- callback
- promise
- async/await

If you have no other choice or just want to handle asynchronous operations, use **callback**. Even then the code is completely manageable and understandable.

When there are multiple chained (or dependent) asynchronous operations and if you try to use callback in this situation, you'll quickly end up in **callback hell**. In order to avoid this, **Promises is preferred,** which is a great tool for keeping operations organized and predictable.

**async/await** is also a great tool if you don't really want or need to use observables, but want to use Promises. You can write "synchronous" code using async/await and manage Promise chains more easily.

# REPL Console

The REPL (READ, EVAL, PRINT, LOOP) is a computer environment similar to shells (Unix/Linux) and command prompts in Windows. Node.js comes with an inbuilt REPL environment when installed. This system is a very useful way of interacting with the user by issuing commands/expressions that are used.

- `Read`: This operation reads input from the user and parses it into JavaScript data structures, storing them in memory.
- `Eval`: The parsed JavaScript data structure is evaluated against the result.
- `Print`: Finally, the result is printed after evaluation.
- `Loop`: This is used to Loop the input command.

Press *Ctrl+C* twice to exit the NODE REPL environment.

# Getting Started with the REPL

To work in NODE's REPL environment, open a terminal (UNIX/LINUX) or command prompt (Windows), type `node`, and press Enter to start the REPL.

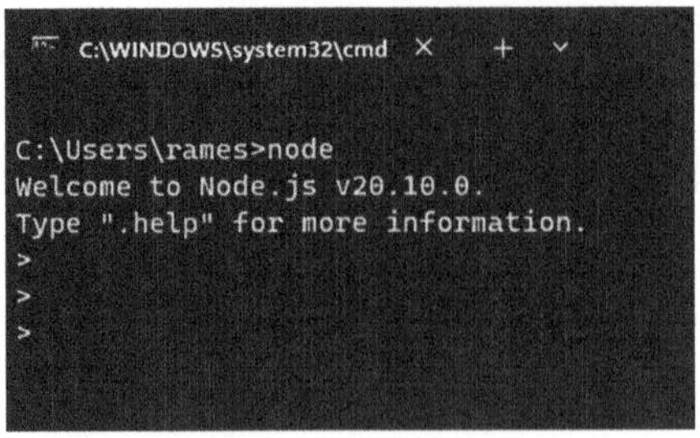

**Figure 1.24**: *Starting REPL terminal*

## Here are some of the examples of using REPL:

- ### Simple Arithmetic operations

Basic maths operations can be performed, such as addition, subtraction, multiplication, and division, as shown in the following figure:

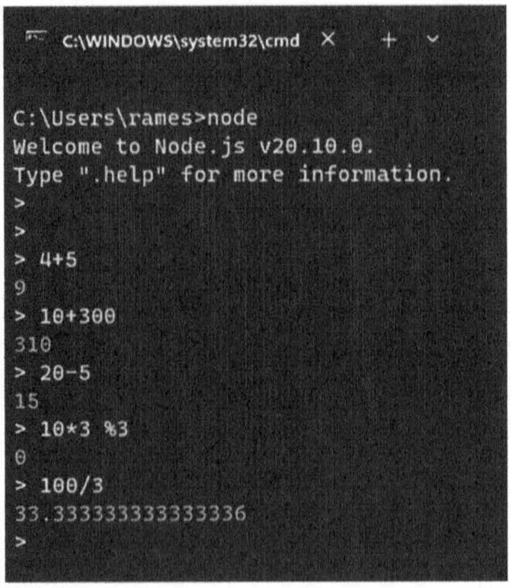

**Figure 1.25**: *Arithmetical operations in REPL*

The REPL can be used to perform operations on strings. Concatenate the following strings in your REPL by typing:

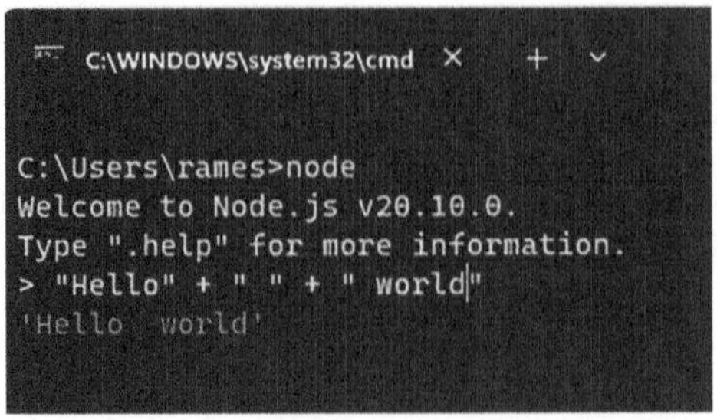

**Figure 1.26**: *String operations in REPL*

- **Calling functions**

We write functions to handle specific tasks that can perform complex operations. REPL provides an easy way to handle these methods. In JavaScript, we commonly use the global **console.log()** method to print messages. Regular JavaScript functions can also be written to solve a problem and work on complex logic.

In the following example, we have written the **addTwoNumbers()** function, which accepts two arguments and produces an output sum of 30.

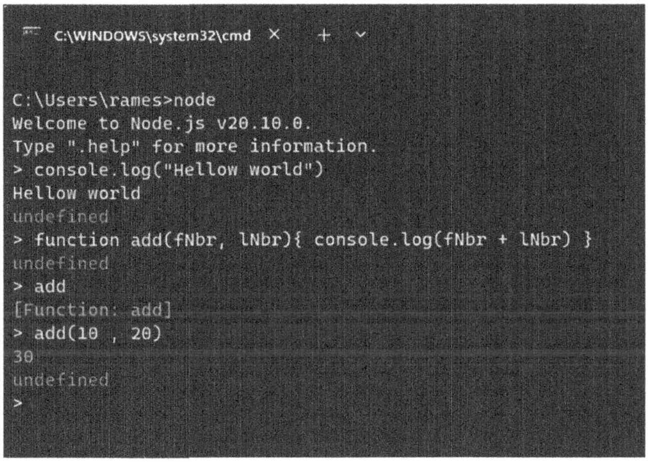

**Figure 1.27**: *Sum operations using a function call in REPL*

- **Using variables**

We can use variables to store values and use them at a later point while performing operations.

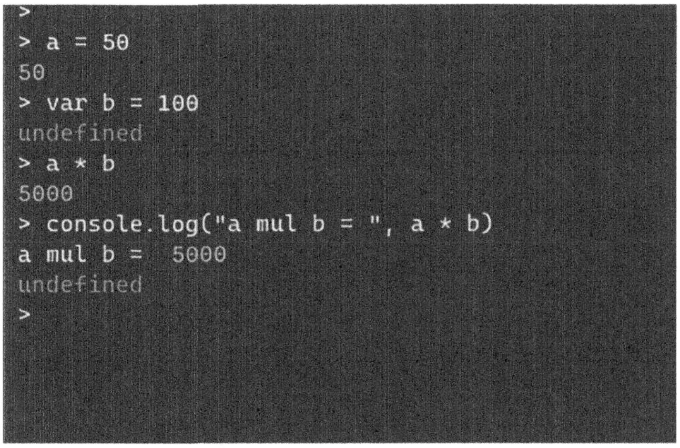

**Figure 1.28**: *Using variables in REPL*

- **Loops and Multiline expressions**

We can use multiline expressions to write loops and other statements that cannot be written in a single line. For example, when we use a do while loop for iteration, then we must write all the statements in different lines as follows:

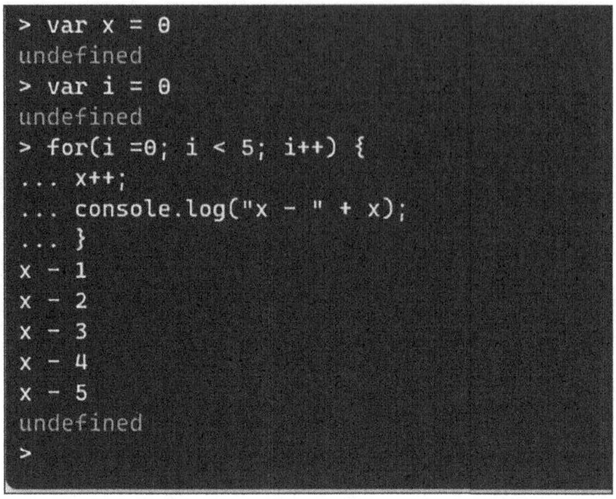

```
> var x = 0
undefined
> var i = 0
undefined
> for(i =0; i < 5; i++) {
... x++;
... console.log("x - " + x);
... }
x - 1
x - 2
x - 3
x - 4
x - 5
undefined
>
```

*Figure 1.29*: Loops and Multiline expression in REPL

- **Using underscore variable**

We can use _ variable to get the last result from Node REPL. Let's create two variables and perform some arithmetic operations.

```
var x = 10;

var y = 20;

var z = 0;

x + y;

z = _ * 100;
```

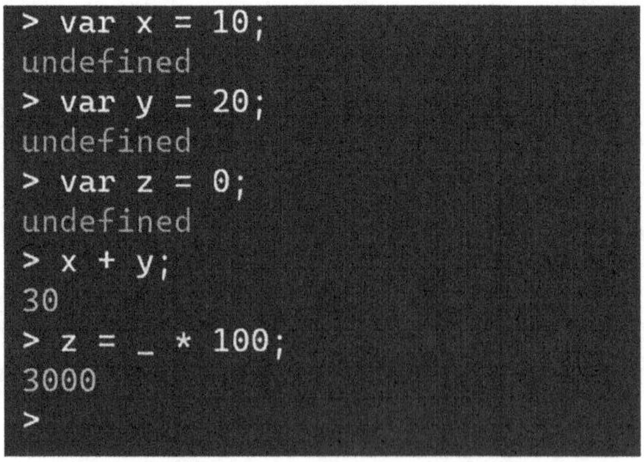

```
> var x = 10;
undefined
> var y = 20;
undefined
> var z = 0;
undefined
> x + y;
30
> z = _ * 100;
3000
>
```

*Figure 1.30*: Using Underscore in REPL

- **Using dot commands**

There are some special commands that start with a dot (.) and are used to perform some of the core functions of the REPL command line tool, as follows:

- `.help`: Shows the dot commands help.
- `.editor`: Enables editor mode, allowing you to write multiline JavaScript code with ease. Once in this mode, press Ctrl-D to run the code you wrote.
- `.break`: When inputting a multi-line expression, entering the .break command will abort further input, similar to pressing ctrl-C.
- `.clear`: Resets the REPL context to an empty object and clears any multi-line expression currently being input.
- `.load`: Loads a JavaScript file relative to the current working directory.
- `.save`: Saves all you entered in the REPL session to a file (specify the filename).
- `.exit`: Exits the REPL (same as pressing Ctrl-C two times).

# Using NPM and Package.json

A package manager is defined as **a system or set of tools used to automate installing, upgrading, configuring, and using the software**. Most package managers are used for discovering and installing developer tools on the local machine or production servers.

Maven is one of the package managers from Java, which is used for automating the process of installation, upgradation, and removal of system dependencies for a given application.

A package manager also deals with bundling of packages and distribution of software.

*NPM is the default package manager for the* **Node.js** *JavaScript runtime* **environment** *maintained by npm, Inc. It consists of a* **command line** *(CLI tool) program, also called as npm, and an online database (***npm registry***) for hosting public(free) and private(paid) packages (https://www.npmjs.com/).*

Some of the important NPM commands are explained here.

# Init

This command is used to initialize an empty node.js project with a pre-configured **package.json** file having either a default option or user-defined values.

```
PS D:\Practice\HelloWorld> npm init
This utility will walk you through creating a package.json file.
It only covers the most common items, and tries to guess sensible defaults.

See `npm help init` for definitive documentation on these fields
and exactly what they do.

Use `npm install <pkg>` afterwards to install a package and
save it as a dependency in the package.json file.

Press ^C at any time to quit.
package name: (helloworld) sample
version: (1.0.0)
description: This is sample node application
entry point: (app.js)
test command: npm run
git repository:
keywords: Node Introduction
author: Ramesh
license: (ISC)
About to write to D:\Practice\HelloWorld\package.json:

{
  "name": "sample",
  "version": "1.0.0",
  "description": "This is sample node application",
  "main": "app.js",
  "scripts": {
    "test": "npm run"
  },
  "keywords": [
    "Node",
    "Introduction"
  ],
  "author": "Ramesh",
  "license": "ISC"
}
```

*Figure 1.31: NPM init command sample output*

# Install

This command is used to install all the dependencies that the project needs inside the **node_modules** folder at the root of the application where **package.json** resides.

## Installing Single Package

We can install a single package if required to include any module dependencies. For this command, we have multiple flags that can be added along with the package name:

- **--save**

  When we use the save flag, a package entry is added to the **package.json** file's dependencies section (which includes packages required for the project to run effectively in production environments). When we install any package without specifying any flag, its entry gets added to the dependencies section.

- **-save-dev**

  This will install and add the current module entry to the **package.json** file's `devDependencies` section (which includes packages only used for project development propose).

- **--no-save**

  This will only install modules but does not add any entry to the **package.json** file dependencies.

- **--save-optional**

  This will install the module along with adding the entry to the `optionalDependencies` section of the package.json file.

- **--no-optional**

  This will prevent optional dependencies from getting installed.

```
PS D:\Practice\HelloWorld> npm i express --save
npm notice created a lockfile as package-lock.json. You should commit this file.
npm WARN sample@1.0.0 No repository field.

+ express@4.18.2
added 57 packages from 42 contributors and audited 57 packages in 5.368s

7 packages are looking for funding
  run `npm fund` for details

found 0 vulnerabilities

PS D:\Practice\HelloWorld> []
```

*Figure 1.32*: NPM *install command sample output*

# Update

This command will check all the packages for any newer version that might be available following the given versioning constraints.

- **Update <package-name>**

  This command will only update a single package.

- **Versioning**

  NPM also helps in managing versions, which means we can specify any higher or lower versions, and its dependencies accordingly get installed with compatible versions.

- **Running tasks**

  This command is very useful in running any specific scripts like build, starting the server, or running unit tests.

  ```
  "scripts": {
      "start-dev": "node dev.server.js",
      "start": "node prod.server.js"
    }
  ```

- **Uninstall**

  This command helps to uninstall modules from a given project or application.

- **Publish**

  This command is used to publish packages from your local dev machine to the npm registry for sharing purposes. Once published this can be downloaded by others and used in their project.

- **Login**

  This command is used to log into the **npm.js** (https://www.npmjs.com/) account of the official website.

# Attributes of Package.json

Following is a detailed list of **attributes** defined inside **package.json**:

- **name**: The name of the package, normally the application or module title. There are some restrictions on the name property:
  - Maximum length of 214 URL-friendly characters
  - No uppercase letters
  - No leading periods (.) or underscores (_) (except for scoped packages)
- **version**: The current version of the package of that module. Node.js modules use a Semantic Versioning approach where three different levels of versioning are used. For example, version 2.0.1 is divided into three levels:
  - `Major-X.0.0`
  - `Minor-0.X.0`
  - `Patch-0.0.X`

where X is the current level of the version.

Semantic Versioning (also known as `SemVer`) is a version control system that has evolved in recent years. This is a constant problem for software developers, distribution managers, and consumers. Having a global approach to version management for your software development projects is the best way to keep track of what's happening with your software, such as new tools, extensions, libraries, and visits almost every day. This problem can be solved using Semantic Versioning. Simply put, this is a way to calculate the computer's output.

So, `SemVer` looks like `Major.Minor.Patch`.

- **license:** This identifier is used to describe the kind of licensing under which this package is covered. A few examples that you may recognize are MIT, ISC, and GPL-3.0.
- **description**: Description of the package containing a full description of the modules, helping develop to let users know more about package usages. This also helps search engines like Google or npm search to find relevant packages.
- **homepage**: Homepage of the package where this module or project has been created and hosted.
- **author**: Author of the package, who has created this application.
- **contributors**: Name of the contributors to the package
- **dependencies**: A list of dependencies. Node.js applications are built using multiple modules, which are grouped as dependencies. NPM automatically installs all the dependencies mentioned here in the **node_ module** folder of the package when we run the npm install command.
- **repository**: A repository is an array that holds the location of source code, mostly this will be a publicly hosted repo like GitHub or Bitbucket for open-source projects.
- **main**: The entry point of the module. When we import any module using the required statement, the main property is returned to the Node.js application.
- **Scripts:** This contains a set of user-defined commands that can be executed by Node.js. Some of the core scripts that are used to test, build, and perform code coverage can be added here. We use the `--npm run` command to execute any of the given scripts, or we can also run using **node filename.js**.

```
"scripts": {
    "start": "npm run app.js"
    "test": "npm run test.js"
  }
```

- **keywords**: keywords are collections of text that describe a module. This can help identify any package and related modules.

  Some of the sample keywords inside **package.json**:

```
"keywords": {
    "Node",
    "Introduction"
  }
```

A sample of **package.json** is shown in the following code:

```
{
  "name": "sample",
  "version": "1.0.0",
  "description": "This is sample node application",
  "main": "app.js",
  "scripts": {
    "test": "npm run test.js"
  },
  "keywords": [
    "Node",
    "Introduction"
  ],
  "author": "Ramesh",
  "license": "ISC"
}
```

# The First Console Application Using Node.js

Let's create a simple Node.js application named "Hello World".

Here are the steps:

1. Create an empty folder called "Helloworld".

```
mkdir HelloWorld
cd HelloWorld
HelloWorld> notepad app.js
```

2. Run the npm init command to initialize Node.js.

3. Now create a file name **app.js** inside the HelloWorld folder.

4. Open VS code editor or any text editor like Notepad.

5. Add the following code to print "Hello World" into the console.

**Figure 1.33**: *Hello world application code*

6. Run this application from a terminal by just typing:

```
node app.js
```

7.  You can see the output as "Hello World" in the terminal.

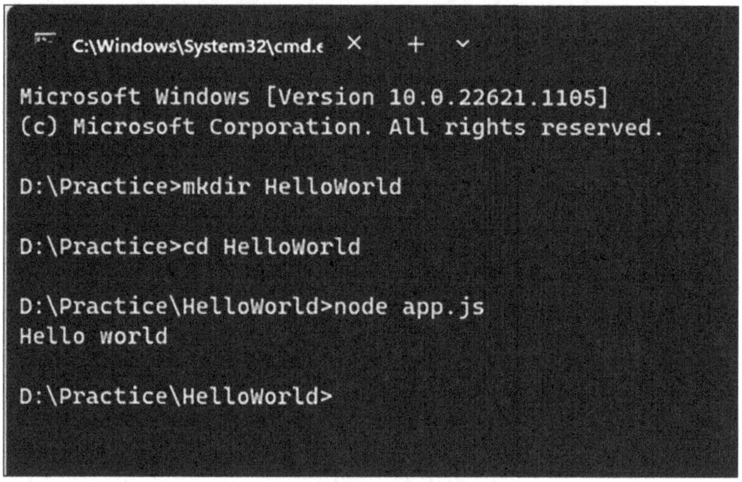

**Figure 1.34**: *Hello world application output*

# The First Web Application Using Node.js

After installing Node.js, we can create our web server and use localhost to run applications using the browser client. Here are the steps:

1.  Create folder **Helloworld**.

2.  Run npm init cmd.

3.  Create a file named app.js inside the **Helloworld** folder.

4.  Add the following code inside the newly created file:

```
var http = require('http');
  http.createServer(function (req, res) {
    res.writeHead(200, { 'Content-Type': 'text/plain' });
    res.end('Hello world!');
  }).listen(3000);
  console.log('Server started on localhost:3000; press Ctrl-C to
terminate....');
```

5.  Now, to install dependencies, run npm install http or npm i http cmd.

6.  Once all the dependencies are installed, you can start your web server using the following `node` command and open http://localhost:3000 in the browser to see the message "`Hello World`".

```
node app.js
```

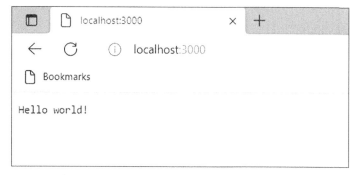

**Figure 1.35:** Hello world web application output

Let's understand that the preceding code is written for a web server:

*   **Importing required models**: We can load any dependencies using the require keywords. For example, in order to create a web server, we need to load the http module, which can be used to create a server:

    ```
    var http = require('http');
    ```

*   **Creating server instance**: We need to create a server instance that can be used to service client's requests. We can use the `createServer()` method, which is exposed from http modules to create our own server instance:

    ```
    http.createServer().listen(3000);
    ```

*   **Request and Response:** The client can make a request using a browser or console, and after performing all the operations, it will return the response back to the browser. For this, we can pass a function with a request and response object inside `creaseServer()`:

    ```
    http.createServer(function (req, res) {}).listen(3000);
    ```

- **Adding Logic:** Inside that create server function, we can add any kind of logic that we want to perform, such as saving data or fetching information from a database or any other source. The following code is used to return "Hello World!" to the browser in the form of plain text:

```
http.createServer(function (req, res) {
            res.writeHead(200, { 'Content-Type': 'text/plain' });
    res.end('Hello World!');
}).listen(3000);
```

# Conclusion

In this chapter, we have learned about the core concepts of Node.js, which are required and serve as the foundation for upcoming chapters. Here, we learned how to install Node.js on our local system and create our first backend server application using the http module of Node.js. We also gained some of the basic understanding of REPL, Event Loop, Asynchronous programming, and more.

The next chapter will reveal most of the concepts of Node.js in more depth, which will boost our confidence in building real-time applications using Node.js.

# Further Readings

The following reference material can be used for further reading and gaining more understanding of Node.js Framework:

- https://www.w3schools.com/nodejs/nodejs_intro.asp
- https://nodejs.org/en/about
- https://en.wikipedia.org/wiki/Node.js
- https://www.youtube.com/watch?v=uVwtVBpw7RQ
- https://nodejs.dev/en/learn/
- https://www.youtube.com/watch?v=yEHCfRWz-EI

## Test Your Node.js Basic Knowledge

1. Which of the following statements is correct about Node.js?

    a. Node.js is Server Side Language

    b.  Node.js is the Client Side Language

    c.  Node.js is both Server Side and Client Side Language

    d.  None of the above

2.  What do you mean by REPL?

    a.  REPL stands for "Read Eval Print Loop"

    b.  REPL stands for "Research Eval Program Learn"

    c.  REPL stands for "Read Earn Point Learn"

    d.  REPL stands for "Read Eval Point Loop"

3.  In which language is Node.js written?

    a.  JavaScript

    b.  C

    c.  C++

    d.  CoffeeScript

4.  What command is used to install the Node.js express module?

    a.  `$ npm install` express

    b.  `node install` express

    c.  `install` express

    d.  None of the above

5.  What do you mean by Callback?

    a.  The callback is a technique in which a method calls back the caller method

    b.  The callback is an asynchronous equivalent for a function

    c.  Both of the above

    d.  None of the above

6.  How can we expose modules in Node.js?

    a.  expose

    b.  module

    c. exports

    d. All of the above

7. Which of the following modules is not a built-in node module?

    a. zlib

    b. https

    c. dgram

    d. fsread

8. Which of the following code prints the platform of the operating system?

    a. `console.log('platform : ' + os.platform);`

    b. `console.log('platform : ' + os.platform());`

    c. `console.log('platform : ' + os.getPlatform());`

    d. None of the above

9. How can we execute the code of the sample.js file?

    a. sample.js

    b. node sample.js

    c. nodejs sample.js

    d. None of the above

10. Which kind of applications can be built using Node.js?

    a. Web Application

    b. Chat Application

    c. RESTful Service

    d. All of the above

# Answers

| | |
|---|---|
| 1 | a |
| 2 | a |
| 3 | a |
| 4 | a |
| 5 | c |
| 6 | c |
| 7 | c |
| 8 | a |
| 9 | b |
| 10 | d |

CHAPTER 2

# Deep Dive into Node.js

## Introduction

This chapter will focus on learning some of the core concepts of Node.js, which will be largely used to build any real-time web applications. We will cover different ways of programming, including Synchronous versus Asynchronous. In this chapter, we are going to learn about different modules of the Node.js framework, such as http, fs, and buffers, and do some hands-on work by creating simple programs.

## Structure

In this chapter, the following topics will be covered:

- Traditional Web Application Architecture
- Architecture of Node.js
- Event Loop
- Non-blocking or Asynchronous I/O
- Core Node Modules

## Traditional Web Application Architecture

Before NodeJS, web applications developed typically followed a **multi-threaded request-response** model. In this model, the server handles all the client requests and, after processing, returns a response to the client. Most of these requests/responses are based on the HTTP/HTTPS protocol. This kind of application is also called three-tier architecture:

- Presentation Layer/Client Layer
- Application Layer/Business Layer
- Data Layer

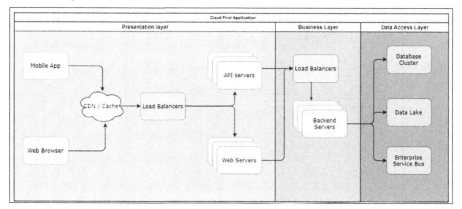

**Figure 2.1**: *Architecture diagram for Traditional*

Following are the processing steps for the request/response model:

- A web server receives a request from a client.
- Thread pools are internally available on the server to service client requests.
- When the web server receives any client request:
  - One thread is assigned from the thread pool to handle requests.
  - This thread performs the following actions:
    - Reading the client's request
    - Processing the client request data
    - Performing any involved IO block operations (if necessary)
    - Preparing the final response
  - The web server in turn sends back responses from the thread to the specific client.

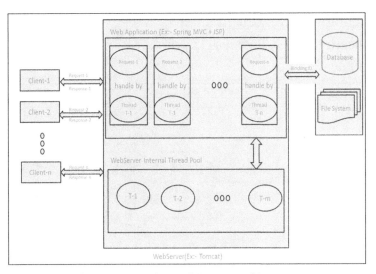

**Figure 2.2**: *Traditional Server Architecture*

Here,

> **n**: number of customers

> **m**: number of thread pool

**Assumptions**:

- All the clients use the system at the same time.
- There is a limited thread pool on the server due to hardware constraints.
- Client-1, Client-2, ..., Client-n are unique customers using this application.

Following are the processing steps for client requests:

- The web server handles Request-1 (Client-1) and assigns this request to thread T-1:
  - Thread T-1 reads Request-1 (Client-1) and processes it
  - Request-2 doesn't need any Blocking – I/O operations
  - Thread T-1 sends back a Response-1 to the server
  - The web server returns this Response-1 to Client-1
- Client-2 makes another Request-2, which is taken by one thread T-2:
  - Thread T-2 processes Request-2
  - This Request-2 does not require any I/O blocking operations
  - Thread T-2 sends back Response-2 to the server
  - The web server alternately sends this Response-2 to Client-2

- The preceding processes continue until Client-n makes a request, and all the available thread inside the thread pool is consumed. This causes blocking operation for subsequent requests.

- Thread T-n requires more time to get free resources, which can be used to process requests and send back responses to the server.

- Client-n must wait longer to get a response from the server once Thread T-n finishes all processing.

- As the thread keeps on processing requests and is freely available for handling the next request, server processes use this thread and keep processing the next client requests.

**Advantages of the Traditional Model:**

- A 3-tier architecture is more secure because the client cannot access the data directly. Even with NodeJS, we will have the same model, replacing NodeJS with Java as our backend server.

- The ability to deploy application servers to multiple machines provides better scalability, better performance, and better reusability.

- You can scale it horizontally and scale each item individually.

- You can offload core performance from the database server and efficiently perform load balancing.

- Data integrity is improved when all data flows through an application server that decides how and who uses the data.

- This modular design allows you to change one layer without affecting other components.

**Disadvantages of the Traditional Model:**

- This system can't handle more simultaneous client requests.

- As time passes, this kind of system becomes less responsive and keeps clients waiting for the response.

- To handle a large number of requests, we might need to increase Server resources, such as memory, networking, and disks.

- The server wastes a lot of time by having an idle CPU due to blocking I/O operations.

# Architecture of Node.js

The core of Node.js works on "Single-Threaded Event Loop" architecture to handle multiple concurrent client requests. Node.js' processing model is based on event-driven and callback mechanisms. This event loop-based mechanism allows Node.js to perform any kind of blocking I/O operations in a non-blocking fashion.

**Key components of the Node.js architecture:**

The following are some of the core components of the Node.js framework:

- **Requirements:** Backend servers can have different kinds of requirements, such as blocking (complex) or non-blocking (simple), depending on the client's actions.

- **Node.js server:** The client makes requests to the server and Node.js processes user requests and returns output to the user.

- **Queue:** Event queue used for storing incoming client requests and passing them in the same order to the event loop.

- **Thread Pool:** The thread pool of any server contains multiple threads that are available at a given point of time to perform the operations that are required to process a request.

- **Event Loop:** The event loop is the core of Node.js architecture, which receives requests from the event queue and sends responses back to the client after processing.

- **External Resources:** External resources like computational, storage, and more are used to handle blocking client requests.

Node.js web servers typically have a workflow very similar to the diagram shown in *Figure 2.3*:

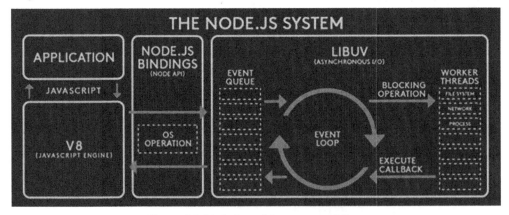

*Figure 2.3: Node.js architecture workflow*

This diagram represents how the Node.js application works behind the scenes. The V8 engine compiles the code you write in your program, and the application code uses binding to communicate with low-level Node.js components. After events are fired from the application code, they are pushed into the event queue in the order in which they were originally fired from the application. The event loop processes all the events, calls their callback functions, and sends them to worker threads for processing until the event queue becomes empty. After the callback function executes, its callback is returned to the event queue, waiting for the event loop to pick it up.

Part of your confusion may stem from the choice of technical terms used in the second diagram. If you look closely, under "NODE.JS BINDINGS", it says "(NODE API)", which unfortunately are two different things. The Node.js API is the user interface for its built-in libraries, while bindings, from a software programming perspective, are bridges between code written in different languages.

A client interacts with a web application by sending requests to a web server, which can be non-blocking or blocking. These requests are as follows:

- Query data
- Deletion of data
- Update data

Node.js takes incoming requests and adds them to an event queue.

Requests are then routed through the event loop, one at a time. Make sure your requirements are simple enough to not require external resources.

The event loop handles simple requests (non-blocking operations), such as I/O polling, and returns responses to the appropriate clients.

One thread in the thread pool is assigned to one complex request. This thread is responsible for accessing external resources, completing specific lock requests, and managing computing power, databases, file systems, and more.

When the task is completed, the response is sent to the event loop and then returned to the client.

The following are the core components that make the Node.js framework incredible:

- **V8:** Google's open-source JavaScript engine written in C++, which is used in Chrome/Chromium browsers. When we talk about browsers, JavaScript code is interpreted on the fly, whereas JavaScript is internally compiled by V8 with just-in-time (JIT) compilation to speed up the execution. This process converts JavaScript code directly into machine code, which turns out to be faster as compared to browsers.

- **libuv:** libuv is written in C and was originally developed to abstract asynchronous non-blocking I/O operations, including asynchronous TCP and UDP sockets. It helps CPU and other resources being used simultaneously while the thread is performing I/O operations like executing database queries, resulting in better and more efficient network resource utilization. This library has mechanisms to handle different services, such as File Systems, Network calls, Child processes, polling, single handling, streaming, and more.

- **Other low-level components**: Components such as c-ares, HTTP parsing, OpenSSL, zlib, and so on, are mostly written in C/C++.

- **Application**: This is where your code, modules, and Node.js built-ins are written in JavaScript (or translated to JS using TypeScript, CoffeeScript, and so on).

- **Binding**: Binding is basically a wrapper around a library written in another language. A language that opens a library for code written in another language so that code written in different languages can communicate.

# Event Loop

The Node JS platform does not follow a multi-threaded stateless request/ response model. Instead, it follows a pattern with a single-threaded event loop. Node.js processing model is primarily based on a JavaScript event-driven model with a JavaScript callback mechanism. You should be aware of JavaScript events and how the callback mechanism works. Before getting into the inner workings of this model, take a look at the diagram in *Figure 2.4*. The core of Node.js's processing model is the **Event Loop**. Once we understand this, Node.js internals are very easy to understand.

This single-threaded process inside Node.js is not possible without an event loop. When a function is called at runtime, it uses an event loop to help group the actions of different tasks using methods like timers, queries, callbacks, and more. These methods are called a phase that uses a FIFO (First In First Out) technique to perform operations smoothly.

The phase methods are explained as follows:

- **Timers:** This is a step that uses a timer call as a threshold to decide when to perform operations like `setInterval()` and `setTimeout()`.

- **Pending Recalls**: These are recalls that are put on hold to be resumed later.

- **Polls:** This is the sequence of electoral events.

- **Checks:** This is a method to perform an action immediately using the `setImmediate()` method.
- **Close callbacks:** This is a way to close open callbacks.

The following steps will be performed by Node.js for processing requests:

- Web server has a limited thread pool for serving client requests.
- The server queues all the requests received by them. This is known as the **Order of Events**.
- The Node JS web server uses only one thread, which is based on event loop, which keeps on checking for any client request in the event queue; otherwise, keeps on waiting indefinitely for incoming requests.
- Once the event queue receives one client request, Node.js starts processing the client request.
  - In case of non-blocking requests, the thread prepares responses and sends them back to the client.
  - Otherwise for some block IO operations, like a database, accessing file system, or external services, it follows a different approach:
    - Check the availability of threads.
    - Assign the client request to a single thread.
    - Request processing happens, including blocking I/O operations, preparing the response, and finally returning it to the event loop.
    - The event loop in turn sends a response to the specific client that made the request.

Here,

$n$: number of customers

$m$: number of thread pool

**Assumptions**:

- All the clients use the system at the same time.
- There is a limited thread pool on the server due to hardware constraints.
- Client-1, Client-2, ..., Client-n are unique customers using this application.

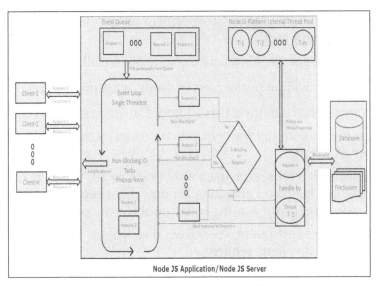

**Figure 2.4**: *Request processing Model for Node.js*

The following are the steps involved in processing client requests:

1. All requests from different clients are put into an event queue by the Node.js web server.

2. Event loop takes these requests one by one and performs the following operations:

   a. Checks whether Request-1 from Client-1 requires any blocking I/O operations or performing complex computation tasks; if so, then it requires a separate thread to handle this kind of request.

   b. If a request is a non-blocking I/O task, the event loop processes all steps and sends Response-1 to Client-1 .

3. Event loop continues to receive further requests from Client-2 Request-2 and performs all the preceding operations.

4. This process is repeated for all the Request-n from Client-n.

5. The event loop selects thread T-1 from the internal thread pool and assigns it to a client request thread T-1.

6. Thread T-1 processes the request and sends Response-n back to Client-n after performing the necessary blocking I/O or computation task.

## Phase Methods in Details

Each stage has a queue/heap that the event loop uses to store callbacks to be executed.

## Timers

JavaScript timer callbacks (`setTimeout`, `setInterval`) are stored on the heap until they are expired. Once expired, timers on the stack, the event loop takes the associated callbacks and starts executing them in an increasing delay sequence until the timer queue is empty. However, the execution of timer callbacks is controlled by the poll phase of the event loop:

```
console.log('Start');
setTimeout(() => {
    console.log('Timeout callback');
}, 2000);
console.log('End');
```

In the preceding code, the `setTimeout()` function is called by a callback that prints `Timeout callback` to the console after 2000 milliseconds (that is, 2 seconds). This function is added to the message queue in the timer step and processed by the event loop after the synchronous code is executed.

**Output**:

```
Start
End
Timeout callback
```

As we can see, "`Timeout callbck`" is printed 2 seconds after "`Start`" and "`End`" are printed because the `setTimeout()` function does not block and its callback is handled by the event loop after execution of the synchronous code.

## Pending callbacks

In this phase, the event loop queries for events such as file and network I/O operations. The event loop processes some request events in the request phase and moves certain events to the wait phase in the next iteration of the event loop. In the wait phase, the event loop adds deferred events to the queue of pending callbacks and fires them. Events in the pending callback phase contain TCP socket errors sent to certain systems. For example, some operating systems defer the handling of ECONNREFUSED error events to this step.

## Idle/Prepare

This is not an official phase mentioned as part of the event loop phases and is mostly used internally to describe some of the backend jobs. At this point, the event loop does nothing and can be used to perform some of the background tasks, including garbage collection and checking for low priority events. It is inactive and preparing to go to the next stage.

## Poll

At this point, the event loop watches for new asynchronous I/O calls. Almost all callbacks, except `setTimeout`, `setInterval`, `setImmediate`, and closure callbacks, are executed.

The event loop does two things at this point:

- If there are already callbacks in the request phase queue, it will fire them until all callbacks are removed from the request phase callback queue.
- If there are no callbacks in the queue, the event loop remains in the request phase for some time and poll for I/O events.

When the transaction loop enters the request phase, it enlivens pending I/O transactions and executes them until the queue is empty or a system-dependent limit is reached. Between the execution of the JavaScript callbacks, the "next ticks" and microtask queues are cleared, just like in the other stages.

The polling phase differs from the other phases in that the event chain sometimes blocks the event chain for some time and polls I/O events until the time expires or the callback limit is reached.

## Check/setImmediate

The event loop executes the `setImmediate` callback in the control phase immediately after the I/O events.

The event loop executes multiple `setImmediate()` calls in the order in which they were created. In the following example, the event loop triggers a call to `fs.readFile()` during the request phase. It then triggers the `setImmediate()` callbacks immediately in the control phase in the same iteration of the event loop.

On the other hand, it handles the next iteration of the event loop in the `setTimeout()` timer step. If you run the `setImmediate()` on the I/O callback, the event loop guarantees that it will run during the control phase in the same iteration of the event loop:

```
const fs = require("fs");
let counter = 0;

fs.readFile("someFilePath", {
    encoding: "utf8"
}, () => {
    console.log(`Reading file, counter = ${++counter}`);

    setImmediate(() => {
        console.log(`setImmediate 1 from I/O callback, counter =
${++counter}`);
    });

    setTimeout(() => {
        console.log(`setTimeout from I/O callback, counter =
${++counter}`);
    }, 0);

    setImmediate(() => {
        console.log(`setImmediate 2 from I/O callback, counter =
${++counter}`);
    });
});
```

## Close Callback

In this closing phase, Node.js executes callbacks to close the events and complete the given iteration of the event loop. When the connector closes, the event loop handles the closed event at that point. When "next ticks" and microtasks are created in this phase, they are processed in the same way as in the other phases of the event cycle. It is worth pointing out that the event loop can be stopped at any stage using the **process.exit()** method. The Node.js process exits, and the event loop bypasses expected asynchronous operations.

# Non-blocking or Asynchronous I/O

This overview discusses the difference between blocking and non-blocking calls in Node.js. While it's related to the event cycle and libs, prior knowledge of these topics is not necessary. Readers are expected to understand the basics of the JavaScript language and the Node.js calling pattern.

**Blocking**

This means that code execution must wait until all the current operations defined within a JavaScript function have been completely executed. This is because the event loop cannot execute JavaScript during the blocking operation.

In Node.js, JavaScript that performs poorly due to being CPU-intensive and does not wait for a non-JavaScript operation, such as I/O, is generally not called blocking. The most commonly used blocking functions in the Node.js standard library are synchronous methods that use slips. Native modules can also have block methods.

All Node.js standard library I/O methods provide asynchronous versions that do not block or accept callback operations. Some methods also have blocking counterparts whose names end in sync.

The following example is a synchronous-style program. It runs from top to bottom on the V8 thread and just chews up some CPU (not ideally blocking):

```
console.log(Date.now().toString() + ': Starting program');
const startTime = Date.now();
let endTime = startTime;
while (endTime < startTime + 20) {
    endTime = Date.now();
}
console.log(Date.now().toString() + ' Program Ends');
```

After looping for 20 milliseconds of CPU time (by constantly checking the system time), the loop terminates. Because there are no callbacks in the event loop, the program ends.

**Non-blocking**

A non-blocking system call is a system call that does not block current code execution. A non-blocking operation does not wait for I/O to complete. If a blocking operation causes the process to be added to the back burner at the operating system level, the process continues instead of executing the non-blocking I/O operation. A non-blocking call initiates an operation and leaves it to the operating system to execute immediately without result.

The main difference between blocking and non-blocking I/O is the behavior of the code execution during the I/O operation. In the blocking I/O, users must wait until data is received before continuing execution, whereas in non-blocking I/O, users don't have to wait for anything, and they continue to do their job!

The main advantage of non-blocking I/O is that it allows users to continue other operations while waiting for the I/O operation to complete. This can be particularly useful when writing concurrent programs where many things are happening at the same time. Non-blocking I/O is a bit harder to write than blocking I/O, but it's also much more efficient and flexible. This is because non-blocking I/O allows users to perform multiple I/O operations simultaneously in any order:

```
'use strict'
console.log(Date.now().toString() + ': Program started');
setTimeout(() => {
    console.log(Date.now().toString() + 'Asynchronous processing
complete.');
}, 2000);
console.log(Date.now().toString() + 'Program ends');
```

**Output**:

```
Program started
Program ends
Asynchronous processing complete.
```

The program executes the following operations:
- Prints the Start message.
- Invokes setTimeout(), setting a timeout of 2000 milliseconds.
- Prints the END message.
- After no less than 2000 milliseconds, the event loop invokes the anonymous callback function provided to setTimeout(), and it runs, showing the Asynchronous processing complete message.

# Bank and Cafe

Let's understand blocking and non-blocking with a real-life example. The following example of a bank and a café serving customers will clear our understanding of blocking versus non-blocking.

**Bank (block)**

Inside the bank, there are separate counters for each department, such as accounts, cashiers, loans, and so on. When you visit the bank, you will notice that there is a line against each counter, and customers go in a specific order when their turn comes.

This banking model of transaction processing works on a basic blocking technique:

- At a given time, one banker can only help one customer.
- The Cashier processes all stages of your transaction in order.
- If the cashier cannot process your transaction and might require supervisor approval, the cashier has to wait for approval before proceeding.
- You will exit the banking window after the entire transaction is completed.

The nature of banking transactions is **synchronous**. The cashier must complete all steps of the transaction alone before they can assist another customer.

**Coffee shop (non-block)**

When you visit a coffee shop, you will place your order at one of the counters by making payment and taking your table. In the background, many cooks will be working together to make your order ready and serve them.

The cafe model of transaction processing is non-blocking:

- A single counter can only assist one customer at a time.
- A cook will prepare one order at a time.
- The counter and cooks share all the steps to complete your order.
- While the cook is preparing your order, the counter is not blocked and can take another customer's order.
- Then, when your order is ready, your name is announced, and you pick your order up.

This nature of the cafe events is an example of **asynchronous**. The counter keeps taking orders, processing payments, and collecting enough information for the customer to report that their order has been fulfilled. The counter worker then helps the next customer, while the behind-the-scenes cooks take care of fulfilling the orders.

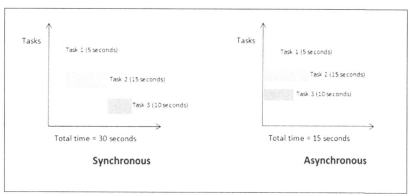

**Figure 2.5**: *Time-lapse for Synchronous versus Asynchronous*

When we compare the overall time taken by execution from both examples, we will notice that order processing at café is much faster as compared to banks.

This applies to the Node.js framework as well, where a single-thread event loop helps to make asynchronous operations and results in faster request processing.

# Core Node Modules

There are various node modules that come along with Node installation and help us to use these features or modules without importing them explicitly.

# Buffers

Buffer objects represent a fixed-length sequence of bytes in Node.js. The Buffer class is a subclass of the Uint8Array JavaScript class and extends it with methods that cover additional use cases. Node.js API accepts simple Uint8Arrays if buffers are supported.

Although the buffer class is available globally, it is still recommended to explicitly reference it via an import or force statement.

Node.js provides a buffer class for storing raw data, which is like an array of integers but corresponds to allocating raw memory outside the V8 heap. The buffer class is used because pure JavaScript is not suitable for binary data. So, when you deal with TCP streams or the file system, you must deal with octet streams.

# Creating Buffers

Following are some of the commonly used methods:

- **Creating an uninitiated buffer of 10 octets**:

  The `buffer.alloc()` method creates a new buffer of any size. When you use this method, you specify the size of the buffer in bytes. The following code will create a buffer of size 10 bytes:

  ```
  var buf = new Buffer.alloc(10);
  console.log(buf);
  ```

  **Running**:

  ```
  PS D:\Demo\Chapter-2\buffer> node .\create_buffer.js
  ```

  **Output**:

  ```
  <Buffer 00 00 00 00 00 00 00 00 00 00>
  ```

- **Creating a buffer from an array**:

  ```
  var buffer = new Buffer.from([10, 20, 30, 40, 50]);
  console.log(buffer)
  ```

  **Running**:

  ```
  PS D:\Demo\Chapter-2\buffer> node .\create_buffer.js
  ```

  **Output**:

  ```
  <Buffer 0a 14 1e 28 32>
  ```

- **Creating a buffer from string with optionally encoding type**:

  The `buffer.write()` method writes a string to **a** buffer, which can be useful **if** you need to stream strings **as** buffers. You can write a string to a buffer using the following method:

  ```
  var buffer = new Buffer.from("Learning Node js in depth",
  "utf-8");
  console.log(buffer)
  ```

  **Running**:

  ```
  PS D:\Demo\Chapter-2\buffer> node .\create_buffer.js
  ```

  **Output**:

  ```
  <Buffer 4c 65 61 72 6e 69 6e 67 20 4e 6f 64 65 20 6a 73 20 69
  6e 20 64   70 74 68>
  ```

**Note**: Though "utf8" is the default encoding, you can use any of the following encodings, such as "ascii", "utf8", "utf16le", "ucs2", "base64", or "hex".

# Writing Buffers

The following syntax is used for writing into a Node buffer and returning the number of octets written:

```
buf.write(string[, offset][, length][, encoding])
```

**Parameters**:

The following list of parameters is passed into the write method:

- **string**: This is used to specify the string data to be written to the buffer.
- **offset**: This is used to specify the index of the buffer to start writing at (default value is 0).
- **length**: This is used to specify the number of bytes to write (defaults to buffer.length).
- **encoding**: Encoding to use (default encoding 'utf8').

We will create a new "buffer.js" inside the **Chapter-2** folder and add the following code:

```
var buf = new Buffer.alloc(256);
var len = buf.write("Writing Buffers of Length 256");
console.log("Octets written : "+ len);


PS D:\Demo\Chapter-2\buffer> node .\writing_buffer.js
```

**Output**:

```
<Buffer 00 00 00 00 00 00 00 00 00 00>
<Buffer 0a 14 1e 28 32>
<Buffer 4c 65 61 72 6e 69 6e 67 20 4e 6f 64 65 20 6a 73 20 69 6e
20 64 65 70 74 68>
Octets written: 24
```

# Reading from Buffers

The syntax used here is for reading data from a Node buffer and returning a string in the specified character set encoding:

```
buf.toString([encoding][, start][, end])
```

**Parameters**:

The following list of parameters is passed into the toString method:

- **encoding**: This is used for encoding to use ('utf8' is the default encoding).
- **start:** This is used for the beginning index to start reading (defaults to 0).
- **end:** This is used for end index to end reading (defaults are complete buffers).

```
var buf = new Buffer.alloc(26);
for (var i = 0; i < 26; i++) {
    buf[i] = i + 97;
}
console.log(buf.toString('ascii'));        // outputs:
abcdefghijklmnopqrstuvwxyz
console.log(buf.toString('ascii', 0, 5));   // outputs: abcde
console.log(buf.toString('utf8', 0, 5));    // outputs: abcde
console.log(buf.toString(undefined, 0, 5)); // encoding defaults
to 'utf8', outputs abcde
```

**Running**:

```
PS D:\Demo\Chapter-2\buffer> node .\string_buffer.js
```

**Output**:

```
abcdefghijklmnopqrstuvwxyz
abcde
abcde
abcde
```

# Converting Buffer to JSON

We can convert buffers to JSON objects using the following syntax:

```
buf.toJSON()
```

Create a file **convert_json.js** and add the following code:

```
var buf = new Buffer.from('Converting buffer to json object');
var json = buf.toJSON(buf);


console.log(json);
```

**Running**:

```
PS D:\Demo\Chapter-2\buffer> node convert_json.js
```

**Output**:

```
{
    type: 'Buffer',
    data: [
        67, 111, 118, 101, 114, 116, 105,
       110, 103,  32,  98, 117, 102, 102,
       101, 114,  32, 116, 111,  32, 106,
       115, 111, 110,  32, 111,  98, 106,
       101,  99, 116
    ]
}
```

# Concatenating Buffers

We can use the following method syntax to concatenate Node buffers:

```
Buffer.concat(list[, totalLength])
```

**Parameters**:

The following list of parameters is passed into the `concat` method:

- **list**: Array list of Buffer objects to be concatenated.
- **totalLength**: This is the total length of the buffers when concatenated.

```
var buffer1 = new Buffer.from('Using NodeJS ');
var buffer2 = new Buffer.from('Concatenating buffers');
var buffer3 = Buffer.concat([buffer1,buffer2]);
console.log("buffer3 content: " + buffer3.toString());
```

**Running**:

```
PS D:\Demo\Chapter-2> node buffer.js
```

**Output**:

```
buffer3 content: Using NodeJS Concatenating buffers
```

## Comparing Buffers

We can use the following method syntax to compare Buffers:

```
buf.compare(otherBuffer);
```

**Parameter**:

The following parameter is passed into the compare method:

- otherBuffer: This is a new buffer that will be compared:

```
var buf1 = new Buffer.from('123');
var buf2 = new Buffer.from('678');
var res = buf1.compare(buf2);

if(res < 0) {
    console.log(buf1 +" less than " + buf2);
} else if(res === 0) {
    console.log(buf1 +" is same as " + buf2);
} else {
    console.log(buf1 +" greater than " + buf2);
}
```

**Running**:

```
PS D:\Demo\Chapter-2/buffer> node compare_buffer.js
```

**Output**:

```
123 less than 678
```

## Copying Buffer

This method is very useful when we want to create a new Node buffer by using another buffer, and it is done using the following syntax:

```
buf.copy(targetBuffer[, targetStart][, sourceStart][, sourceEnd])
```

**Parameters**:

The following list of parameters is passed into the copy method:

- **targetBuffer**: Buffer object where source buffer will be copied to the target.
- **targetStart:** Number, Optional, Default: 0
- **sourceStart:** Number, Optional, Default: 0
- **sourceEnd:** Number, Optional, Default: **buffer.length**

```
var sourceBuf = Buffer.alloc(123);
//copy a buffer
var targetBuf = Buffer.from('ABC');
sourceBuf.copy(targetBuf);
console.log("Target Buffer content: " + targetBuf.toString());
```

**Running**:

```
PS D:\Demo\Chapter-2\buffer> node copy_buffer.js
```

**Output**:

```
Target Buffer content: 123
```

# Events

The real power of Node.js comes from the events core module, which helps to perform asynchronous operations. We define an **EventEmitter** object that raises an event, which causes attached listeners to be executed.

In Node.js, many core modules inherit the **EventEmitter** class, including the HTTP module, enabling them to execute code asynchronously.

The following code demonstrates the usability of Event in a Node.js application:

- The events module is included or imported using the **require()** function:

```
const EventEmitter = require('events');
```

- We create a new object of the **EventEmitter** class:

```
const emitter = new EventEmitter();
```

- We attach event listeners using the **on()** method:

```
emitter.on('saved', () => {
    console.log(`A saved event occurred.`);
});
```

Here, we have created an event named **saved** and attached a listener that executes the callback function automatically when invoked.

In order to trigger an event, we call the **emit()** method defined on the emitter class:

```
emitter.emit('saved');
```

The complete code can be saved to a file at events/index.js:

```
const EventEmitter = require('events');
const emitter = new EventEmitter();
emitter.on('saved', () => {
    console.log(`A events saved called.`);
});
```

**Running**:

```
PS D:\Demo\Chapter-2\events> node index.js
```

**Output**:

```
A saved event occurred.
```

# Emit an event with arguments

We can also pass some data into the **emit()** method as a second argument, and the same can be subscribed to by the **on()** method.

The following code provides an examples of how we can pass data into the **emit()** function:

```
const EventEmitter = require('events');
const emitter = new EventEmitter();
emitter.on('saved', (arg) => {
    console.log(`A saved event called with arguments: name:
```

```
    ${arg.name}, id: ${arg.id}`);
});


emitter.emit('saved', {
    id: 1,
    name: ‹John Doe›
});
```

**Running**:

```
PS D:\Demo\Chapter-2\events> node .\event_with_args.js
```

**Output**:

```
A saved event called with arguments: name: John Doe, id: 1
```

# Detach an event listener

To detach an event listener from an event, the **off()** method of the `EventEmitter` object would be used. For example:

```
const EventEmitter = require('events');
const emitter = new EventEmitter();
// declare the event handler
function log(arg) {
    console.log(`A saved event occurred having args, name: ${arg.
name}, id: ${arg.id}`);
}


// attach the event listener to the saved event
emitter.on('saved', log);


// emit the saved event
emitter.emit('saved', {
    id: 1,
    name: 'Test'
```

```
    });

    // remove the event listener
    emitter.off('saved', log);

    // no effect
    emitter.emit('saved', {
        id: 2,
        name: 'ABC'
    });
```

**Running**:

```
    PS D:\Demo\Chapter-2\events> node .\detach_events.js
```

**Output**:

```
    A saved event occurred having args, name: Test, id: 1
```

In this example, after detaching the event listener from the event, the event listener is not called when the saved event is emitted.

## Extend the EventEmitter class

The following example shows how to extend the **EventEmitter** class:

```
    const EventEmitter = require('events');

    class Salary extends EventEmitter {
        constructor(basic, tax) {
            super();
            this._basic = basic;
            this._tax = tax;
        }
        set basic(newBasic) {
            if (newBasic !== this._basic) {
```

```
                this.emit('BasicChanged', {
                    tax: this._tax,
                    oldBasic: this._basic,
                    newBasic: newBasic,
                    adjustment: ((newBasic - this._basic) * 100 /
    this._basic).toFixed(2)
                });
            }
        }
        get basic() {
            return this._basic;
        }
        get tax() {
            return this._tax;
        }
    }


    const sal = new Salary(1000, 10);


    sal.on('BasicChanged', (arg) => {
        console.log(`The salary has changed ${arg.adjustment}%`);
    })


    sal.basic = 1720;
```

The Salary class extends the **EventEmitter** class. It has two properties: basic and tax.

When the basic changes, the salary setter emits the **BasicChanged** event with an object.

The following code shows how to use the Salary class:

```
    const sal = new Salary(1000, 10);


    sal.on('BasicChanged', (arg) => {
```

```
        console.log(`The salary has changed ${arg.adjustment}%`);
    })


    sal.basic = 1720;
```

**Running**:

```
    PS D:\Demo\Chapter-2\events> node .\extends_events.js
```

**Output**:

```
    The salary has changed 72.00%
```

**Summary**

- Node.js events module provides you with the **EventEmitter** class that allows you to manage events in the node application.
- Use the **on()** method of the **EventEmitter** object to register an event handler for an event.
- Use the **emit()** method of the **EventEmitter** object to emit an event.

# File System

The File System module is one of the important modules used in Node.js applications for performing any I/O operation, such as reading/writing with files on a local disk.

File System (**fs**) module is imported using the following syntax:

```
    var fs = require("fs")
```

In the fs module, most of the methods are synchronous and asynchronous.

# File Reading

Let's create a file named **fileSystem.js** and copy the following code:

```
    // Synchronous read
    var data = fs.readFileSync('data.txt');
    console.log("Synchronous reading data from file:
    " + data.toString());
```

Here, we are reading data synchronously from the file and printing it on the console:

```
// Asynchronous read
fs.readFile('data.txt', function (err, data) {
    if (err) {
        return console.error(err);
    }
    console.log("Asynchronous reading data from file: " + data.
toString());
});
```

In this example, we are reading data asynchronously from the file and printing it on the console.

To run the program, open **cmd** and use the following code:

```
PS D:\Demo\Chapter-2> node fileSystem.js
```

**Output**:

```
internal/fs/utils.js:269
    throw err;
    ^


Error: ENOENT: no such file or directory, open 'data.txt'
    at Object.openSync (fs.js:462:3)
    at Object.readFileSync (fs.js:364:35)
    at Object.<anonymous> (D:\Demo\Chapter-2\fileSystem.js:12:15)
    at Module._compile (internal/modules/cjs/loader.js:1015:30)
    at Object.Module._extensions..js
(internal/modules/cjs/loader.js:1035:10)
    at Module.load (internal/modules/cjs/loader.js:879:32)
    at Function.Module._load (internal/modules/cjs/loader.
js:724:14)
    at Function.executeUserEntryPoint [as runMain]
(internal/modules/run_main.js:60:12)
    at internal/main/run_main_module.js:17:47 {
  errno: -4058,
```

```
    syscall: ‹open›,
    code: ‹ENOENT›,
    path: ‹data1.txt›
}
```

You will get an error since the data file is not yet created:

```
Error: ENOENT: no such file or directory, open 'data.txt'
```

Let's create a file named *data.txt* and add the text "This is a sample text file.", and then run the same cmd again:

```
PS D:\Demo\Chapter-2> node fileSystem.js
```

**Output:**

```
Synchronous reading data from file: This is a sample text file
Asynchronous reading data from file: This is a sample text file
```

# File Open

Syntax for opening a file in asynchronous mode is as follows:

```
fs.open(path, flags[, mode], callback)
```

**Parameters:**

The following list of parameters is passed into the open method:

- **path:** This is a string value for the filename, including the path.
- **flags:** There are many flags that can be used to specify the behavior of the file to be opened.
- **mode:** This is used to set the file mode. Its default value is 0666 (readable and writable).
- **callback:** We define a function that gets two arguments (err, fd).

Following is the list of flags that can be used to define the behavior of the file open operation:

| Flag | Description |
|------|-------------|
| r | Open file for reading; an exception occurs if the file does not exist |
| r+ | Open file for reading and writing; an exception occurs if the file does not exist |

| rs | Open file for reading in synchronous mode |
|---|---|
| rs+ | Open file for reading and writing, telling the os to open it synchronously (see notes for **'rs'** about using this with caution) |
| w | Open file for writing; the file is created (if it does not exist) or truncated (if it exists) |
| wx | Like 'w' but fails if the path exists |
| w+ | Open file for reading and writing; the file is created (if it does not exist) or truncated (if it exists) |
| wx+ | Like 'w+' but fails if the path exists |
| a | Open file for appending; the file is created if it does not exist |
| ax | Like 'a' but fails if the path exists |
| a+ | Open file for reading and appending; the file is created if it does not exist |
| ax+ | Open file for reading and appending; the file is created if it does not exist |

***Table 2.1**: List of flags for file open*

Create a file and add the following code to check file opening functionality:

```
console.log("Going to open file!");
fs.open('input.txt', 'r+', function(err, fd) {
    if (err) {
        return console.error(err);
    }
    console.log(«File opened successfully!»);
});
```

**Output**:

```
Data File opened successfully!
Asynchronous reading data from file: This is sample text file
```

# File Information

We can use the following syntax to get more detailed information about files:

```
fs.stat(path, callback)
```

**Parameters:**

The following list of parameters is passed into the stat method:

- **Path:** This is string having filename including path.
- **Callback**: This is the callback function that gets two arguments (err, stats), where stats is an object of fs.Stats type.

| Method | Description |
|---|---|
| stats.isfile() | Returns true if the file type is of a simple file |
| stats.isdirectory() | Returns true if the file type is of a directory |
| stats.isblockdevice() | Returns true if the file type is of a block device |
| stats.ischaracterdevice() | Returns true if the file type is of a character device |
| stats.issymboliclink() | Returns true if the file type is of a symbolic link |
| stats.isfifo() | Returns true if the file type is of a FIFO |
| stats.issocket() | Returns true if the file type is of a socket |

*Table 2.2: List of methods for file stat operation*

Let's create a **file filesystem/index.js** and add the following code:

```
var fs = require("fs");
console.log("Going to get file info!");
fs.stat('sample.txt', function (err, stats) {
    if (err) {
        return console.error(err);
    }
    //console.log(stats);
    console.log(«Displaying file info successfully...»);
    // Check file type
    console.log(«check if File - « + stats.isFile());
```

```
        console.log(«check if Directory - « + stats.isDirectory());
    });


    PS D:\Demo\Chapter-2> node fileSystem.js
```

**Output**:

```
    Data File opened successfully!
    Displaying file info successfully...
    check if File - true
    check if Directory - false
```

# HTTP

The http module is a core module of Node designed to support several features of the HTTP protocol.

The following example shows how to use the http module:

First, create a new file called server.js and include the http module by using the **require()** function:

```
    const http = require('http');
```

Second, create an HTTP server using the **createServer()** method of the http object:

```
    const server = http.createServer((req, res) => {
        if (req.url === '/') {
            res.write(«<h1>Hello, Node.js!</h1>»);
        }
        res.end();
    });
```

The **createServer()** accepts a callback that has two parameters: HTTP request (**req**) and response (**res**). Inside the callback, we send an HTML string to the browser if the URL is / and end the request.

Third, listen to the incoming HTTP request on the port 5000:

```
server.listen(5000);
console.log(`The HTTP Server is running on port 5000`);
```

**Output**:

```
PS D:\Demo\Chapter-2> node http-server.js
The HTTP Server is running on port 5000
```

***Figure 2.6***: *Running node HTTP server*

# Path

The Node.js path module is used to handle and transform file paths. This module can be imported by using the following syntax:

```
var path =  require ("path");
```

The following is the list of methods used in the path module:

| Index | Method | Description |
|-------|--------|-------------|
| 1. | `path.normalize(p)` | It is used to normalize a string path, taking care of '..' and '.' parts |
| 2. | `path.join([path1][, path2][, ...])` | It is used to join all arguments together and normalize the resulting path |
| 3. | `path.resolve([from ...], to)` | It is used to resolve an absolute path |
| 4. | `path.isabsolute(path)` | It determines whether the path is an absolute path. An absolute path will always resolve to the same location, regardless of the working directory |

| 5. | `path.relative(from, to)` | It is used to solve the relative path from "**from**" to "**to**" |
|---|---|---|
| 6. | `path.dirname(p)` | It returns the directory name of a path. It is similar to the **unix dirname** command |
| 7. | `path.basename(p[, ext])` | It returns the last portion of a path. It is similar to the **Unix basename** command. |
| 8. | `path.extname(p)` | It returns the extension of the path, from the last '.' to the end of the string in the last portion of the path. if there is no '.' in the last portion of the path or the first character of it is '.', then it returns an empty string |
| 9. | `path.parse(pathstring)` | It returns an object from a path string |
| 10. | `path.format(pathobject)` | It returns a path string from an object, the opposite of the **path.parse** method |

**Table 2.3**: *Methods defined on path objects*

Create a file named **path/index.js**:

```
var path = require("path");
// Normalization
console.log('normalization : ' + path.normalize('some path to
normalize'));
// Join
console.log('joint path : ' + path.join('/text', 'path-1',
'path-2'));
// Resolve
console.log('resolve : ' + path.resolve('text_path_example.js'));
// Extension
console.log('ext name: ' + path.extname('text_path_example.js'));
```

**Running**:

```
PS D:\Demo\Chapter-2\path> node index.js
```

**Output**:

```
normalization : some path to normalize
joint path : \text\path-1\path-2
resolve : D:\Demo\Chapter-2\path\text_path_example.js
ext name: .js
```

# Process

Node.js process is a global object, an instance of **EventEmitter**, that can be accessed from anywhere. This is used to get information about any process, including process ID, architecture, platform, version, and more. Process objects can be used to kill processes and perform various operations on behalf of the operating system.

Following is a list of commonly used properties of Node.js Process:

| Property | Description |
| --- | --- |
| arch | What is the process architecture: 'arm', 'ia32', or 'x64' |
| args | Returns commands line arguments as an array |
| env | Returns user environment |
| execPath | Absolute pathname of executable that started process |
| exitCode | Define a number that will process exit code |
| pid | Define process id of the process |
| platform | What is the platform of the process: 'darwin', 'freebsd', 'linux', 'sunos', or 'win32' |
| release | Returns the metadata for the current node release |
| Stdout | Writable stream to stdout |

| Stdin | Writable stream to `stdin` |
|---|---|
| version | Returns value of `NODE_VERSION` |
| versions | Returns the node version and its dependencies |

**Table 2.4**: *List of properties Node Process*

Let's create a file named **process/index.js** and add the following code:

```
console.log(`To get Process Architecture: ${process.arch}`);
console.log(`To get Process PID: ${process.pid}`);
console.log(`To get Process Platform: ${process.platform}`);
console.log(`To get Process Version: ${process.version}`);
```

**Running**:

```
PS D:\Demo\Chapter-2\process> node index.js
```

**Output**:

```
To get Process Architecture: x64
To get Process PID: 38212
To get Process Platform: win32
To get Process Version: v12.19.1
```

Node.js process functions are displayed in *Table* 2.5:

| Function | Description |
|---|---|
| cwd() | This method will return path of current working directory |
| hrtime() | This method will return the current high-resolution real time in a [seconds, nanoseconds] array |
| memoryUsage() | This method will return an object having information of memory usage |
| process.kill(pid[, signal]) | This method is used to kill the given pid |
| uptime() | This method will return the Node.js process uptime in seconds |

**Table 2.5**: *List of Node.js Process function*

Following is the code to print current working directory and uptime of process:

```
console.log(`Current directory: ${process.cwd()}`);
console.log(`Uptime: ${process.uptime()}`);
```

**Running**:

```
PS D:\Demo\Chapter-2\process> node index.js
```

**Output**:

```
Current directory: D:\Demo\Chapter-2\process
Uptime: 0.0289348
```

# Stream

As per Node.js official documentation:

> A **stream** is an abstract interface for working with streaming data in Node.js. The node:stream module provides an API for implementing the stream interface. There are many stream objects provided by Node.js. For instance, a request to an HTTP server and process.stdout are both stream instances.

Streams can be readable, writable, or both. All streams are instances of **EventEmitter**.

We can access the stream module using the following syntax:

```
const stream = require('node:stream');
```

The **node:stream** module is useful for creating new types of stream instances. It is usually not necessary to use the **node:stream** module to consume streams.

There are four types of streams in Node.js:

- **Readable:** This stream is used for read operations.
- **Writable:** This stream is used for write operations.
- **Duplex:** This stream can be used for both read and write operations.
- **Transform:** This is used to return computed output stream according to input.

Each type of stream is an Event emitter instance and throws several events at different times.

The following are some commonly used events:

- **Data:** This event is triggered when data is available to read.
- **End:** This event is fired when there is no more data available to read.
- **Error:** This event is fired when there is any error in receiving or writing data.
- **Finish:** This event is fired when all data has been flushed to the underlying system.

# Reading from Stream

Let's create a new file named **reading.js** and add the following code:

```javascript
var fs = require("fs");
var data = '';


// This is used to Create a readable stream
var readerStream = fs.createReadStream('input.txt');


// This will set the encoding to be utf8.
readerStream.setEncoding('UTF8');


//This is used to Handle stream events data
readerStream.on('data', function (chunk) {
    data += chunk;
});


//This is used to Handle stream events end
readerStream.on('end', function () {
    console.log(data);
});


//This is used to Handle stream events error
readerStream.on('error', function (err) {
    console.log(err.stack);
});
```

**Running**:

```
PS D:\Demo\Chapter-2\streams> node .\reading.js
```

**Output**:

```
PS D:\Demo\Chapter-2> node stream.js
Program Ended
This is sample text file
```

# Writing to Stream

Create a file named **writing.js** and add the following code:

```
var fs = require("fs");
var data = 'This is example of writing data using Node.js
stream.';

// This will create a writable stream
var writerStream = fs.createWriteStream('output.txt');

// This is used to write the data to stream with given encoding
of utf8
writerStream.write(data, 'UTF8');

//This is used to mark the end of file and finish writing
writerStream.end();

// This will handle stream events finish
writerStream.on('finish', function () {
    console.log(«Writing data completed.»);
});

// This will handle stream events error
```

```
writerStream.on('error', function (err) {
    console.log("Error while writing data.");
    console.log(err.stack);
});
```

**Running**:

```
PS D:\Demo\Chapter-2\streams> node .\writing.js
```

**Output**:

```
Writing data completed.
```

You can check the generated file as **output.txt**:

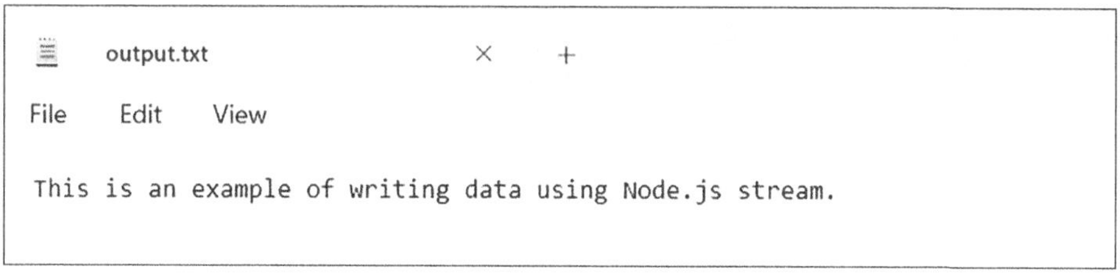

*Figure 2.7*: *Output of file writing*

# Piping Stream

Piping is a process that is used to pass output of any stream operation as input to the next stream operation. There is no limit on piping operation.

Let's understand with an example of writing content.

We will create the following two files.

**input.txt**

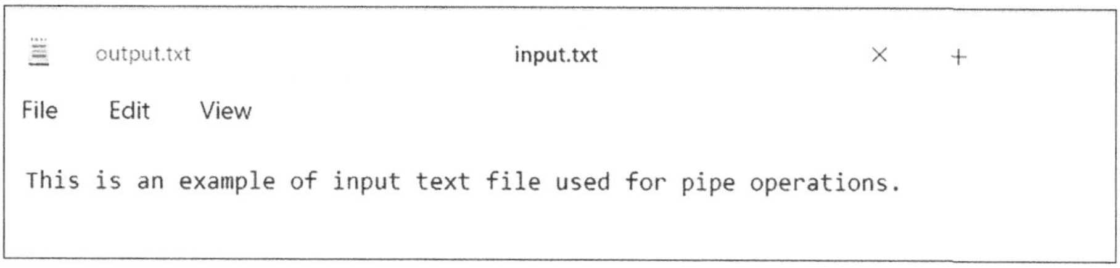

*Figure 2.8*: *Input file text*

The following is the **output.txt** file that contains the output stream:

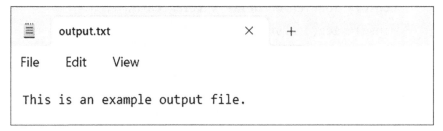

**Figure 2.9**: *Output file text*

```
var fs = require("fs");

// This will create a readable stream
var readerStream = fs.createReadStream('input.txt');

// This will create a writable stream
var writerStream = fs.createWriteStream('output.txt');

// This will read input.txt file and write data to output.txt file
readerStream.pipe(writerStream);

console.log("Operation Completed");
```

**Running**:

```
PS D:\Demo\Chapter-2\streams> node .\piping.js
```

**Output**:

After running the preceding program, we will notice that the output file has changed its content and is overwritten using input file data.

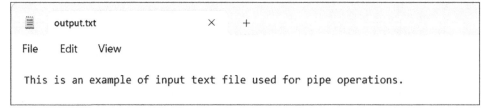

**Figure 2.10**: *Output changed after using pipe*

# Chaining Stream

Chaining streams in Node.js is a process of creating a chain of multiple stream operations by passing output of one stream to another stream. This is achieved with the piping operation that we discussed earlier.

Let's understand how to compress a file and then decompress the same file using chaining of multiple operations with the following example.

**To Compress the file:**

Let's add the following code in a file named **chaining_file_compressed.js**:

```
var fs = require("fs");
var zlib = require('zlib');
// Compress the file input.txt to input.txt.gz
fs.createReadStream('input.txt')
    .pipe(zlib.createGzip())
    .pipe(fs.createWriteStream('input.txt.gz'));
console.log("Given File is Compressed.");
```

**Running:**

```
PS D:\Demo\Chapter-2\streams> node .\chaining_file_compressed.js
```

**Output:**

```
Given File is Compressed.
```

After running this program, you will notice that the input.txt file is compressed and a new file **input.txt.gz** is created.

**To Decompress the file:**

Let's add the following code in a file named chaining_file_decompressed.js:

```
var fs = require("fs");
var zlib = require('zlib');
// Decompress the file input.txt.gz to input.txt
fs.createReadStream('input.txt.gz')
    .pipe(zlib.createGunzip())
    .pipe(fs.createWriteStream('input.txt'));
console.log("Given File is Decompressed.");
```

**Running**:

```
PS D:\Demo\Chapter-2\streams> node .\chaining_file_decompressed.js
```

**Output**:

```
Given File is Decompressed.
```

# Conclusion

This chapter focused on understanding some of the core modules of the Node.js Framework. We also discussed Node.js architecture in detail to have an understanding of how different components work together to create such an incredible framework. We took a deep dive into understanding core components working like event loop, libuv, V8 engine, and the single-threaded application architecture.

Furthermore, we covered some of the core modules, including events, process, HTTP, path, and more, with coding examples and tried to understand how to write some basic code in Node.js using the Visual Studio Code editor.

In the next chapter, we will cover more about the HTTP server and get introduced to **Express.js,** one of the popular frameworks for developing backend server applications.

# Questions

1.  What method is used to return the current working directory of the process?

    a.  `cwd()`

    b.  `pwd()`

    c.  `cmd()`

    d.  None of these

2.  What **cmd** can kill a process in Node.js using the keyboard shortcut?

    a.  Ctrl + C

    b.  Ctrl + B

   c.  *Ctrl + K*

   d.  *Ctrl + T*

3.  Which of the following are examples of NodeJS stream types?

   a.  Writable

   b.  Duplex

   c.  Readable

   d.  All of the above

4.  Which of the following are built-in node modules?

   a.  `zlib`

   b.  `https`

   c.  `dgram`

   d.  All of the above

5.  Which of the following operations is required to be used for path-specific operations?

   a.  `os` module

   b.  `path` module

   c.  `fs` module

   d.  None of the above

## Answers

| 1 | a |
|---|---|
| 2 | c |
| 3 | d |
| 4 | d |
| 5 | c |

# CHAPTER 3

# Introducing Express.js

## Introduction

This chapter will introduce Express.js and cover some of the basic topics about Express that will help you in creating your first web server. We will also go through some of the key concepts such as routing, request and response objects, middleware, and serving static files.

## Structure

In this chapter, the following topics will be covered:

- Express.js Overview
- Express Installation
- How Express.js Works
- Adding Routes in Express
- Request and Response Object
- Using Middleware Inside the Route
- Serving Static Files
- Express.js Application Generator

## Express.js Overview

Express.js is an open-source framework for developing web applications using the Node.js ecosystem. It helps encapsulate complex code and helps developers write code focused on applications.

We can create single-page, multi-page, or hybrid websites by using Express.js. Express.js being lightweight can be used to develop server-side web applications that are highly scalable and maintainable.

We can build any enterprise application using a JavaScript-based technology called the MEAN or MERN software stack. MEAN stands for MongoDB, Express.js, Angular/React, and Node.js. Recently, the MEVN stack has also emerged and gained popularity among the developer community. This stack includes MongoDB, Express.js, Vue.js, and Node.js.

Express.js is mostly used for the backend and provides some of the core components such as routing, sessions, HTTP requests, error handling, logging, and more.

# Key Features of Express.js

The following are the key features of using Express.js:

- **Middleware**

  Express.js has the cool feature of using any inbuilt middleware or custom-defined middleware to manage the request and response pipeline processing. This helps to organize and encapsulate some of the reusable components across applications. For example, we can implement a centralized way for handling errors and logging logic throughout the application.

- **Routing Module**

  Express.js has a highly advanced routing mechanism that is used for managing URLs as well as performing state management for applications. Using these routing modules, we can define static as well as dynamic routes that can used to build highly scalable real-time applications. The route method accepts URL and callback functions, which are used to handle req and response.

  ```
  // return message "hello world" when request is made to the root
  of application
  app.get('/', (req, res) => {
      res.send('hello world')
  })
  ```

- **Templating Engine**

  There are various templating engines that can be used along with Express.js to help developers create HTML dynamic content on the server. Templating engines help teams to rapidly build web apps that can be divided into several components. Some of the popular templating engines include Ejs, Jade, Pug, Mustache, HandlebarsJS, Jinja2, and Blade.

- **Debugging**

  Debugging is the process of identifying and removing errors from the web applications. Developing server-side applications involves writing complex business logic, and debugging helps identify issues easily before they are deployed to any environment.

  Some of the general debugging tools include:

  - Console.log
  - Node inspector
  - DevTools
  - Chrome debugging tools

- **Logging**

  Node.js logging is very useful for developers, starting from the building to debugging web applications. Logging provides lots of information about the applications' behavior and errors along with exceptions happening while clients use the system. These logs also help product management in planning new features for the future. Express.js can easily integrate with logging frameworks, providing detailed insight into activities and issues happening within the system. There are many open-source Node.js tools that can provide logging support, including Pino, Winston, Bunyan, Morgan, Loglevel, Log4js, Roarr, Tracer, and more.

- **Authentication/Authorization**

  Web applications are used over the internet and we need to make sure our applications are safe and secure to be used by clients. Node.js provides great tools for implementing Authentication/Authorization. Some of the popular packages used for this purpose include `jsonwebtoken`, `bcryptjs`, and `passportjs`.

# Benefits of Express.js

Following are some of the key benefits of Express.js, which has made this Framework so popular:

- **Easy to learn and develop**

  It is very easy to learn the Express.js framework, which is based on JavaScript.

  With the popularity of TypeScript, we can develop our Node application in TypeScript as well.

- **Less maintenance**

  Applications developed using Node.js and Express.js are easy to maintain over a period of time with minimum effort.

- **Lightweight and fast development**

  Express.js is a very lightweight framework, and we can quickly create our backend server with less code and deploy it in real-time. This has helped teams build their applications with less complexity and greater productivity.

- **Automated deployments**

  With the help of DevOps, we can easily automate the builds and deployment of server applications developed using Express.js with minimum configurations.

- **Community support**

  Being popular among the developer community, there are lots of support and content available related to Express.js over various platforms such as Stackoverflow, and more.

- **Open-source tools and packages**

  We have seen that there are many Node module packages available in NPM that reduce our rework, improve productivity, and help deliver features and products as soon as possible.

# Installing Express.js

Following are the steps to create our first backend server using **Express.js**:

1.  Create a file named **server.js** inside the folder:

    ```
    D:\demo\app\
    ```

2.  Add the following code inside the newly created file:

    ```
    const express = require('express');
    const app = express();
    app.get('/', (req, res) => {
        res.send('Hello, My server using Express');
    });
    const server = app.listen(8081, function () {
        var host = server.address().address;
        var port = server.address().port;
        console.log($"Server is listening at http://{host}:{port}")
    });
    ```

3.  Open the terminal or **cmd** to install dependencies using the *npm i* command:

    ```
    PS D:\Demo\app> npm i
    npm WARN sample@1.0.0 No repository field.
    +express@4.18.2
    added 1 package from 8 contributors and audited 57 packages in
    0.764s
     7 packages are looking for funding
      run `npm fund` for details
     found 0 vulnerabilities
    ```

**Running**:

```
PS D:\Demo\app> node server.js
```

**Output**:

```
Server is listening at http://:::8081
```

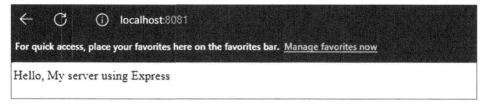

**Figure 3.1**: *Application running in the browser*

# How Express.js Works

There are four stages in which the Express.js application works:

- Creating a new Express application
- Adding new routes
- Starting an HTTP server on any given port
- Handing request/response

In the preceding example, we have created code to print the basic message "Hello, My server using Express" on the browser window. Let's understand each of the important lines of code:

- Importing express module:

  ```
  const express = require('express');
  ```

- Creating our application object using **express()**:

  ```
  const app = express();
  ```

- Adding a default GET route to listen to the incoming request.

  Express routing is used to handle all the client requests, and we can hook these routes with the Express application.

  - We have defined **get()** route, which will be the root of our web application, and a callback function has also been added to handle **res/req**. For all routes that are defined in Express, a callback function must be provided to handle all the requests from the client. After processing, the response object is returned:

    ```
    app.get('/', (req, res) => {


    });
    ```

Inside the callback function of a route, we will return our response to the client in the form of String, JSON, or any other format. This is done by calling the **res.send()** method:

```
res.send('Hello, My server using Express');
```

- We use the **listen()** method to bind and listen to the connection on the specified host and port. This method is used to start our backend server, which handles requests by clients using specific server URLs:

```
app.listen([port[, host[, backlog]]][, callback])
```

The following parameters are defined for the listen method:

- ○ **Port**: Defines the port on which the application listens.
- ○ **Host (optional)**: Specifies the IP address of the host on which the application will listen. You can only specify a host if you specify a port.
- ○ **Backlog (optional)**: Specifies the maximum queue length for pending connections. You can define the delay if you have specified a port and host.
- ○ **Callback (optional)**: Defines an action to run when the application starts listening on the specified port.

- For output, a notification message is printed (Server is listening at **http://:::8081**) in the console about the successful startup of server applications:

```
var server = app.listen(8081, function () {
    var host = server.address().address;
    var port = server.address().port;


    console.log("Server is listening at http://%s:%s", host,
port)
});
```

# Adding Routes in Express

Routing is a technique used to define an application's endpoints (URIs) to respond to client requests.

Express app object contains all the required route information and corresponding HTTP method definitions, such as **app.get()**, to handle GET requests sent from the client.

We define a callback function known as "**handler functions**", which are called when a client sends a request and proceeds by Express.js application. In other words, every time a client makes a request to the server, the **Express.js** routing mechanism matches defined routes, and callback functions are triggered to process requests.

The following code is an example of a very basic route:

```
const express = require('express')
const app = express()


// return message "hello world" when request is made to the root
of application
app.get('/', (req, res) => {
  res.send('hello world')
})
```

# Request/Response Object

Express.js has pre-defined method arguments for handling Request and Response objects. These are the parameters that are accepted by the callback function as per the following syntax:

```
app.get('/', (req, res) => {
    res.send('hello world')
})
```

### Request Object Properties

The following are some of the properties associated with request objects:

| | Properties | Description |
|---|---|---|
| 1. | req.app | This holds a reference to the instance of the Express application |
| 2. | req.baseurl | This is the URL path on which a router instance was mounted |
| 3. | req.body | This is a key-value pair that is passed along with the request body from the client |

| 4. | `req.cookies` | This property is an object that contains cookies sent by the request used by cookie-parser middleware |
|---|---|---|
| 6. | `req.hostname` | This is the hostname from the "**host**" HTTP header |
| 7. | `req.ip` | This is the remote IP address of the request |
| 8. | `req.params` | This object has properties mapped to the named route params. For example, if we have route /employee/:id, then the "**id**" property is available as req.params.id. This object defaults to {} |
| 9. | `req.path` | It contains the path part of the request URL |
| 10. | `req.protocol` | This is a request protocol string, "**http**" or "**https**", when requested with TLS |
| 11. | `req.query` | An object containing a property for each query string parameter in the route. For example, if we have route /employee?isActive=false, then the "**isActive**" property is available as req.query.isActive. This object defaults to {} |
| 12. | `req.route` | This is a string value that represents the currently matched route |
| 13. | `req.secure` | This is a boolean flag; if a TLS connection is established, we set the flag as true |

**Table 3.1**: *List of request object properties*

Following are some of the examples of **Express.js** request object methods:

```
req.accepts('html');
//=>?html?
req.accepts('text/html');
// => ?text/html?
req.accepts('application/json');
// => ?application/json?

req.get('Content-Type');
// => "text/plain"

req.param(name [, defaultValue])
```

```
// ?name=sasha
req.param('name')
// => "sasha"
```

## Response Object Methods

The methods on the response object send a response to the client and terminate the request-response cycle.

Following are some of the methods of response objects:

|    | Method | Description | Syntax |
|----|--------|-------------|--------|
| 1. | res.append() | Append specified value to the HTTP response heard field | res.append(field [, value])<br><br>res.append('Warning', '199 Miscellaneous warning'); |
| 2. | res.attachment() | Send a file as an attachment in the HTTP response | res.attachment([filename])<br><br>res.attachment('path/to/js_pic.png'); |
| 3. | res.cookie() | Set a cookie name to value | res.cookie(name, value [, options])<br><br>res.cookie('Section', { Names: [ABC, XYZ] }); |
| 4. | res.clearCookie() | Used to clear the cookie specified by name | res.clearCookie(name [, options])<br><br>res.clearCookie('name', { path: '/user }); |
| 5. | res.download() | This transfers the file as an attachment and prompts the user to download the file | res.download(path [, filename] [, fn])<br><br>res.download('/invoice-03.pdf'); |
| 6. | res.json() | Send a JSON response | res.json([body])<br><br>res.json({ data: [] }) |

| 7. | res.jsonp() | Send a JSON response with JSONP support | `res.jsonp([body])`<br>`res.jsonp({ data: [] })` |
|---|---|---|---|
| 8. | `res.redirect()` | Redirect a request | `res.redirect([status,] path)`<br>`res.redirect('http://test.com');` |
| 9. | `res.render()` | Render a view template | `res.render(view [, locals] [, callback])`<br>`res.render('index');` |
| 10. | `res.send()` | Send a response of various types | `res.send([body])`<br>`res.send({ some: 'json' });` |
| 11. | res.sendFile() | Send a file as an octet stream | `res.sendFile(path [, options] [, fn])`<br>`res.sendFile(fileName, options, function (err) {`<br>`    // ...`<br>`});` |
| 12. | `res.status()` | Set the response status code and send its string representation as the response body | `res.status(code)`<br>`res.status(400).send('Bad Request');` |

*Table 3.2*: *List of response object properties*

Following are the examples of response objects of **Express.js**:

```
res.append('Link', ['<http://localhost/>',
'<http://localhost:3000/>']);
res.append('Warning', '199 Miscellaneous warning');


res.attachment('path/to/js_pic.png');


res.cookie('name', 'Aryan', { domain: '.xyz.com', path: '/admin',
secure: true });
res.cookie('Section', { Names: [raj, sunil, ajay] });
```

```
res.cookie('Cart', { items: [1,2,3] }, { maxAge: 900000 });

res.download('/report-12345.pdf');

res.end();
res.status(404).end();

res.json(null)
res.json({ name: 'ajeet' })

res.links({
    next: 'http://api.example.com/users?page=5',
    last: 'http://api.example.com/users?page=10'
 });

res.redirect('http://example.com');

res.send(new Buffer('hoooo'));
res.send({ some: 'json' });
res.send(' Sample string ');

res.set('Content-Type', 'text/plain');

res.set({
  'Content-Type': 'text/plain',
  'Content-Length': '1233434',
})
```

# Using Middleware in Express

Express heavily relies on routing and middleware, which are, in themselves, like a web framework. When a client makes a request to the Express server, a series of middleware functions gets called, which process logic such as authentication, transforming params, and many more things.

Middleware functions are defined as callback functions that are responsible for handling and processing client requests before Node.js executes route logic.

The following tasks are performed by middleware functions:

- Execute any logic
- Transform request and the response objects
- End the request-response cycle
- All middleware functions are called in sequence

**Important Note**

> Because of any reason the current middleware function does not complete the entire request-response cycle, at the end, it should always call **next()** to pass control to the next middleware function, or else the request will remain on hold.

The following types of middleware are used inside the Express application:

# Application-level middleware

This middleware is used to bind to an instance of the app object by using the **app.use()** and **app.METHOD()** functions.

The following function is executed every time the Express app receives a request, and prints the time in the console when the request was made:

```
const express = require('express');
const app = express();


app.use((req, res, next) => {
  console.log('Time Log when request is made:', Date.now());
  next();
})
```

The following example shows a middleware function mounted on the /employee/:id path and executed whenever a client makes a request to http://example.com/employees:/id:

```
app.use('/employee/:id', (req, res, next) => {
    console.log('Request What http method Type used:', req.method);
```

```
        res.send("Employee with id - ",req.params.id);
    })
```

In the next example, we will try to call a series of middleware and use the **next()** method to execute them in sequence:

```
app.use('/employee/:id?isActive=true', (req, res, next) => {
    console.log('Request URL:', req.params.id);
    next()
  }, (req, res, next) => {
    console.log('Request Type:', req.query.isActive);
    next()
})
```

---

**Important Note**

When we define multiple routes for the same route path like /employees/search, then only the first one will get called and all others will get ignored.

If we want to skip the rest of the middleware functions, we can call **next('route')** to pass control to the next route. This will only work if routes are loaded by using the **app.METHOD()** or **router.METHOD()** functions.

---

We can also declare in middleware as an array for reusability.

Let's understand the following example having route as **/order/:id** path:

```
const express = require('express')
const app = express()

// middleawre used for authenticating request
function authMiddleware(req, res, next) {
    console.log('Authentication of request will happen');
    next();
}

// middleare used for logging application information
```

```
function logMiddleware(req, res, next) {
  console.log('Request logging will take care here');
  next();
}


// We are creating array of middleware which will be exuected be-
fore request processing
const logStuff = [authMiddleware, logMiddleware]


// Get request using logStuff array of middlewares
app.get('/order/:id', logStuff, (req, res, next) => {
  res.send('Order detail...');
})


const server = app.listen(8081, function () {
  var host = server.address().address;
  var port = server.address().port;


  console.log(`Server is listening at http://${host}:${port}`)
});
```

Here, we wanted to use two middleware:

- Authentication middleware
- Logging middleware

We can configure both at the same time in the form of an array syntax of middlewares. So, when the client makes calls to the URL **'order/2312'**, both middleware will execute in a synchronous manner, one after another. Finally, the request processing will happen.

# Router-level middleware

Router-level middleware is used similarly to application-level middleware. The only difference is that it is bound to an instance of **express.Router()** method.

The following example code explains the difference between Application- versus Router-level middleware:

```
// Router level middleware
const express = require('express');
const app = express();
const router = express.Router();

// a middleware function with no mount path. This code is executed
for every request to the router
router.use((req, res, next) => {
    console.log('Time:', Date.now())
    next()
})

// handler for the /order/:id path, which renders a special page
router.get('/order/:id', (req, res, next) => {
    res.render('order detail page')
})

// mount the router on the app
app.use('/', router)

// use the router and 401 anything falling through
app.use('/customer/settings', router, (req, res) => {
    res.sendStatus(401).redirect('error page')
  })
```

In this example, we have used both application-level middleware and router-level middleware. Here, routes that are used with **express.Router()** are router-level, whereas those used with **app.use()** are application-level.

# Error-handling middleware

Error handling inside Express.js refers to detecting and handling errors that occur simultaneously and synchronously. Express includes a default error handler, so you don't need to start by creating your own custom error-handling mechanism.

Error-handling middleware follows the concept of passing the error as the first argument, and because of this, the first argument is always **err** among the four mandatory arguments. These arguments include **err**, **req**, **res**, and **next**.

If we don't pass any of these arguments, it will be interpreted as regular middleware, and this will cause the error handler to fail.

```
app.use((err, req, res, next) => {
    console.error(err.stack);
    res.status(500).send('internal server error');
})
```

# Built-in middleware

Starting with version 4.x, the middleware functions that were previously included with Express are now treated as third-party packages and installed separately.

Express has the following built-in middleware functions:

- **express.static**

  This is used to serve static assets such as HTML files, images, and so on.

- **express.json**

  This is used to parse incoming requests with JSON payloads.

- **express.urlencoded**

  This is used to parse incoming requests with URL-encoded payloads.

# Third-party middleware

When we need to add additional support or functionality, we use third-party Express apps.

In the following example, the **body-parser** middleware function is used to parse different data formats passed as arguments inside the body of the request:

```
$ npm install body-parser


const express = require('express')
```

```
const app = express()
const bodyParser = require('body-parser')


// load the body-parsing middleware added to express app
app.use(bodyParser())
```

# Serving Static Files

Web applications that are developed using Node.js and Express.js require serving static files such as images, CSS, and JavaScript. This can be done using the **express.static** built-in middleware function that comes along with Express:

```
const express = require('express')
express.static(root, [options])
```

Where the root argument specified from which location to serve static assets.

The following example will enable you to load static content from '**public**' directory inside your application:

```
app.use(express.static('public'))
//Now, following listed files can be loaded from public directory:
http://localhost:3000/images/kitten.jpg
http://localhost:3000/css/style.css
http://localhost:3000/js/app.js
http://localhost:3000/images/bg.png
http://localhost:3000/hello.html
```

We can also create a virtual path prefix for mapping files to different locations that don't physically exist on the server:

```
app.use('/static', express.static('public'))
 //this will help us to serve files that are in the public directory
from the /static path prefix.
 http://localhost:3000/static/images/kitten.jpg
http://localhost:3000/static/css/style.css
http://localhost:3000/static/js/app.js
```

```
http://localhost:3000/static/images/bg.png
http://localhost:3000/static/hello.html
```

# Express Application Generator

We can generate our Express application automatically using an application generator tool known as **express-generator**.

The following command can be used to install the **express-generator** tool:

```
PS D:\Book\Building-Real-Time-application-using-Node.js\chap_03\
demo-app> npx express-generator
```

**Output**:

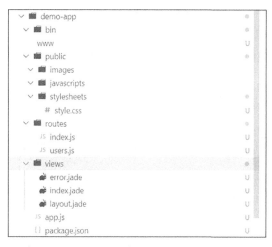

*Figure 3.2*: *Output of Express Generator tool*

We can view all the command options using the **-h** flag.

The following list of commands is available with the **express-generator** tool:

| Flag | Full version | Description |
|------|--------------|-------------|
| -h   | --help       | How to use information |
| -e   | --ejs        | Adds **ejs** engine support |
|      | --hbs        | Adds handlebars engine support |
|      | --pug        | Adds pug engine support |

| -H | -- hogan | Adds **hogan.js** engine support |
|----|----------|----------------------------------|
|    | --no-view | Generate without view engine support |
| -v | --view <engine> | Add view <engine> support (**ejs**, **hbs**, **pug**, **jade**, **twig**) |
|    |          | Default to jade |
| -c | --css <engine> | Add Stylesheet <engine support> (**less**, **stylus**, **compass**, **sass**) |
|    |          | Default to plain CSS |

*Table 3.3*: *List of cmd for Express Generator tool*

# Conclusion

This chapter covered some of the basics of Express.js and showed how we can use this framework to build lightweight backend application servers. We also explored core functionalities of the Express framework, such as routing, using middlewares, and HTTP methods.

In the next chapter, we will cover some of the basics of Restful services and learn how to use Express along with the HTTP module to create our own RESTful APIs.

# Questions

1. Which of the following NodeJS modules splits up a web address into readable parts?

   a. Express

   b. Cors

   c. URL

   d. None of the above

2. _____ is a software service that allows two or more applications to talk to each other.

   a. REST

   b. API

    c.  Both A and B

    d.  None of the above

3.  What are the different methods defined in Express routes?

    a.  **GET**

    b.  **POST**

    c.  **PUT**

    d.  All of the above

4.  What is the use of writing a middleware function in Express?

    a.  To transform request and response

    b.  To read data

    c.  To write data

    d.  None of the above

5.  How do we install the Express framework in Node.js?

    a.  npm install express

    b.  node install express

    c.  install express

    d.  None of the above

## Answers

| 1 | a |
|---|---|
| 2 | c |
| 3 | d |
| 4 | a |
| 5 | a |

# CHAPTER 4
# Creating REST API and Routing

## Introduction

This chapter will introduce RESTful APIs and guide us in creating our backend server using the HTTP Node.js module. We will delve into more detail about different routing methods such as GET, POST, PUT, and DELETE. Additionally, we will learn how to perform request validations, response transformation, and error handling. The chapter will also shed some light on CORS request processing and some standards that we should follow while creating a backed server using HTTP.

## Structure

In this chapter, the following topics will be covered:

- Introduction to RESTful Services
- Creating the First HTTP Server
- Adding Routes for **GET**, **POST**, **PUT**, and **DELETE**
- Request Validations
- Response Transformation
- CORS Request Handling with Express
- API Error Handling

# Introduction to RESTful Services

RESTful web services are defined as loosely coupled, lightweight web services that are used to build APIs for web or mobile-based applications. The REST is based on a stateless communication protocol, typically HTTP protocol.

Representational State Transfer (REST) is a well-known and established architectural style for developing client-server applications. REST primarily focuses on transferring representations of resources through requests and responses. Here, everything like data or operations is considered a resource and can be accessed usually on the web using Uniform Resource Identifiers (URIs).

Following are some examples of well-defined REST resources:

- The current weather conditions of a place
- Account information about the user
- Any static resource like an image or HTML page

The client can perform specific operations including:

- Searching specific resources using patterns
- Creating a new resource
- Modifying the existing resource by updating its information
- Deleting the resource entirely

The following principles motivate RESTful applications to be simple, lightweight, and fast:

- **Identifying resources by URI**

  A RESTful web service exposes a set of resources that identify objects for interacting with clients. Resources are identified using URIs, which provide a global address space for locating resources and services.

- **Unified UI**

  Resources are handled by the four fixed create, read, update, and delete functions: `PUT`, `GET`, `POST`, and `DELETE`. `PUT` creates a new resource, which can then be deleted with the `DELETE` command. `GET` retrieves the current state of a resource in some representation. `POST` transfers the new state to the resource. For more information, refer to Responding to HTTP Methods and Requests.

- **Self-describing messages**

  All the RESTful Services follow similar standards for any interaction with client servers. Each request has its own set of information, such as request payload, authentication headers, and other configurations, which is required by the server to identify any resource with proper permissions. Once a request is received by the server, it performs all the necessary background checks before processing the request. The request also contains HTTP protocol-specific information, which is used by the network layer to pass data in a secure way over the network using HTTPS protocol.

- **Cacheable resource**

  Caching is a mechanism by which we can store API responses, either in the client's browser or on the server itself using technologies like Redis or Memcache. When a client makes an API request to the server, cached data is returned quickly instead of performing a database query and returning an actual response. This helps to improve the performance of the application and also decreases network utilization by avoiding certain API calls from client applications running on browsers.

- **Stateless**

  REST APIs are stateless, meaning that any client interaction with the server is independent of each request and response cycle. Each request has all the information that is required by the server to process a given request and return a specific response.

  Stateless transfer helps to reduce memory usage for both client and server by reducing the additional effort to store and retrieve stateful information for each request.

# Benefits of RESTful APIs

RESTful APIs include the following benefits:

- **Scalability**

    Systems developed using REST APIs can scale efficiently because of client-server optimized interactions and the stateless behavior of HTTP protocol.

- **Flexibility**

    RESTful web services follow some of the best design patterns and help to build them separately. These services help to decouple most of the backend components so that different teams can work separately and independently.

- **Manageability**

    Server applications based on RESTFul web services are easy to maintain and do not affect the client application in case of any changes. Normally, these web services are broken into multiple layers and changes can be done to each other without affecting them. For example, changes can be made to the database layer without rewriting the application's business logic.

- **Technology Independent**

    REST APIs are independent of what technology is used behind the scenes. We can write both client and server applications in different programming languages without affecting our API design.

# Different Kinds of HTTP Verbs

Following are the nine HTTP methods typically associated with RESTful web development and most commonly used for building web applications:

- **GET**

    The most common HTTP method is GET. The purpose of the GET method is simply to retrieve data from the server. It is used to request the following resources, which include static content like a web page or HTML file, image, video, JSON/XML document, CSS, and JavaScript files.

    The GET request method is considered a safe operation, which means that it should not change the state of any resources on the server.

- **PUT**

    The HTTP PUT method is used to completely replace or create the resource identified by the given URL. If there is a resource in the URL returned by the PUT method, the representation of the resource is completely replaced. If the resource does not exist at this URL, a new resource is created.

    PUT operations are said to be unsafe but idempotent.

- **POST**

    The POST HTTP request method sends data to the server for processing. The data sent to the server is usually in the following format:

o   Web form input fields

o   XML

o   JSON data

The **HTTP** configuration allows the developer to decide on the type of processing of the data sent by the **HTTP POST** method. Prototypical uses of the **POST** method include:

o   Post a message on the message board

o   Save data from HTML forms to a database

o   Calculate the result based on the information given

POST is not considered a safe operation because it can update the server state and cause potential side effects to the server state at startup. Also, the **HTTP POST** method does not need to be idempotent, meaning it can leave data and resources on the server in a different state each time it is called.

- **DELETE**

  The **HTTP DELETE** method is self-explanatory. After execution, the resource indicated by the **DELETE** function is deleted from the server.

  As with PUT operations, the **HTTP DELETE** method is idempotent and unsafe.

- **PATCH**

  The **PATH HTTP** method is independently added to the Hypertext Transfer Protocol and allows updating existing resources partially. For example, it is significantly more efficient to send a small partial payload to the server, which requires an update rather than a complete resource representation.

- **HEAD**

  The **HTTP HEAD** method is used to simply return the metadata of the resource on the server. This HTTP request method returns all headers associated with the given URL resource but does not actually return the resource.

- **OPTIONS**

  A server does not need to support all **HTTP** methods for every resource it manages. Some resources support **PUT** and **POST** operations. Other resources only support **GET** operations.

The `HTTP OPTIONS` method returns a list of supported and enabled `HTTP` methods.

- **TRACE**

  The `TRACE HTTP` method is used for diagnostics, debugging, and troubleshooting. It simply returns a diagnostic trace that records information about the request-response cycle.

  The contents of the trace are often just an echo of the various request headers sent by the client from the server.

- **CONNECT**

  The connect function is used to connect to a server-side resource. The most common target of the `CONNECT HTTP` method is a proxy server that the client must access to tunnel from the local network.

# Idempotency of Different HTTP Verbs

Idempotency is a property of certain functions or API requests that ensures that performing an operation multiple times produces the same result as if it was executed only once.

Idempotency is crucial for APIs because it ensures consistent results even when a resource is called multiple times due to network outages or duplicate requests. Non-idempotent operations can cause unintended side effects, such as the creation of additional resources or unexpected changes, which pose a significant risk when data accuracy is critical.

Idempotency in HTTP verbs simplifies error handling, concurrency control, debugging, and monitoring of operations while using APIs. This improves the user experience by maintaining consistency and predictability even in the face of network failures and request retries over distributed applications.

HTTP methods such as `GET`, `HEAD`, `PUT`, `DELETE`, `OPTIONS`, and `TRACE` are considered idempotent. They can be retried or performed multiple times without causing unwanted side effects.

`POST` is not inherently idempotent, which means making the same `POST` request multiple times can produce different results or create multiple data entries on the backend server.

# How RESTful APIs Work

Following are the general steps for any REST API calls happening between the client and server:

1. Client or browser configures API request with property payload and Header

2. The client makes an AJAX request

3. Server received request

4. Request processing happens at the server

5. The response returned to the client

6. The client handles responses and presents them to users

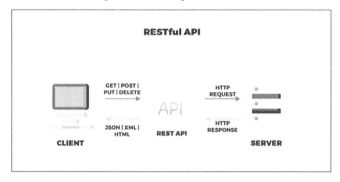

*Figure 4.1*: RESTful API working model

# Creating the First HTTP Server

The following steps are used to create our backend server using the HTTP module:

1. **Importing HTTP Module**

   This is the first step where we will import the required HTTP module into our backend application using the **require** keyword.

   Let's create a **http_basic.js** file inside the **chap_04** directory and add the following code:

   ```
   var http = require('http');
   ```

2. **Creating Configuration**

Now add some of the variables that will be used for setting up configuration for our server like host, port, and more:

```
const host = 'localhost';
const port = 8000;
```

3. **Creating Server Process**

For creating our backend server using the HTTP module, we need to call createServer() method defined on the HTTP module, which we can access using the above **http** variable:

```
const server = http.createServer();
```

This will create a server instance and store inside *server* variables for further usage. In order to start a server process, we need to call the **.listen()** method defined on the server instance:

```
server.listen(port, host, () => {
    console.log(`Server is running on http://${host}:${port}`);
});
```

4. **Request Handler**

We need to create a handler function, requestHandler(), which will be used to handle all the client requests and process responses:

```
const requestHandler = function(req, res) {}
```

The **requestListener** function expects two arguments: **req** and **res**. For the **req**, we can access the request object sent by the client, and for **res**, we can access the corresponding response object that will be returned to the client.

5. **Request Processing**

In the **requestHandler()** method, we use the **req** argument to check for the body request params and the **res** argument to send back a response to the client:

```
const requestHandler = function(req, res) {
    if(req.body){
```

```
            console.log(`Request body`, req.body);
    }
    res.send("Hello World from Node.js HTTP Server");
}
```

6. **Running Server**

   We will run the server and see the output on the browser:

   ```
   Hello World from Node.js HTTP Server
   ```

# Adding Routes

### GET

The **GET** method is used to access resources or send data using a specified URL on the server. The client can cache **GET** requests and send parameters in the RESTful API request to instruct the server to filter data before sending:

```
// returns the list of students
app.get('/students', function (req, res) {
    res.json(students);
});
```

### POST

A request is used to send data to a server, such as adding a new row to the backend database table or saving a file using file upload for any website. The **POST** method is used to create new items or resources for the backend server. In REST CRUD meaning, it performs the create operation:

```
// add student
let students = [];
app.post("/students", function (req, res) {
    var student = req.body;
    students.push(student);
    res.json({ message: "Record Added" });
});
```

## PUT

The **PUT** method is mostly used to update an existing resource or data that was already created in the past.

In the **PUT** method, the resource is first identified by the URL, and if it exists, it is updated; otherwise, a new resource is created. In simple terms, we can say that if the resource exists, then update it; else, create a new resource.

Clients use **PUT** to update existing resources on the server. Unlike POST, sending the same **PUT** request multiple times in a RESTful web service gives the same result:

```
// update student by id
app.put("/students/:id", function (req, res) {
    var id = req.params.id;
    var student = req.body;
    // updating user with the specific id
    for (var i = 0; i < students.length; i++) {
        if (students[i].id == id) {
            students[i] = student;
            break;
        }
    }
    res.json({ message: "Record Updated" });
});
```

## PATCH

Similar to the **PUT** method, **PATCH** is used to send data to update an "existing resource" on the server. However, there is an important difference between PUT and PATCH: PATCH only makes partial changes to a record instead of overwriting the entire record, which happens in the case of **PUT**.

The following code shows the implementation of the **PATCH** method in JavaScript:

```
// patch resource
app.patch("/students/:id", function (req, res) {
    var id = req.params.id;
    var student = req.body;
    for (var i = 0; i < students.length; i++) {
```

```
        if (students[i].id == id) {
            // replacing only specific properties
            for (var key in student) {
                students[i][key] = student[key];
            }
            break;
        }
    }
    res.json({ message: "Record Updated using patch" });
});
```

### DELETE

DELETE request is used to remove the resource, such as file, image, or data, from the database.

A DELETE request is meant to change the server state after some resource is removed. If the user does not have appropriate authentication, the request will fail and the user might get an unauthorized error:

```
// deleting resource
app.delete("/students/:id", function (req, res) {
    var id = req.params.id;
    for (var i = 0; i < students.length; i++) {
        if (students[i].id == id) {
            students.splice(i, 1);
            break;
        }
    }
    res.json({ message: "Record Deleted" });
});
```

# Using Swagger with Node.js

Swagger is a set of tools that can be used to build backend APIs very easily. Primarily intended for API documentation following OpenAPI specification,

Swagger provides tools to help in all phases of API development, including designing, developing, documenting, and testing.

The OpenAPI specification is a specification used to create interfaces for describing, producing, consuming, and rendering RESTful APIs, sometimes also known as the swagger specification.

Following is an example of swagger documentation about defining a set of APIs for a blog post web application:

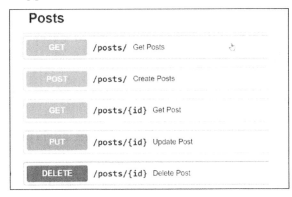

*Figure 4.2*: *Example of RESTful API Methods using Swagger docs*

# Setting up Swagger in Node.js

The easiest way to get started with Swagger Docs in Node.js and Express server is to use **swagger-ui-express** package, which is available in NPM. This package allows us to transfer documents based on the JSON/YAML file provided by the developer.

Firstly, we need to create a sample project and then install **swagger-ui-express** via NPM.

Let's add the following code in app.js:

```
var express = require('express');
var app = express();
app.get('/', function (req, res) {
    res.send('Hello, My server using Express');
});


var server = app.listen(8081, function () {
```

```
        var host = server.address().address;
        var port = server.address().port;


        console.log("Server is listening at http://%s:%s", host, port)
    });
```

After running the application, we will get the output:

```
    Hello, My server using Express
```

The next step is to install express, `swagger-ui-express`, and `ymaljs` package using NPM:

```
    npm install --save express
    npm install --save swagger-ui-express
    npm install --save ymaljs
```

Once we have installed all the dependencies, we will update our server code to read the configuration about Swagger and generate the documentation URL:

```
    /* .... */
    var swaggerUi = require('swagger-ui-express');
    var YAML = require('yamljs');
    const swaggerDocument = YAML.load('./swagger.yaml');


    /* .... */


    var express = require('express');
    var app = express();


    app.use('/api-docs', swaggerUi.serve, swaggerUi.setup
    (swaggerDocument));


    app.get('/', function (req, res) {
        res.send('Hello, My server using Express');
    });
```

```
var server = app.listen(8081, function () {
   var host = server.address().address;
   var port = server.address().port;


   console.log("Server is listening at http://%s:%s", host, port)
});
```

Now, when we try to browse our Swagger URL using http://localhost:8081/api-docs/

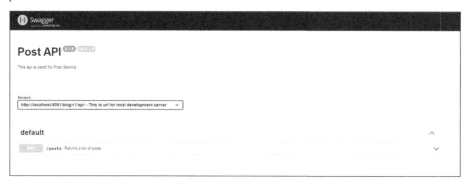

**Figure 4.3**: *Demo for setting up Swagger with Node.js*

# Request Validations

Validation is required for all kinds of RESTful services that prevent clients from sending unwanted data to the server. When we receive a request to create a user, we must validate the content being sent inside the request. We must return the correct error response to the client if a request is invalid.

In order to add validation support to Express applications, we might need to understand some of the middleware responsible for performing validation, as follows:

- **body-parser**: This is a Node.js request-body parsing middleware that is responsible for parsing the incoming request-body before handlers logic is executed, and all the client data can be accessed through the req.body attribute.

- **Express Validator**: Express Validator is a Node.js middleware that uses the validator.js library responsible for validation and sanitization using inbuilt functions. In other words, Express Validator is a middleware library that helps to validate your server-side data.

# Validating Request Body

Let's take an example of user registration, where the input must be sent from the client to our server, which includes the following data:

| Field | Requirement |
|---|---|
| Full name | A string with a length in the range of 2 and 50 |
| Email address | It must be a valid email address |
| Password | It must be a string containing only letters and numbers with a minimum of 8 characters |
| Password confirmation | It must be equal to the password field |

*Table 4.1*: List of properties sent for user registration

Create a **validation.js** file and add the following code:

```
const { check } = require('express-validator');
exports.registrationValidation = [
    check('name', 'Name is required').not().isEmpty(),
    check('email', 'Please include a valid
email').isEmail().normalizeEmail({ gmail_remove_dots: true }),
    check('password', 'Password must be 8 or more alphanumeric
characters').isLength({ min: 8 })
]
```

Here, we are putting together all the validation requirements for user registration, such as:

- What should be mandatory and optional fields?
- What should be the length of each field?
- What are valid characters that will be accepted?
- What is the error message that needs to be returned in case of invalid input?

Let's create a **http_request_validation.js** file to test the validation function and add the following backend server code:

```
const express = require('express');
const bodyParser = require('body-parser');
const validator = require('./validator');
const {
    validationResult
} = require('express-validator')

const app = express();

app.use(express.json());
app.use(bodyParser.json());
app.use(bodyParser.urlencoded({
    extended: true
}));

app.post('/register', validator.registrationValidation,
(req, res, next) => {
    // your registration code
    const errors = validationResult(req);
    if (errors.isEmpty()) {
        // in case request params meet the validation criteria
        console.log('User registration is done');
        res.send("User registration successfull");
    }

    res.status(400).json({
        errors: errors.array()
    })
});
```

```
app.listen(3000, () => console.log('Server is running on port
3000'));
```

To check the validation function, we will pass the following data using Postman:

```
{
    name: "John DOE",
    email: "john.doe@gmail.com",
    password: "Aes",
    confirmPassword: "Aest03Luxi74",
}
```

For the preceding data, `registrationValidator()` function will check for a given input and validate against validation definitions provided by us for user registration. If the client passes the correct input, then user registration will continue and logic defined inside the POST method will be executed. Otherwise, in case of invalid input, the client will get an error response back from the validator function.

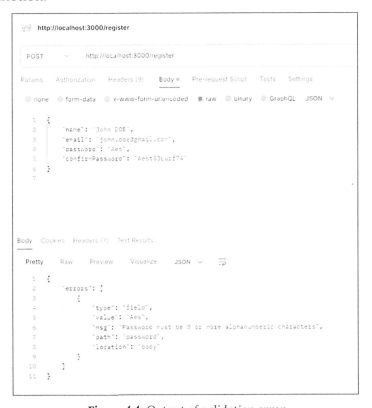

***Figure 4.4****: Output of validation error*

# Request Transformation

This is a process to convert our incoming requests into different forms that are accepted by the server. For example, clients can send requests to backend servers through different platforms like desktop, web, and mobile apps.

For example, a client has a requirement to convert incoming requests from JSON to XML, and for this, we can use two popular middleware, **body-parser** and **xml2js**:

```
const express = require('express');
const bodyParser = require('body-parser');
var mung = require('express-mung');
var parseString = require('xml2js').parseString;


let app = express();


app.use(bodyParser.json());
app.use(bodyParser.raw({ type: () => true }));


// ... everything we have above goes here ...
//Request Data Transformation
app.use((req, res, next) => {
    if (/\/xml$/.test(req.headers['content-type'])) {
        parseString(req.body.toString(), function (err,
result) {
            console.dir(result);
            req.body = result;
        });
    }
    next();
});
```

The preceding code should look very familiar, as it is similar to what we have already written to create our backend server. Here, we are using the **body-parser** to parse requests using the **use()** function defined on the application object that is created using Express. The **body-parser** analyzes incoming requests to know if JSON body content matches the content type defined in the request header.

Now, the most important question arises: why do we need to use the **bodyParser.raw()** line at all? This happens when a client hits our API with a different type of information. It can be XML or something else! The **raw()** middleware allows us to be flexible in our gateway to add more content types in the future:

```
//Request Data Transformation
app.use((req, res, next) => {
    if (/\/xml$/.test(req.headers['content-type'])) {
        parseString(req.body.toString(), function (err, result) {
            console.dir(result);
            req.body = result;
        });
    }
    next();
});
```

This middleware works for all RESTful method types and checks the content-type attribute defined in the request header each time. If the middleware finds that there is **/xml** at the end of the header, our middleware function takes the "raw" body data (which is actually a buffer) and **xml2js** converts the JSON into an actual JavaScript object, replacing **req.body** with that object.

This operation is very similar to what **bodyParser.json()** does when the content-type is defined as **application/json**.

In the given transformation middleware function defined earlier, we can do many things with the data before it reaches the Express route and process logic.

**Figure 4.5**: *Output of request transformation XML to JSON*

# Response Transformation

In Express backend services, handling incoming requests is a simple process, and most of the time Express itself provides all the necessary tools that can help us in performing request transformation.

When we convert outgoing responses to the desired format, as expected by the client, it requires more work and effort. To understand this process, let's take one of the simple use cases of converting JSON response to XML using **express-mung** package.

Response transformation can be done in the following steps:

1. **Installing express-mung package**

2. **Adding Middleware to the default route**

Once we add this middleware, requests are forwarded to their endpoints before actual application logic gets executed. The reason we need to perform this operation before our route code execution is that we need to attach the response object's data stream to prevent it from being returned to the client before the "communication" is complete:

```
//Response Data Transformation
app.use(mung.json((body, req, res) => {
    console.log("xml", /\xml$/.test(req.url));
    if (/\xml$/.test(req.url)) {
        var builder = new xml2js.Builder();
        var xml = builder.buildObject(body);
        return xml;
    }
}));
```

The preceding code checks the request URL for **xml** keyword. If the test succeeds, the response body is converted from the default JSON to XML and returned a response to the client.

In this example, if a client has made a request using URL **/api/sample**, it would receive the default JSON response. However, if a client requires data in the form of XML, then they can make a request using **/api/sample/xml**, and the same JSON data will be transformed into XML before being returned to the client.

3. **Setting correct Response header**

For Express to make corrections correctly and identify what content needs to be sent back to the client, we also need to change the Content-Type header of the response. We can use a separate middleware provided by the **mung** package to change the header:

```
app.use(mung.headers((req, res) => {
    if (/\xml$/.test(req.url)) {
        res.set('Content-Type', 'text/xml');
    }
}));
```

After we have made this change, the client can send the proper header while making the request, and the backend Express application will process the request accordingly, sending back a response in the form of XML.

**Figure 4.6**: *Output of response transformation JSON to XML*

# Understanding HTTP Status Codes

An HTTP status code is the server's response to a browser request. When you visit a website, your browser sends a request to the website's server, and the server then responds to the browser's request with a three-digit code: the HTTP status code.

These status codes are the Internet equivalent of a conversation between your browser and a server. They communicate when things between the two of them are A-okay, when touch and go, or when something is off. Understanding status codes and their usage will help you quickly diagnose website errors and minimize website downtime. You can even use some of these status codes to help search engines and people find your site. For example, a 301 redirect tells bots and humans that the page has permanently moved somewhere else.

The first digit of each three-digit status code begins with one of five digits, 1 through 5; you may see it expressed as 1xx or 5xx to indicate status codes for that area. Each of these areas contains a different class of server responses.

Some of the common HTTP status code categories are as follows:

- **1xx**: Informational responses mean the server is considering or processing the request.
- **2xx**: Success response means that the request was completed and successfully processed by the server, returning the expected response to the browser.
- **3xx**: Redirect means that you will be redirected. The request was received, but there is some kind of redirect to another website.
- **4xx**: Request errors, which include page not found, page could not be accessed, or don't have permission to view content.
- **5xx**: Server errors mean that the request was made correctly but the server was unable to process the request due to some error.

Following are some of the common HTTP status codes:

| HTTP Code | Title | Description |
| --- | --- | --- |
| 200 | OK | Request has succeeded |
| 201 | Created | Request has been fulfilled and resources are created |
| 202 | Accepted | Request has been accepted for processing but not completed |
| 204 | No Content | Server has successfully fulfilled the request and no content is returned to the browser |
| 301 | Moved Permanently | Target resource has been assigned a new permanent URI and all future references to this resource must use one of the enclosed URIs |
| 302 | Found | Target resource resides temporarily under a different URI |
| 400 | Bad Request | Server cannot or will not process the request due to malformed request syntax, or invalid request |
| 401 | Unauthorized | Request does not have authentication credentials for the target resource |
| 403 | Forbidden | Server understood the request but refused to authorize it |

| 404 | Not Found | Server was unable to find relevant request |
| 405 | Method Not Allowed | Method not supported by the target resource |
| 500 | Internal Server Error | The Server encountered an unexpected condition while processing the request |
| 501 | Not Implemented | Server does not support the functionality required to fulfill the request |
| 502 | Bad Gateway | Gateway or proxy return error, while the server was waiting to process the request |
| 503 | Service Unavailable | Server is currently unable to handle the request due to maintenance or service was down |
| 504 | Gateway Timeout | Gateway or proxy did not receive a timely response from an upstream server |

*Table 4.2*: *List of HTTP Status Codes*

# CORS Request Handling with Express

**What is CORS?**

CORS stands for Cross-Origin Resource Sharing. It allows clients to make API service calls by overriding some of the security applied to an API. This is done by bypassing the **Access-Control-Allow-Origin** headers, which tell browsers which origins can be accessed by a given API.

**In other words**, CORS is an inbuilt browser security feature, which restricts clients or users from making cross-origin HTTP requests from one server to another server and specifies what all domains can access your resources.

**How does CORS work?**

We can deploy frontend applications either combined or separately on different servers, which are based on either N-Tier application architecture or a Microservice. Depending on which model we follow to design our application, we can have two options to handle requests across different servers and enable clients to make requests.

- The client and server have the same origin.

  In this case, the resource can be accessed from the same domain because all application code has been deployed on the same server. You are trying to access your server's resources like static HTML, images, files, or dynamic data using APIs. The same server is processing the request.

- The client and the server have different origins.

  Here, applications are deployed across different servers like frontend applications deployed on XYZ server and backend API services on server ABC. When a client makes a request through a frontend application running on a client browser, an application fails to load data from API calls on different servers due to a cross-origin request policy defined on the client browser.

This is a browser default security policy and prevents applications from making requests that are from different domains.

CORS helps applications by enabling them to allow access to resources on different servers. CORS adds an **access-control-allow-origins** header to the response object and the client can specify which origins are allowed for a given application. The browser on the client machine looks at this header and decides whether or not the response is safe to deliver to the client.

# Configuring CORS with Express

Let's create a simple Express HTTP server endpoint that serves a GET response:

```
const express = require('express');
const app = express();
const users = [{
        Name: 'test', phone: 324234234
}];
app.get('/users', (req, res) =>{
    res.send(users);
});
app.listen(6069);
```

Start the server with npm nodemon.

Go to **http://localhost:6069/users** in your browser.

In this example, CORS is enabled by default because we are currently serving the request from the same domain, and the client making this request from the same domain.

Now, let's try to get the users to use the search command by creating a dummy HTML page and making an AJAX call using JavaScript:

```html
<!DOCTYPE html>
<html lang="en">
<head>
    <title>Document</title>
    <script>
        function run() {

            // Creating Our XMLHttpRequest object
            let xhr = new XMLHttpRequest();

            // Making our connection
            var url = 'http://localhost:6069/users';
            xhr.open("GET", url, true);

            // function execute after request is successful
            xhr.onreadystatechange = function () {
                if (this.readyState == 4 && this.status == 200) {
                    console.log(this.responseText);
                }
            }
            // Sending our request
            xhr.send();

        }
        run();
    </script>
</head>
<body>
```

```
</body>

</html>
```

Let's start the backend server by running the following command:

```
PS D:\Book\Building-Real-Time-application-using-Node.js\chap_04>
node .\express_cors.js
```

After running, you will get an error saying the **CORS module is not found**.

```
PS D:\Book\Building-Real-Time-application-using-Node.js\chap_04> node .\express_cors.js
internal/modules/cjs/loader.js:834
  throw err;
    at require (internal/modules/cjs/helpers.js:74:18)
    at Object.<anonymous> (D:\Book\Building-Real-Time-application-using-Node.js\chap_04\express_cors.js:23:14)
    at Module._compile (internal/modules/cjs/loader.js:1015:30)
    at Object.Module._extensions..js (internal/modules/cjs/loader.js:1035:10)
    at Module.load (internal/modules/cjs/loader.js:879:32)
    at Function.Module._load (internal/modules/cjs/loader.js:724:14)
    at Function.executeUserEntryPoint [as runMain] (internal/modules/run_main.js:60:12) {
  code: 'MODULE_NOT_FOUND',
  requireStack: [
    'D:\\Book\\Building-Real-Time-application-using-Node.js\\chap_04\\express_cors.js'
  ]
}
PS D:\Book\Building-Real-Time-application-using-Node.js\chap_04> []
```

**Figure 4.7**: *Output of running CORS cmd*

Run the following command to install CORS locally:

```
PS D:\Book\Building-Real-Time-application-using-Node.js\chap_04> npm i cors
npm WARN sample@1.0.0 No repository field.

+ cors@2.8.5
added 2 packages from 2 contributors and audited 87 packages in 1.055s

8 packages are looking for funding
  run `npm fund` for details

found 0 vulnerabilities

PS D:\Book\Building-Real-Time-application-using-Node.js\chap_04> []
```

**Figure 4.8**: *Output of installing CORS locally*

Open http://localhost:3000/ in your browser and make the following AJAX request from the browser console.

Make sure the server is running before performing the preceding query.

```
function run() {

    // Creating Our XMLHttpRequest object
    let xhr = new XMLHttpRequest();

    // Making our connection
    var url = 'http://localhost:5001/users';
    xhr.open("GET", url, true);

    // function execute after request is successful
    xhr.onreadystatechange = function () {
        if (this.readyState == 4 && this.status == 200) {
            console.log(this.responseText);
        }
    }
    // Sending our request
    xhr.send();
}
run();
```

**Figure 4.9**: *JavaScript code to make AJAX call*

We are looking for information about users from a backend server running on another origin, but the origin of this URL is not allowed to receive a response from this server. That's why it throws a CORS error.

**Figure 4.10**: *Output of CORS error in the browser*

In order to resolve this error, we might need to add a CORS header to the server and give http://localhost:3000/ access to the server response. Add the following information to the index.js file:

```
app.use(cors({
    origin: 'http://localhost:3000/'
}));
app.get('/users', cors(), (req, res, next) => {
    res.send(users);
});
```

If you run the application again, it should work fine, and you will see the following output in the console:

**Figure 4.11**: *Application output in the console*

This means that you only have access to our server resources. You can have several of these multiple sources, as shown:

```
const cors = require('cors');
app.use(cors({
    origin: ['http://localhost:3000/', 'https://www.google.com/']
}));
```

However, an API can be public, and these resources can be accessed by interfaces and servers from various origins. The following code block ensures that all pages can use the users:

```
app.use(cors({
    origin: '*'
}));
```

The * symbol is used to create a CORS header, and any origin can now receive a response from that localhost server without throwing a CORS error.

We can add specific RESTful methods, including **GET**, **POST**, **DELETE**, **UPDATE**, and **OPTIONS** while configuring **CORS** response:

```
app.use(cors({
    methods: ['GET', 'POST', 'DELETE', 'UPDATE', 'PUT', 'PATCH']
}));
```

# API Error Handling

Error handling refers to the process of catching and handling errors that occur while Express handles request and process logics. Express comes with a default error handler, which is used for most cases, eliminating the need to write any extra code to handle errors. We need to make sure that Express catches any type of errors that occur while executing route logic using error handling middleware.

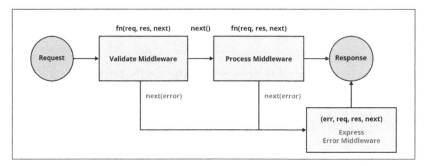

*Figure 4.12*: *Express error handling mechanism*

For example, the following code can be used to throw an error directly:

```
app.get('/', (req, res) => {
    throw new Error('BROKEN') // Express will catch this on its
own.
})
```

### Error Using Route Manager Functions

One way to handle errors in Express applications is to apply error-handling logic directly into individual route functions. Inside the route, we can check for specific error conditions or use try-catch to automatically handle all errors.

Following is an example of error handling in the route manager function:

```
const express = require('express');
const app = express();
// handle post request for path /employees
app.post('/employees', (request, response) => {
  const name = request.body.name;
  // Check for error condition
```

```
    if (name == null) {
      // Error handling logic: log the error
      console.log("input error")
      // Error handling logic: return error response
      response.status(400).json({ message: "Mandatory field: name is
    missing" })
    } else {
      const empCreationResponse = { result: "success" }
      // return success response
      response.json(empCreationResponse)
    }
  })
```

Here, we are checking for an error condition, that is, the name is a required input in the request payload, and returning the error whenever the name is not provided in the request payload

The following example uses a try-catch block to handle errors:

```
app.get('/employees', async (request, response) => {
  try{
    const apiResponse = await axios.get("http://localhost:3001/
  employees");
    const jsonResponse = apiResponse.data;
    console.log("response " + jsonResponse);
    response.send(jsonResponse);
  } catch(error) {
    // return error response
    response.status(500).json({ message: "Error in invocation of
  API: /employees" });
  }
})
```

In this code, we have seen how to log the error in the catch block and return an error message with error code 500 in the HTTP response to the client.

It seems like a very simple use case, but this way of adding error-handling logic into every route function is not a clean approach.

Next, we try to handle this more cleanly using Express middleware, as explained in the following sections.

**Express' Built-in Default Error Handler**

When we use the Express framework, a default error handler function is defined that catches and handles errors in our web application:

```
const express = require('express');

const app = express();

// handle get request for path /users with error

app.get('/userswitherror', (request, response) => {

  // throw an error with status code of 400

  let error = new Error(`processing error in request at
${request.url}`)

  error.statusCode = 400;

  throw error;

})

const port = 3000;

app.listen(port, () => console.log(`Server listening on port
${port}.`));
```

When we run this code, we get an error with **status  code 400** and an error message: **Processing error in request**.

Here, we don't need to handle this error because this is being handled by the default Express's error handler.

However, this default error handler is not a very good and user-friendly way to provide detailed information about the error to the client. This can be greatly improved by Error handling using middleware functions.

**Error Handling Using Middleware Functions**

When an error occurs, we call **next(error)**  and pass the error object as input to the next middleware function, which is defined as an error handler function:

```
const express = require('express');

const axios = require("axios");

const app = express();

const errorHandler = (error, request, response, next) => {
```

```
        console.log(`error ${error.message}`)
        const status = error.status || 400
        // send back an easily understandable error message to the
    caller
        response.status(status).send(error.message);
    }
    app.get('/users', async (request, response) => {
        try {
            const apiResponse = await axios.get("http://
    localhost:3001/users");
            const jsonResponse = apiResponse.data;
            response.send(jsonResponse);
        } catch (error) {
            next(error); // calling next error handling middleware
        }
    })
    app.use(errorHandler);
```

Here, we are using a try-catch block to just catch errors when something wrong happens, but the actual implementation of error handling is being done inside **errorHandler()** function.

Middleware error handling functions are defined in the same way as other middleware functions, but they accept an **error** object as the first input parameter, followed by a **request**, a **response**, and the **next** object parameter as follows:

```
    const errorHandler = (error, request, response, next) => { }
```

# Conclusion

In this chapter, we have focused on learning some of the core concepts related to RESTful API services and how we can create a backend Node.js Service from scratch. We also covered important concepts like request/response handling by creating our own HTTP server.

In the next chapter, we will learn about one of the popular NoSQL databases, **MongoDB**. Here, we will try to explain some of the core concepts of MongoDB and perform some practical tasks related to installing and connecting to MongoDB on the local system.

# Further Readings

You can use the following online resources to gain more understanding of RESTful API services:

- https://www.tutorialspoint.com/restful/index.htm
- https://aws.amazon.com/what-is/restful-api/
- https://www.digitalocean.com/community/tutorials/restful-web-services-tutorial-java
- https://developer.ibm.com/articles/ws-restful/
- https://restfulapi.net/

# CHAPTER 5

# Working with MongoDB

## Introduction

In this chapter, we will delve deeper into working with databases while building web applications using the Node.js tech stack. Here, we will cover some basics about one of the popular databases from the NoSQL world, **MongoDB.** We will learn how to connect and create some entities using available Node packages like Mongoose or Mongo client.

## Structure

This chapter will cover some of the following topics related to MongoDB:

- Introducing Database
- SQL vs. NoSQL
- MongoDB
- Installation of MongoDB Locally
- Creating the First Connection to the Database
- Performing Database Operation Using Mongo-CLI

## Introducing Database

The term database represents a set of tools that are used to organize the collection of information. Alternatively, we can describe a database as an electronic framework that helps to store, process, and update information in digital format.

The database is one of the foundations in building any kind of web application that handles data in an organized and controlled way.

Let's understand from *Figure 5.1*:

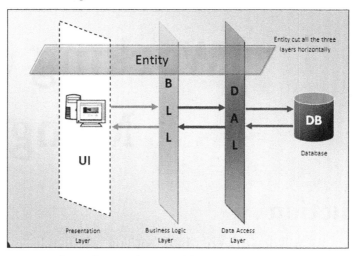

**Figure 5.1**: *Database used for persistent storage*

As you can see from the preceding diagram, databases help in storing data permanently and can be retrieved whenever required over the network using Application Programming Interface (APIs). A client running an application using a browser, represented by the Presentation Layer, requests a backend server to process data and return a response. During this process, requests go through various layers like Presentation, Business, and Data Access layers. When it comes to accessing data, services are writing a Data Access layer that talks to the database and returns the required information to the business layer, which runs specific logics before returning the final response to the client.

# Use Case of Database

Banking applications are required to save thousands of real-time data for their customers. For developing these kinds of applications, banks normally use transactional databases like SQL Server, which provides an easy way to store relational data with proper relationships among entities.

For example, the following figure shows how banking applications store information related to accounts, branches, customers, employees, and loans using different tables:

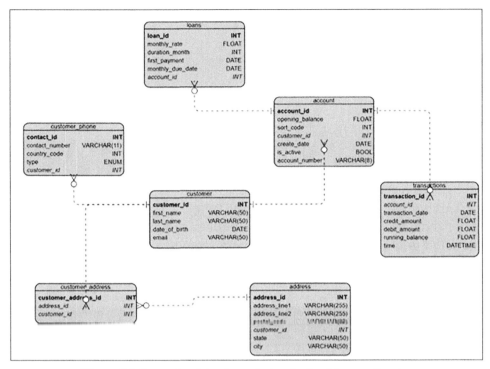

***Figure 5.2***: *Example of database design for Banking application*

# Types of Database

There are two main types of database collections, which can be further divided into multiple subcategories.

### Relational database

Data are organized or stored in tables with rows and columns in these types of databases. Here, each row is a record and each column is a field label. This structure makes it easy to query and manipulate data using Structured Query Language (SQL).

For example, suppose you want to plot weather data at a specific date or time. In that case, you can create it like this:

- Table: Weather
- Columns: Date
- Rows: Time of day
- Data points: Fahrenheit

Some popular SQL database systems are as follows:

- Oracle
- Microsoft SQL Server
- PostgreSQL
- MySQL
- MariaDB

**Non-Relational database**

A non-relational database, also known as a NoSQL database, is a type of database that does not use a traditional table-based relational structure. In contrast, non-relational databases use different data models, such as key-value, text, column family, and graph. This allows greater data storage and management flexibility, especially for large-scale, distributed, and unstructured data. Let's look at the different unrelated data models individually to break them down.

The popular NoSQL databases include the following:

- MongoDB
- Google Cloud Firestore
- Cassandra
- Redis
- Apache HBase
- Amazon DynamoDB

The following are the main differences between SQL and NoSQL:

| Relational database | Non-relational database |
|---|---|
| These databases have fixed, static, or predefined schema | They have a dynamic schema |
| These databases are not suited for hierarchical data storage | These databases are best suited for hierarchical data storage |
| These databases are best suited for complex queries | These databases are not so good for complex queries |
| Vertically scalable | Horizontally scalable |
| Follows ACID property | Follows CAP (consistency, availability, partition tolerance) |
| Examples: MySQL, PostgreSQL, Oracle, MS-SQL Server, and so on | Examples: MongoDB, GraphQL, HBase, Neo4j, Cassandra, and so on |

*Table 5.1: Difference between SQL and NoSQL*

# Advantages of Using Databases

Some of the main advantages of using databases are as follows:

- Reduced data redundancy
- Reduced updating errors and increased consistency
- Greater data integrity and independence from application programs
- Improved data access to users through the use of host and query languages
- Improved data security
- Reduced data entry, storage, and retrieval costs

# Disadvantages of Using Databases

The following are the disadvantages of using databases:

- Increases application design complexity
- Additional cost of buying hardware or license
- Additional Data security is required to maintain information secure
- Database compatibility with the application

# Database Management System (DBMS)

Database Management System (DBMS) is a collection of tools that help clients access databases, control stored information, manipulate information, and generate reports. The database engine inside DBMS enables data access, locking, and modification of desired data. The database schema defines the logical structure of the database in which data will be stored. The DBMS ensures concurrency, security, data integrity, and consistent data management across multiple databases.

# Usage of DBMS

A DBMS is widely used for the following management tasks:

- Change management
- Performance monitoring and tuning
- Security
- Backup and recovery
- Logging and monitoring the activities of databases and the applications that use them

A DBMS provides tools for clients to get a centralized view of data that multiple users can access with a certain set of permissions and privileges. The DBMS can apply user-level privileges to limit the data visible to the end client.

Some of the key DBMS tools available in the market are as follows:

- **MySQL Workbench**

  MySQL Workbench is an optional downloadable tool that provides additional support for MySQL tools. Oracle provides this tool for free to manage MySQL databases. We can use this tool to complete many data management tasks, but it is primarily used to improve data modeling techniques and SQL development.

- **Microsoft Server SQL Management Studio**

  Microsoft Server SQL Management Studio is a free tool that allows users more design options using graphical tools when creating tables and graphs for their data. This helps to record your system when new data is created or existing data is updated. The tool also creates database diagrams that show the complete database design and its structure and help you modify data, tables, columns, and relationships.

- **SQL Developer**

  SQL Developer is an open-source DBMS tool that helps you create, design, and perform other database management tasks. This tool is used for data management in Oracle databases and helps manage end-to-end database applications. SQL Developer is a very lightweight and fast tool that can be used on any system without many performance issues.

- **PgAdmin**

  PgAdmin4 is a powerful database management solution for PostgreSQL database. This is a very simple and useful tool for any application that uses PostgreSQL as the main database. It is an open-source tool that offers an easy-to-use interface and is compatible with all major operating systems.

- **MongoDB Compass**

  The MongoDB project provides a powerful graphical user interface called MongoDB Compass. Compass allows us to access most of the features provided by the MongoDB database engine through a visual interface. This tool helps to explore databases, collections, and individual documents, create interactive queries, manipulate existing documents, and design build pipelines through a single interface.

# Types of Data Models in DBMS

The DBMS can be divided into five major types based on data models:

- **Hierarchical Model**

  This kind of DBMS utilizes the **parent-child** relationship of putting away information and is seldom used these days. Its structure is like a tree, with hubs speaking to records and branches speaking to areas. The Windows registry utilized in Windows XP is an illustration of a progressive database. Arrangement settings are put away as tree structures with nodes.

- **Network Model**

  This sort of DBMS underpins many-to-many relations. This ordinarily comes about in complex database structures. RDM Server is an illustration of a database administration framework that actualizes the organized model.

- **Relational Model**

  This sort of DBMS characterizes database connections within the shape of tables, also known as relations. Unlike organizing DBMS, RDBMS does not bolster numerous connections. Social DBMS ordinarily has pre-defined information sorts that it can support. This is the most prevalent DBMS sort within the advertisement. Illustrations of social database administration frameworks incorporate MySQL, Prophet, and Microsoft SQL Server databases.

- **Object-oriented Model**

  This sort bolsters the capacity of new data sorts. The information to be put away is within the frame of objects. The objects to be put away within the database have qualities (that is, sexual orientation and age) and strategies that characterize what to do with the information. PostgreSQL is an illustration of an object-oriented social DBMS.

- **Entity-Relationship Model (ER)**

  In this type of ER database model, objects of interest are grouped together into entities as relationships, and their properties are grouped into assets. These relationships are used as glue to connect different entities together to form a complete database. The ER model is designed in such a way that relationships are used to describe entire functional or business logic so that multiple stakeholders can understand.

# Advantages of DBMS

Here are some of the advantages of DBMS:

- DBMS offers an assortment of procedures to store and recover data.
- DBMS serves as a proficient handler to adjust the desires of different applications utilizing the same data.
- It ensures uniform organization methods for data.
- Application software engineers never uncover subtle elements of information of data representation and storage.
- A DBMS employs various robust capacities to store and recover information efficiently.
- It offers information astuteness and security.
- The DBMS infers judgment limitations to induce a high level of security against denied access to data.
- DBMS plans concurrent access to the information in such a way that only one client can access the same information at a time.
- Reduced application advancement time.

# Disadvantages of DBMS

DBMS may offer a bounty of preferences, but it has certain flaws:

- The cost of equipment and programs of a DBMS is very high, which increases the budget of your organization.
- Most database administration frameworks are regularly complex frameworks, so the preparation for clients to utilize the DBMS is required.
- In a few organizations, all information is coordinated into a single database, which can be harmed because of electric disappointment, or the database is debased on the capacity media.
- Use of the same program at a time by numerous clients in some cases leads to the misfortune of a few data.
- DBMS can't perform modern calculations.

# ACID Properties in DBMS

Databases are meant to have constant changes in data, and every DBMS system needs to make sure that they handle all changes gracefully without corrupting data. Once the data has been modified, its integrity must be maintained. This is very important because when data integrity has been compromised, the entire dataset is corrupted, and in turn, it puts the entire database in an inconsistent state. The contents of a database can be accessed and modified as part of a single logical unit of operation called a **Transaction**.

These transactions access data through read-and-write operations. To ensure consistency, data transactions must always remember certain characteristics called **ACID** (atomicity, consistency, isolation, and durability).

The following are the key ACID properties that DBMS software should follow:

- **Atomicity**

  Atomicity refers to database operation where all transactions happen simultaneously or none of them happen at all. In the DBMS system, transactions can't be completed partially in parts. Each transaction is considered a separate process, and it may be marked as a complete or incomplete transaction once DBMS has processed the entire operation.

  Only two situations can happen here:

  - **Acceptance**: When a transaction has been completed, and all the changes are committed to the database, the entire change request is accepted, maintaining data integrity.
  - **Rollback**: When any transaction fails, DBMS doesn't commit any changes to the database, and we won't see any changes that were made.

- **Consistency**

  We need to maintain reliability requirements for certain databases to ensure consistency before and after transfers. Data integrity must be maintained by the DBMS software, ensuring the protection of all data changes at all times. Data integrity is very important when transactions occur because it ensures the consistency of the data stored in the database just before and after a transaction has been completed. When one or more clients request any information, accurate data has to be delivered each time.

- **Isolation**

  When multiple clients use web applications from different locations, multiple transactions can be performed simultaneously, so that the database conditions are not identical. In most of these cases, separate or unrelated transactions happen that can cause problems. Changes made by one transaction are not visible to any other transactions unless changes specific to that transaction are saved successfully. Isolation plays an important role when transactions are executed concurrently by making sure that all the transaction happens separately and requests are processed in the order they were called.

- **Durability**

    Durability in a DBMS means ensuring that data remains in the database after a task is completed. The data must be robust enough to continue working even if the system crashes or errors occur while the application used. However, after any incident has occurred, the recovery manager is now responsible for ensuring the integrity of the database. Each time data is modified, we must commit the configuration or data changes using the `COMMIT` command. Durability ensures that data updates and changes are written and saved to disk after the transaction has been completed successfully.

# Basics of MongoDB

Here, we are going to cover some of the basic topics about MongoDB.

MongoDB is an open-source NoSQL database administration program. NoSQL (Not as it were SQL) is utilized as an elective to conventional social databases. NoSQL databases are very valuable for working with expansive sets of disseminated information. MongoDB is an instrument that can oversee document-oriented data and store or recover information.

MongoDB is utilized for high-volume information capacity, making a difference when organizations store expansive sums of information while still performing quickly. Organizations moreover utilize MongoDB for its ad-hoc questions, ordering, stack adjusting, conglomeration, server-side JavaScript execution, and other features.

Structured Inquiry Dialect (SQL) is a standardized programming dialect used to oversee social databases. SQL normalizes information as patterns and tables, and each table incorporates a settled structure.

Instead of utilizing tables and lines as in social databases, as a NoSQL database, the MongoDB design is made up of collections and records. Records are made up of key-value sets, MongoDB's essential unit of information. Collections, identical to SQL tables, contain archive sets. MongoDB offers bolster for many programming dialects, such as C, C#, Go, Java, Python, Ruby, and Swift.

# RDBMS versus MongoDB

The following are some of the key differences between RDBMS and MongoDB:

- RDBMS is typically based on schema structure, while MongoDB is document-oriented.

- RDBMS supports complex transactions using join between related entities or tables, while MongoDB does not support complex transactions using join operations.

- MongoDB performance is very good in terms of searching as compared to RDBMS. This is possible because all documents are stored in BSON format, and the new format helps in better parsing of data.

- MongoDB allows a very flexible and scalable document structure, whereas in RDBMS, the table and schema structure are fixed, maintaining relationships between tables.

- In RDBMS, all data is stored in a table, whereas a collection is used in MongoDB to store documents.

- MongoDB provides a "**_id**" field, which is a 12-byte hexadecimal number that ensures the uniqueness of each document. For the same, we use the primary key inside the RDBMS database.

# Key Components of MongoDB Architecture

Following are a few of the common terms used in MongoDB:

- **_id**: This is a mandatory field in every MongoDB document and represents a unique MongoDB document, similar to the primary key in the SQL database. When we create a new document, an **_id** field is automatically created if not provided.

- **Collection**: This is a way of grouping MongoDB documents. A collection is the equivalent of a table which is used to store information in SQL databases. For example, when we want to store employee information, we will create an employee collection and add employee-related documents.

- **Cursor**: This is a pointer to the result set of a query. Clients can iterate through a cursor to retrieve results.

- **Database**: This is a container for all collections, similar to RDBMS where databases store tables. When we create multiple databases, each database has its own set of files on the file system. A MongoDB server can store multiple databases.

- **Document**: A document in a MongoDB collection stores information very similar to rows inside a table in an SQL database. The document is stored in JSON format and consists of fields in key and value pairs.

- **Field**: These key-value pairs are used to store all the information in the JSON document. In the following example, we are storing user information, including name, age, groups, and more:

```
{
    "name": "sue", //Field to store name value
    "age": 25,       // Field to store age
    "status": "A",
    "groups":["news", "sports"]
}
```

- **JSON**: JavaScript Object Notation has become the default standard for data representation, which is supported by multiple languages and platforms.

```
{
    "data": [
        {
            "code": "altel10",
            "item_name": "Water Bottle",
            "price": 39750,
            "type": "plastic",
            "status": "active"
        },
        {
            "code": "altel10",
            "item_name": "Water Bottle",
            "price": 39750,
            "type": "plastic",
            "status": "active"
        }
    ]
}
```

*Figure 5.3*: *JSON object in MongoDB*

- **BSON**: BSON stands for **Binary JSON**. BSON's binary structure encodes different information types and lengths, making navigation and searching faster than JSON. BSON adds some basic non-JSON data types, such as dates and binary data. Without BSON, MongoDB would lose some important native support.

Following are sample JSON objects and their BSON responses, which are stored in the MongoDB database:

```
{"hello": "world"} →
\x16\x00\x00\x00           // total document size
\x02                       // 0x02 = type String
hello\x00                  // field name
\x06\x00\x00\x00world\x00  // field value
\x00                       // 0x00 = type EOO ('end of object')
```

# How MongoDB Works

MongoDB is a perfect database for clients who want to develop web applications that are really fast, real-time, and mostly work with raw data. MongoDB stores all information in the form of collections and documents that are easily searchable.

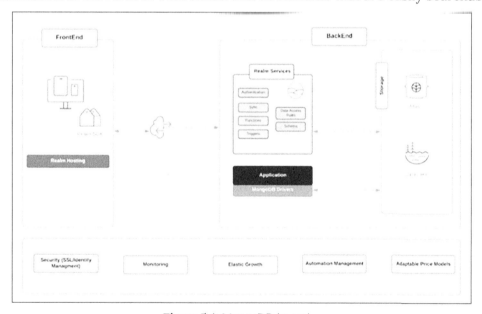

**Figure 5.4**: *MongoDB in action*

Every database engine has a very complex internal architecture that allows it to perform multiple tasks at the same time and handle all requests efficiently. MongoDB working can be divided into basically two layers:

- Application Layer
- Data Layer

The Application Layer has two subparts: the first part, which we can call the Frontend or application interface, is used by the user, and the second part is the actual backend server. The frontend or user interface is used by the users to access MongoDB via the web or mobile. The backend system contains the server that is used to run the logic using controllers or the Mongo shell, which communicates queries to the MongoDB server.

When a client makes a request, the MongoDB server receives the requests and forwards all the received requests to the MongoDB storage engine. The MongoDB server itself does not read or write data directly to files or to disk or memory. After passing the received requests to the storage engine, the storage engine is responsible for reading or writing data to a file or memory, which basically manages the data.

## Features of MongoDB

The following are the different features of MongoDB:

- **Replication**: A reproduction set is two or more MongoDB occurrences utilized to supply tall accessibility. Replica sets are made of essential and auxiliary servers. The primary MongoDB server performs all the examined and composed operations, whereas the auxiliary reproduction keeps a copy of the information. In the event that an essential reproduction falls flat, the auxiliary reproduction is at that point used.

- **Scalability**: MongoDB supports vertical and flat scaling. Vertical scaling works by including more control to an existing machine, whereas even scaling works by adding more machines to a user's resources.

- **Load adjusting**: MongoDB handles stack adjusting without the requirement for a separate, dedicated stack balancer, either through vertical or horizontal scaling.

- **Schema-less:** MongoDB could be a schema-less database, which suggests the database can oversee information without requiring a blueprint.

- **Document**: Information in MongoDB is put away in records with key-value sets rather than lines and columns, which makes the information more flexible when compared to SQL databases.

## Advantages of MongoDB

MongoDB brings many advantages to tables. The following are the key benefits:

- It is cheaper and easier to maintain MongoDB databases.

- MongoDB has flexible data allocation, flexible data models, and automatic recovery, which helps to reduce operating costs.

- It is open source and cheaper for developers.

- MongoDB databases use smaller database storage, so they cost less per gigabyte for data storage and processing.

- It supports built-in caching that improves data retrieval performance.

- MongoDB has no problems when data models and formats are changed whenever required, without causing any issues to existing applications.

- MongoDB provides many useful features, making it an easy-to-use NoSQL database.

## Disadvantages of MongoDB

Though there are a few profitable benefits to MongoDB, there are some drawbacks:

- **Continuity**: With a programmed failover methodology, the client has one or more nodes within the MongoDB cluster. In the event of a failure, the other node will naturally start and continue to serve requests. This switch guarantees progression, but it's not instantaneous – it can take up to a minute or more.

- **Write limitations**: MongoDB's single master node limits how quickly information can be written to the database due to limited capacity.

- **Consistency of data**: MongoDB, being a NoSQL database, does not give full referential integrity, that is, like any SQL database, we have foreign key constraints that help to maintain data integrity among different objects in the database.

## Installing MongoDB on Windows

To install MongoDB on Windows, follow these steps:

1. Download MongoDB Community Server from the link or install the 64-bit version for Windows using the following link:

https://fastdl.mongodb.org/windows/mongodb-windows-x86_64-6.0.6-signed.msi

**Figure 5.5**: *Installing MongoDB on Windows*

2.  Open Setup after the download is completed:

**Figure 5.6**: *Starting MongoDB setup file*

3.  Accept the End-User Licence Agreement:

**Figure 5.7**: *Accept terms and conditions*

4. Choose Setup Type:

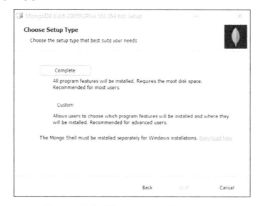

**Figure 5.8**: *Choose complete setup*

5. Choose `Complete` and click `Next`:

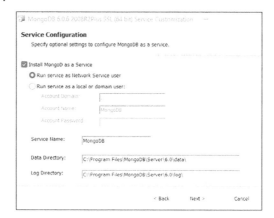

**Figure 5.9**: *Starting MongoDB setup file*

6. Ignore Compass Setup for now:

**Figure 5.10**: *Skipping compass setup*

7. Click **Install** to install all of the components:

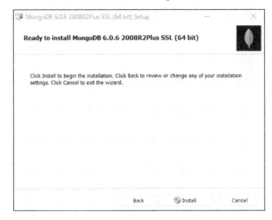

**Figure 5.11**: *Install setup*

8. Installation in progress:

**Figure 5.12**: *Setup Progress*

9. Click **Finish** to complete the installation:

**Figure 5.13**: *Finish setup*

# Creating our First Connection to MongoDB

In MongoDB, drivers are used for creating connections between client applications and the database. The MongoDB database has native support for some of the popular drivers for connecting to backend applications. The driver for JavaScript has out-of-the-box support.

Navigate to "**C:\Program Files\MongoDB\Server\6.0\bin**" and double-click mongod.exe:

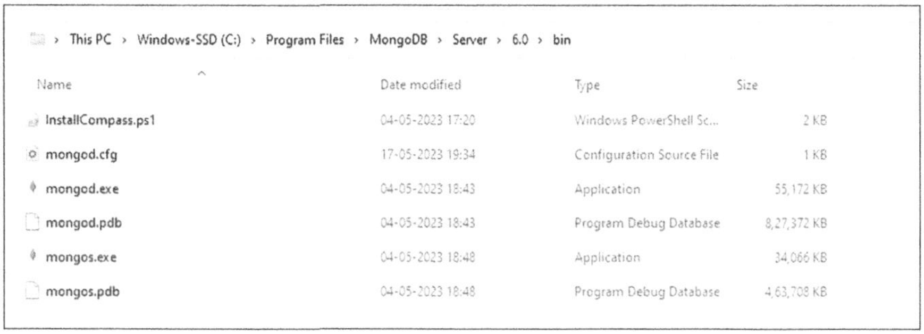

*Figure 5.14: Locate MongoDB Setup file*

When you open mongod.exe for the first time, you will get the following error:

Missing pass '**c:/data/db**':

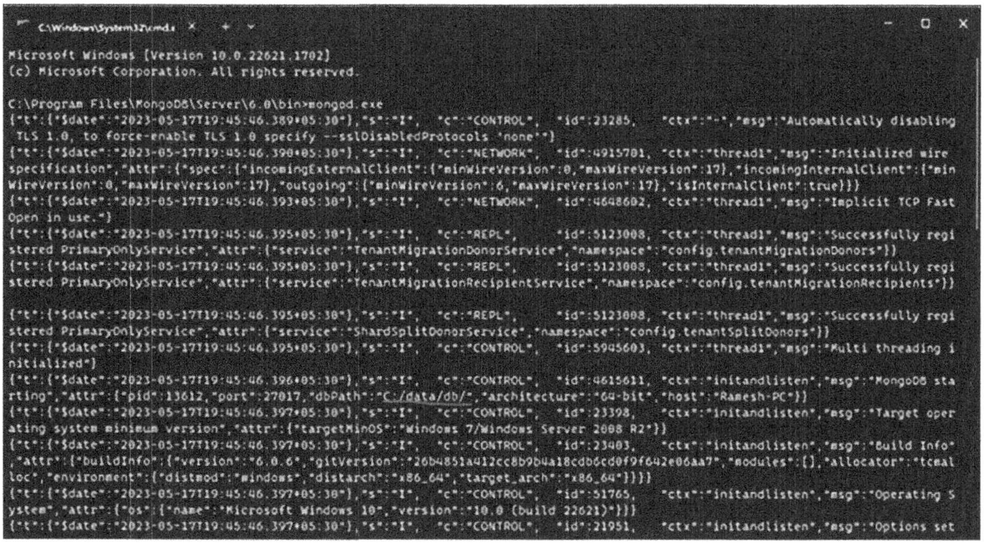

*Figure 5.15: Starting MongoDB server with an error response*

After manually creating the directory **c:/data/db**, try running the MongoDB application again:

**Figure 5.16**: *Start of server with message Waiting for connection*

# Mongo Shell for MongoDB

MongoDB Mongo shell is an intelligent tool that uses a JavaScript interface that permits everyone to connect with the MongoDB server through the command line. The shell can be utilized either for data manipulation or performing any kind of administrative operations

Here are the key features that Mongo shell offers:

- Helps run all MongoDB queries from the Mongo shell.
- Allows manipulation of information and performing organization operations.
- Uses the JavaScript API to issue commands.
- Enables monitoring all kinds of information using Mongo shell.

## Installing the Mongo Shell

To install Mongo Shell on your system, download the archive file from MongoDB download **mongosh-1.8.2-win32-x64.zip**, and copy it to a location in your file system.

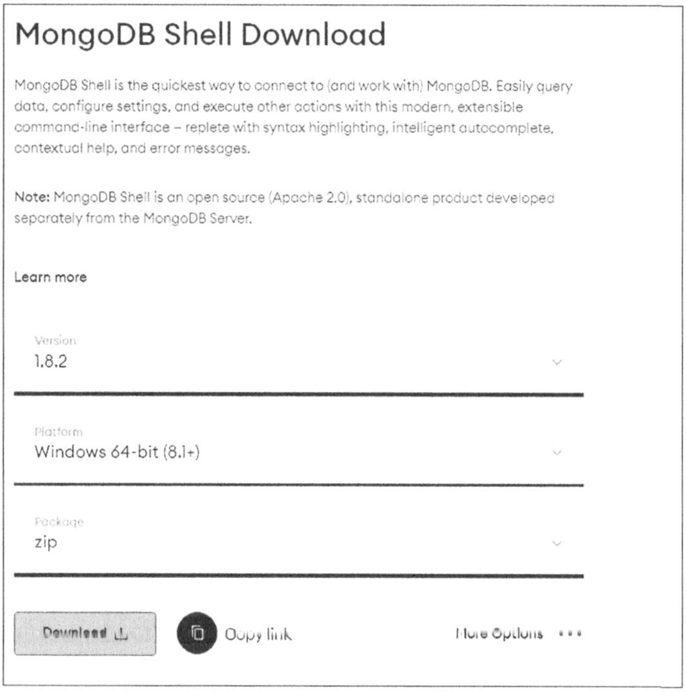

**Figure 5.17**: *Download Mongo shell*

# Connecting to MongoDB Database

Once you've downloaded and extracted the Mongo shell files, you can use the Mongo shell to connect with a MongoDB server that is up and running.

**Note:** It is required that your server is already running before you connect with it through the shell. You can start the server in CMD using the following command:

```
> net start mongoDB
```

**Figure 5.18**: *Download Mongo shell*

# Running Mongo Shell Application

Navigate to the following path and double-click **mongosh.exe** to start the Mongo shell application:

D:\Software\mongosh-1.8.2-win32-x64\mongosh-1.8.2-win32-x64\bin

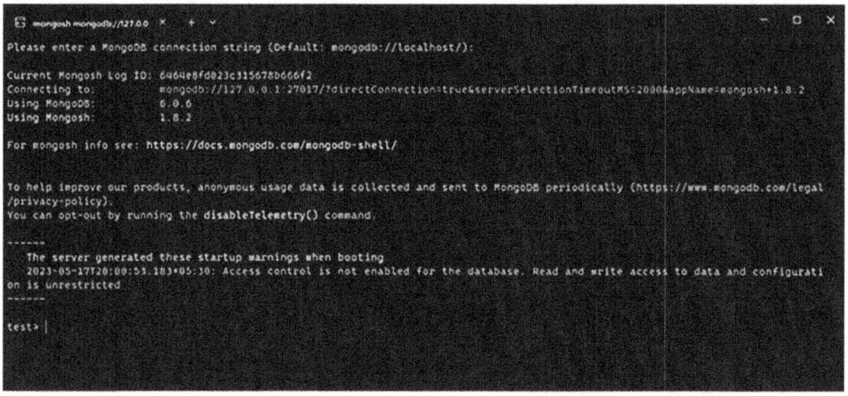

**Figure 5.19**: *Running and connecting to Mongo Shell*

Now, you are in the Mongo shell.

# Basic Commands for Mongo Shell

Now it's time to work with the Mongo shell. First, we will learn some basic commands that will help you to get started with using MongoDB.

Run the **db** command to see the database you are currently working with:

> db

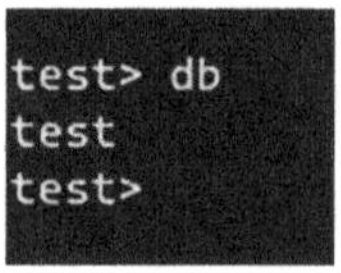

**Figure 5.20**: *Output of db query*

Run the **use** command to switch to a different database. If you don't have a database, learn how to create a new database:

> use employee

**Figure 5.21**: *Output of use employee cmd*

You can create collections and insert data with the following command:

`db.employee.insertOne( { name: "John" } );`

Where

- **db** refers to the current database in use.
- **employee** is the collection name.
- **insertOne** is the method to insert a document to the collection.

```
test> db
test
test> use employee
switched to db employee
employee> db.employee.insertOne({name : 'John'})
{
  acknowledged: true,
  insertedId: ObjectId("6464ea67023c315678b666f3")
}
employee>
```

*Figure 5.22*: *Output of use employee insertOne cmd*

Use the **find** method to fetch data in a collection:

`db.employee.find({})`

```
test> use employee
switched to db employee
employee> db.employee.find({})
[ { _id: ObjectId("6464ea67023c315678b666f3"), name: 'John' } ]
employee>
```

*Figure 5.23*: *Output of use employee find cmd*

Use the **show dbs** command to Show all databases:

```
employee> show dbs
admin      40.00 KiB
config     84.00 KiB
employee   40.00 KiB
local      72.00 KiB
employee>
```

*Figure 5.24*: *Output of use show dbs cmd*

One important command that will help you work with the Mongo shell easily is the **help** command. Run the help command to get a list of help options available in the Mongo shell.

# Introduction to MongoDB Compass

MongoDB Compass is a powerful MongoDB GUI tool that allows users to analyze the content of stored data without any prior knowledge of MongoDB's query syntax. When exploring data in a visual environment, you can use the MongoDB Compass GUI to optimize operations, manage indicators, and implement text validation.

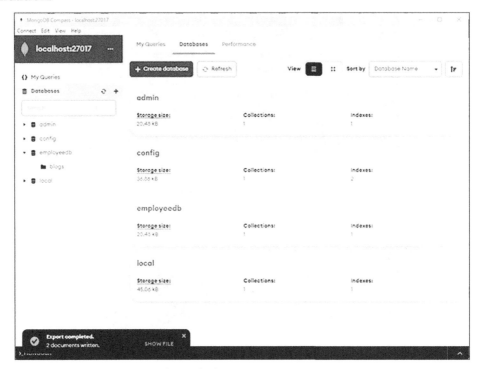

*Figure 5.25*: *MongoDB Compass*

# Installation of Compass on Windows

The following step will help in the installation of MongoDB Compass on Windows:

1. Download from https://www.mongodb.com/try/download/compass

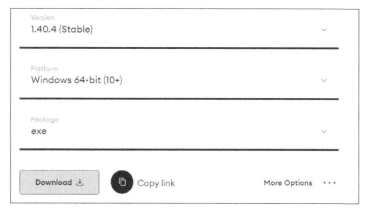

**Figure 5.26**: *Download MongoDB compass*

2. Run the Compass GUI from the downloaded file **mongodb-compass-1.40.4-win32-x64.exe**

**Figure 5.27**: *Download MongoDB compass*

3. Click Start to create a new connection to localhost.

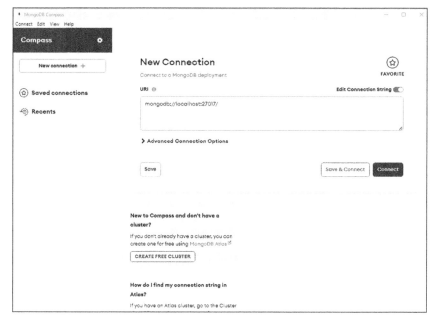

***Figure 5.28**: Download MongoDB compass*

4. Successfully connected to the MongoDB server at localhost:27017.

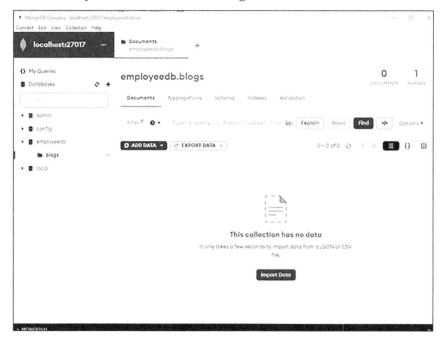

***Figure 5.29**: Download MongoDB compass*

5. Run your first query on MongoDB Compass to find all blogs.

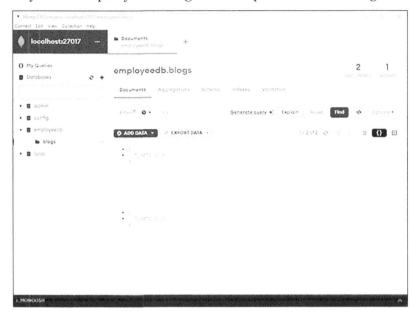

*Figure 5.30*: *Running first query on MongoDB compass*

# Conclusion

This chapter covered some of the key concepts of the MongoDB database, which is gaining popularity in recent times. We also explored how to set up MongoDB on a local system and create our own database. At the end of this chapter, we tried to use some of the queries and shell commands that are available with the MongoDB native console application, also known as **Mongo Shell**.

In the next chapter, we will cover some of the bases of **data persistence** and learn how to save and retrieve data using the popular package, Mongoose.

# Further Readings

You can use the following online resources to gain more understanding of MongoDB:

- https://learn.mongodb.com/learning-paths/introduction-to-mongodb
- https://www.youtube.com/watch?v=lBBtq3Oawqw
- https://intellipaat.com/blog/what-is-mongodb/
- https://www.tutorialspoint.com/mongodb/index.htm

# CHAPTER 6
# Data Persistence

## Introduction

In this chapter, we will learn more about the data persistence technique used in Node.js applications and explore some of the popular ORM tools like Mongoose or MongoClient which help us to define the schema and use them to perform all CRUD operations on behalf of the Node.js web application.

## Structure

This chapter will cover the following topics related to storing data inside the MongoDB server:

- Understanding ORM Tool
- Introduction to Mongoose
- Characteristics of Mongoose
- Advantages of Mongoose
- Disadvantages of Mongoose
- Key Terminologies
- Schema and Model
- Connecting to MongoDB through Mongoose
- Basic CRUD Operations
- Real-world Example

## Understanding ORM Tool

An ORM tool is software designed to help OOP developers interact more easily with relational databases.

These tools use one of two strategies:

- **Active record pattern**: These tools are used to map data into the object structure of the programming code and manage the data using classes and structures in the code.
- **Data mapping pattern**: This type of tool is used to separate the business logic (in objects) from the underlying database, allowing the same programming logic to be reused and simplifying database modification.

Some of the best ORM tools available in the market generate high-quality code without affecting application performance. They also facilitate easy database migration and provide opportunities to improve data schemas. They also help in speeding up development, reduce development costs, and improve application security by reducing the possibility of SQL injection and other types of attacks.

# Introduction to Mongoose

Mongoose is a Node.js-based object data modeling (ODM) library for MongoDB. It is similar to Object Relational Mappers (ORMs) such as SQLAlchemy, Hibernate, and Entity Framework.

For traditional SQL databases, Mongoose addresses the challenge of allowing developers to implement a specific schema at the application level. In addition to formula enforcement, Mongoose also provides various hooks, model validation, and other features designed to make MongoDB easier.

Mongoose is an ODM library built on MongoDB's native controller for Node.js projects. Thanks to ready-made hooks, it allows you to save time when writing the basis of MongoDB validation, casting, and business logic.

# Characteristics of Mongoose

The following are some of the important characteristics of Mongoose:

- **Schemas**: MongoDB is a schemaless database. This allows documents to have different types of fields with different data types. While this enhances the flexibility of the data model, it can cause problems in the long run.
- **Validation**: Mongoose provides built-in schema validation, saving us from writing code to validate data added to the MongoDB controller.

- **Instance Methods**: Mongoose makes it easy to define and manage custom methods defined in the schema definition for a specific object or document. Mongoose also includes pre- and post-storage functions for data models.
- **Retrieving Results**: Updated documents and query results can be easily retrieved using Mongoose. For update requests, Mongoose returns the modified object itself, while the parent controller returns the object, flags, and the number of modified documents.

# Advantages of Mongoose

The following are the benefits that Mongoose provides:

- The chained functions make code flexible and readable.
- It eliminates the need to use named collections.
- It performs bulk operations to add default values to properties and data validation.
- The formula is easier to define.
- It has features like type casting, data validation, query construction and many more.

# Disadvantages of Mongoose

The following are the disadvantages that Mongoose has:

- It doesn't support transactions.
- It lacks triggers, something that makes life easier in relational database management systems (RDBMS).
- The abstraction comes at the cost of performance as compared to the MongoDB driver.

# Key Terminologies

### Collections

Collections in Mongo are equivalent to tables in relational databases. They can contain multiple JSON documents.

### Documentation

Documents correspond to SQL records or rows of data. Although a SQL row can refer to data from other tables, Mongo documents usually combine them in a document.

## Fields

Fields, also called properties or attributes, are similar to columns in an SQL table. In the following code, first name, last name, email and phone, topics are all fields.

```
{
    "fname": "sue",            //Field to store firstname value
    "lname": "test",           //Field to store lastname value
    "email": "sue.test@gmail.com", // Field to store email
    "phone": "56756756756",        // Field to store phone
    "topics":["news", "sports"]    // Field to store list of fav
topic
}
```

## Diagram

Although Mongo is schema-free, SQL defines the schema through the table definition. A Mongoose schema is a document data structure (or document format) enforced through the application layer.

## Schematic types

While Mongoose schemas define the overall structure or format of a document, SchemaTypes define the expected data type (string, number, boolean, and more) for individual fields. You can also provide useful options necessary to make a field non-optional, setting a default value for a field, and more.

## Models

Models are higher-order constructors that take a schema and create a document instance corresponding to the records in the relational database.

# Schema and Model

**Referencing Mongoose**: This is the same as the one we used while connecting our database, which implies that defining schema and model does not require an explicit connection to the database.

```
let mongoose = require('mongoose');
const { Schema } = mongoose;
```

**Schema definition**: We define a schema to decide the properties of the object including default values, data types, if required, and more.

```
let mongoose = require('mongoose');
const { Schema } = mongoose;
const employeeSchema = new Schema({
    // String is shorthand for {type: String}
    name:  String,
    dob: { type: Date, default: Date.now },
    address:   String,
    phone: String
});
```

Here, **employeeSchema** defines a few basic properties for an employee.

We've defined the following  properties:

- name: **String** SchemaType
- dob: **Date** SchemaType and its default value is set to **Date.now (current date)**
- address: **String** SchemaType
- phone: **String** SchemaType

In Mongoose, there are 8 SchemaTypes:

- Array
- Boolean
- Buffer
- Date
- Mixed (A generic/flexible data type)
- Number
- ObjectId
- String

**Creating and exporting a model**: To use the schema defined, we need to convert blogSchema into a model we can work with. To do this, we will use the following code:

```
let mongoose = require('mongoose');

const { Schema } = mongoose;

const employeeSchema = new Schema({
    // String is shorthand for {type: String}
    name:   String,
    dob: { type: Date, default: Date.now },
    address:    String,
    phone: String
});

// Creating a Model
let employee = mongoose.model('Employee', employeeSchema);

// Exporting the created module
module.exports = employee;
```

We can use this `Employee` model to easily perform operations like create, read, update, delete, and more from our database.

# Connecting to MongoDB through Mongoose

We will perform the following steps to connect our application to the MongoDB database.

1.  Create a new folder and initialize the project using the `npm init` command.

```
PS D:\Book\Building-Real-Time-application-using-Node_fork.js\chap_06> npm init
This utility will walk you through creating a package.json file.
It only covers the most common items, and tries to guess sensible defaults.

See `npm help json` for definitive documentation on these fields
and exactly what they do.

Use `npm install <pkg>` afterwards to install a package and
save it as a dependency in the package.json file.

Press ^C at any time to quit.
package name: (chap_06) test
version: (1.0.0)
description:
entry point: (moongoose_code.js)
test command:
git repository:
keywords:
author:
license: (ISC)
About to write to D:\Book\Building-Real-Time-application-using-Node_fork.js\chap_06\package.json:

{
  "name": "test",
  "version": "1.0.0",
  "description": "",
  "main": "moongoose_code.js",
  "scripts": {
    "test": "echo \"Error: no test specified\" && exit 1",
    "start": "node server.js"
  },
  "author": "",
  "license": "ISC"
}

Is this OK? (yes)
PS D:\Book\Building-Real-Time-application-using-Node_fork.js\chap_06> []
```

*Figure 6.1*: *Npm Init command*

2. Install the latest version of Mongoose with the npm install mongoose command.

```
PS D:\Book\Building-Real-Time-application-using-Node_fork.js\
chap_06> npm install mongoose --save
```

```
PS D:\Book\Building-Real-Time-application-using-Node_fork.js\
chap_06> npm install mongoose --save
```

```
PS D:\Book\Building-Real-Time-application-using-Node_fork.js\chap_06> npm install mongoose --save
npm WARN mongodb@5.5.0 requires a peer of @aws-sdk/credential-providers@^3.201.0 but none is installed. You must install peer dependencies y
ourself.
npm WARN mongodb@5.5.0 requires a peer of mongodb-client-encryption@>=2.3.0 <3 but none is installed. You must install peer dependencies you
rself.
npm WARN mongodb@5.5.0 requires a peer of snappy@^7.2.2 but none is installed. You must install peer dependencies yourself.
npm WARN test@1.0.0 No description
npm WARN test@1.0.0 No repository field.

+ mongoose@7.2.2
added 24 packages from 64 contributors and audited 47 packages in 3.511s
found 4 vulnerabilities (2 moderate, 1 high, 1 critical)
  run `npm audit fix` to fix them, or `npm audit` for details
PS D:\Book\Building-Real-Time-application-using-Node_fork.js\chap_06> []
```

*Figure 6.2*: *Npm install mongoose command*

The preceding command will install version 7 of the Mongoose library.

# Database connection

Create a file **server.js** under the **chap_06** folder and add the following code:

```
const express = require("express");
const Employee = require("./employee_schema");


// Create an express application.
const app = express();
app.use(express.json());


// Create a POST endpoint to receive data from the user.
app.post("/", async (req, res) => {
    // Destructuring data from body of request.
    const {
        name,
        dob,
        address,
        phone
    } = req.body;

    try {
        // Create a new employee.
        const employee = new Employee({
            name: name,
            dob: dob,
            address: address,
            phone: phone
        });

        // Insert the employee in the database.
        await employee.save();
```

```
        res.send("Employee Saved Successfully.");
    } catch (err) {
        console.log(err);
        res.json(err);
    }
});


app.listen(8080, function (err) {
    if (err) console.log(err);
    console.log("Server listening on 8080");
});
```

In the preceding code, `require('mongoose')` call creates an instance of the Mongoose class and returns it. We then save our MongoDB connection server and database name as a string in the server and database object, respectively. `mongoose.connect()` is the minimum need to connect the database with the app.

Now, since we have successfully connected our database connection, let's run the database.js with the following line of code:

```
PS D:\Book\Building-Real-Time-application-using-Node_fork.js\
chap_06> node server.js
```

We have connected our app with the **employeedb** database using Mongoose.

# Basic Mongoose Operations

In this section, we will learn how to perform some of the basic Mongoose CRUD operations on the MongoDB database. Here we will learn to establish a connection with the MongoDB NoSQL database using `mongoose.connect()` method.

Let us understand how to perform Mongoose CRUD operations.

## Create operation

The first method to create a document is using the `save()` method.

When we want to create or save new entries of a JSON object, we use the `save()` method on that object. This method will save the newly created document in the MongoDB database.

**save()**

```
// Create a new employee.
    const employee = new Employee({
        name: name,
        dob: dob,
        address: address,
        phone: phone
    });


    // Insert the employee in the database.
    await employee.save();
```

**insert()**

The second method, **insert()** and insertMany() are also used for inserting individual objects or an array of records.

The only difference is that the former returns the number of inserts and confirmation about the record inserted. In contrast, **insertMany()** returns the record id and inserted record.

```
    Employee.collection.insert(
        [ {
            name: name,
            dob: dob,
            address: address,
            phone: phone
        },{
            name: name,
            dob: dob,
            address: address,
            phone: phone
        }]
    )
```

**create()**

Similar to the **save()** method, even the **create()** method is used to create new model documents in Mongoose. However, it is shorthand to make one or more documents in the database

```
Employee.create([NewEmployee1,NewEmployee2,NewEmployee3])
  .then((data)=>{
    resolve(data);
  }).catch((err)=>{
    reject(err);
})
```

# Retrieve operation

Mongoose CRUD Operations gives us three simple ways to retrieve or read any data from the MongoDB database: **find()**, **findOne()**, and **findById()**.

The **find()** method returns everything in the database that matches the query.

```
Employee.find([query],[callback])
```

The **findOne()** method returns only the first matching record.

```
Employee.findOne([query],[fieldsToReturn],[callback])
```

Lastly, the **findById()** method returns a single object in the MongoDB database based on the id you provide.

```
Employee.findById(id,[fieldsToReturn],[callback])
```

# Update operation

Update operation looks for an existing record in the database, retrieves it, and then modifies the same record according to the query provided. For achieving this, we can use the inbuilt **FindByIdAndUpdate()** method to update a certain record by giving its record Id.

```
if (mongoose.Types.ObjectId.isValid(id)) {
    Employee.findByIdAndUpdate(id, {
        $set: {
            name: employee.name
        }
    }, {
        new: true
    }).then((docs) => {
        if (docs) {
            resolve({
                success: true,
                data: docs
            });
        } else {
            reject({
                success: false,
                data: "no such employee exist"
            });
        }
    }).catch((err) => {
        reject(err);
    })
} else {
    reject({
        success: "false",
        data: "provide correct key"
    });
}
```

For condition-based updating, you can use the **update()** method; you can even update multiple files by making the multi flag true.

```
Employee.update({_id:id},
{$set:{name:employee.name,state:employee.state}},
    {multi:true,new:true})
     .then((docs)=>{
       if(docs) {
         resolve({success:true,data:docs});
       } else {
         reject({success:false,data:"no such employee exist"});
       }
    }).catch((err)=>{
       reject(err);
    })
```

## Delete operation

There are two methods to delete or remove a record – **remove()** and **findOneAndRemove()**. While **remove()** deletes all the records from MongoDB that satisfy the given condition, the **findOneAndRemove()** method removes only one record based on the Id you give.

```
Employee.findOneAndRemove(id,options,callback);
```

# Real-world Example

Let's create one API application based on Node.js and Mongoose.

### Creating the application

We will create a new **Demo** folder inside D:/ and run the following cmd to initialize the new node project.

```
npm init
```

The output of the preceding command gives a new **package.json** file with the following details.

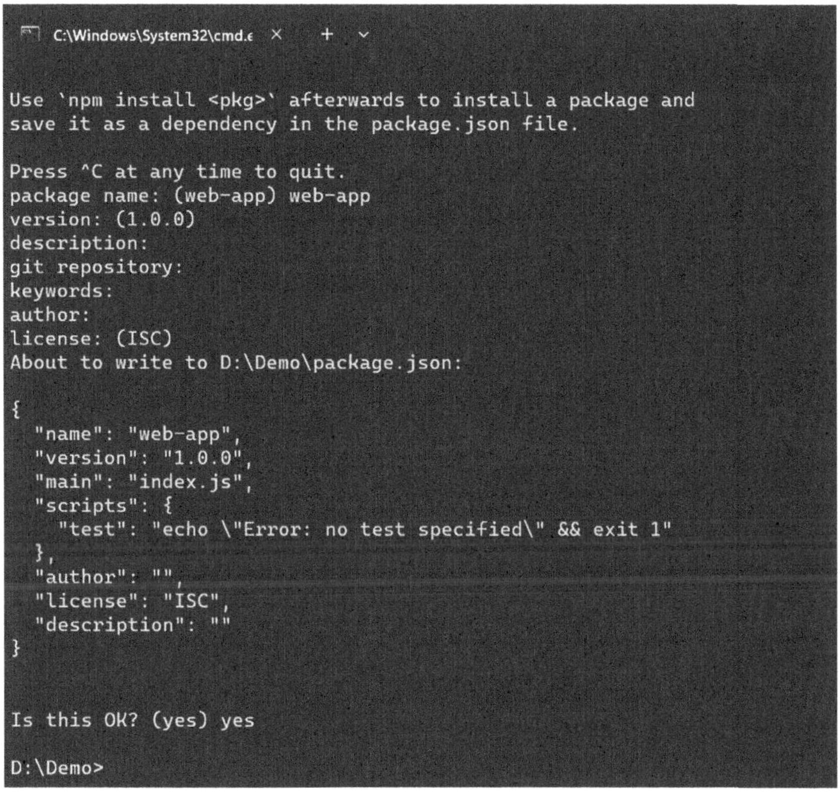

*Figure 6.3*: *Npm Init command to create a new application*

We will create an entry point for our web server using a file called **server.js**.

**Install dependencies**

We will need some of the popular node packages in order to build our applications such as:

- express,
- mongoose
- body-parser

We can install the preceding package using the following command:

```
npm install express body-parser mongoose --save
```

**Output:**

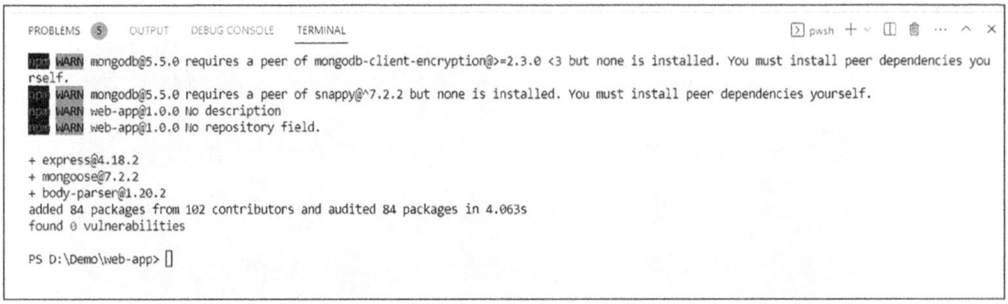

**Figure 6.4**: *Npm install express, mongoose, body-parser*

## Setting up the web server

We will write the basic code which is used to set up our backend server running on Node.js.

```
const express = require('express');
const bodyParser = require('body-parser');


const app = express();


app.use(bodyParser.urlencoded({ extended: true }))


app.use(bodyParser.json())


app.get('/', (req, res) => {
    res.json({"message": "Hello, Webapp running"});
});


app.listen(3000, () => {
    console.log("Server is listening on port 3000");
});
```

Let's understand the preceding code.

Firstly, we imported our core modules which are **express** and **body-parser** modules.

**Express**: Our main web framework that we'll be using for building backend REST APIs.

**Body-parser**: This is a module that is used to parse the request and creates a `req.body` object that we can access in our routes and extract all the information provided by the user.

```
const express = require('express');
const bodyParser = require('body-parser');
```

Second, we create an express app and add two body-parser middlewares in the express's `app.use()` method. A middleware is a function that can execute any code, transform the request object, or return a response.

```
app.use(bodyParser.urlencoded({ extended: true }))
app.use(bodyParser.json())
```

Next, we define a simple route that returns a welcome message to the clients.

```
app.get('/', (req, res) => {
    res.json({"message": "Hello Crud Node Express"});
});
```

At last, we listen to our server running at localhost on port **3000** for incoming connections.

```
app.listen(3000, () => {
    console.log("Server is listening at http://localhost:3000");
});
```

### Configuring and connecting to the database

Let's create a new folder **config** in the root folder of our application and add a new file **db_config.js**:

```
module.exports = {
    url: 'mongodb://localhost:27017/employeedb'
}
```

We'll be able to connect to the MongoDB database using this **db_config.js** file.

Create another file **connection.js** and add the following code where we will actually connect using the mongoose module.

```
const dbConfig = require('./config/db_config.js');
const mongoose = require('mongoose');


mongoose.Promise = global.Promise;

mongoose.connect(dbConfig.url, {
    useNewUrlParser: true
}).then(() => {
    console.log("Database Connected Successfully!!");
}).catch(err => {
    console.log('Could not connect to the database', err);
    process.exit();
});
```

Update code inside the **server.js** file to initialize the connection.

```
const express = require('express');
const bodyParser = require('body-parser');
const Connection = require('./connection');


const app = express();


app.use(bodyParser.urlencoded({ extended: true }))


app.use(bodyParser.json())


app.get('/', (req, res) => {
    res.json({"message": "Hello Crud Node Express"});
});


app.listen(3000, () => {
    // connecting to database once server is running
```

```
        Connection();
        console.log("Server is listening at http://localhost:3000");
    });
```

Now, run the server and check if you are able to connect to the database.

```
    PS D:\Demo\web-app> node server.js
```

**Output:**

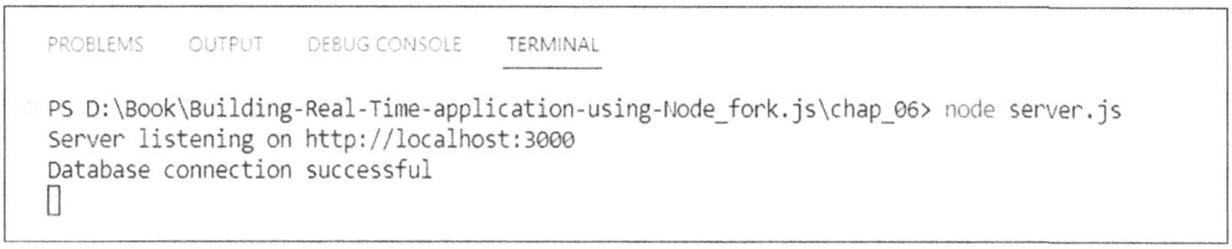

*Figure 6.5*: *Output of database connection.*

### Create Mongoose model

Models are fancy constructors compiled from Schema definitions. An instance of a model is called a document. Models are responsible for creating and reading documents from the underlying MongoDB database.

Let's create a folder called **models** inside the /**web-app** folder. Now add the **employee.js** file and add the following code.

```
    var mongoose = require('mongoose');


    // schema definition for Employee entity
    var empSchema = new mongoose.Schema({
        email: {
            type: String,
            required: true,
            unique: true
        },
        firstName: {
            type: String,
            default: ''
        },
        lastName: {
```

```
        type: String,
        default: ''
    },
    phone: String,
    dob: Date
});


//creating Employee model
var employee = new mongoose.model('Employee', empSchema);


module.exports = employee;
```

Next, we will look at the two most important parts: Routes and Controllers.

- **Routing** is the part where the APIs are actually created and hosted.
- **Controllers** are functions which are used to write separate codes for different actions being performed by API and are imported in the routing section to keep the operation handling smoother.

  These controllers can then internally call either directly using models or we can create separate services which abstract internal functionality of the underlying data layer.

These are different kinds of **HTTP** requests defined under **REST** services which are used to handle all the operations called by the user like fetching data, creating new records, and more. They enable interactions between the client and the server and work as a request-response protocol.

The following table list some of the popular HTTP requests:

| Method | Description |
|--------|-------------|
| GET | Used to request data from a specified resource |
| POST | Used to send data to a server to create/ update a resource |
| PUT | Replaces all the current representations of the target resource with the uploaded content |

| DELETE | Removes all the current representations of the target resource given by URI. |
| PATCH | The PATCH method applies partial modifications to a resource |

**Table 6.1**: *HTTP Methods*

Systems like Node JS are mostly based on MVC (Model View Controller) architecture. The idea is that it helps to focus on a specific part of the application and build it on a modular basis.

The key components of the MVC pattern are:

- **Model**: It represents the structure and constraints of the data stored in the database.
- **View**: It is the way the required data is presented to the user as per the need of the user.
- **Controller**: This section controls the requests of the user and generates the appropriate response which is fed to the user.

**Adding controllers**

Inside the **web-app/controllers** folder, let's create Employee.js with the following CRUD functions:

- `create`
- `findAll`
- `findOne`
- `update`
- `remove`

**Note:**

> We have used async and await keywords as the database query takes time and so the asynchronous property of node js comes in.

Let's now look at the implementation of the controller functions one by one.

**Define routes**

When a client sends a request for an endpoint using an HTTP request (GET, POST, PUT, DELETE), we need to determine how the server will respond by setting up the routes.

Create **Employee.js** inside the **web-app/routes** folder and add the following contents:

```
import { Router } from 'express';
import { findAll, findOne, create, update, destroy } from
'../controllers/employee';
const router = Router();
router.get('/', findAll);
router.get('/:id', findOne);
router.post('/', create);
router.patch('/:id', update);
router.delete('/:id', destroy);
export default router;
```

In the last step before trying out our routes, we have to add the route class to the server.js.

```
const EmployeeRoute = require('./app/routes/employee');
app.use('/employee', EmployeeRoute);
```

Now, we can start the **node.js server** and our API is ready.

```
node.js server
```

```
PROBLEMS    OUTPUT    DEBUG CONSOLE    TERMINAL

PS D:\Book\Building-Real-Time-application-using-Node_fork.js\chap_06> node server.js
Server listening on http://localhost:3000
Database connection successful
□
```

*Figure 6.6*: *Output of application running*

# Conclusion

In this chapter, we have learned about some of the tools and techniques used for **data persistence** in Node.js web applications. For performing data persistence, we have many tools available in the market and out of all those, we have explained and used the Mongoose ORM tool. We have seen how we can define models and schemas which are the core of Mongoose ORM tools for building applications using Node.js and MongoDB.

In the next chapter, we will be covering some of the basics of **Template Engines** used in generating dynamic HTML content on the fly and doing data binding using JavaScript.

# Further Reading

- https://hashnode.com/post/how-to-store-persistent-data-in-nodejs-cjl9enle000dlcss2zs8cpchb
- https://www.newline.co/books/fullstack-nodejs/a-complete-server-persistence
- https://www.tabnine.com/code/javascript/modules/node-persist
- https://www.codingame.com/playgrounds/1064/building-a-basic-todo-list-rest-api-in-node-js-with-express/persistence
- https://www.youtube.com/watch?v=U2h8gj-2dPs
- https://www.youtube.com/watch?v=wxbQP1LMZsw

# CHAPTER 7

# Template Engines

## Introduction

In this chapter, we will explore templating engines that are used to generate dynamic HTML content in Node-based web applications.

## Structure

This chapter will cover some of the following topics related to templating engines used in Node.JS:

- Templating engines
- Working of template engines
- Advantages and disadvantages of template engines
- HTML rendering with templates
- Exploring the EJS template engine
- Creating dynamic content using EJS

## Templating engines

Template engines help in generating dynamic HTML templates by writing minimal code. We can also insert data into the HTML template on the server side and generate the final HTML code which will be rendered by the client.

A templating engine used to make static template files in Node-based Web Applications. At runtime, we can write simple logic that replaces the variables in the template file with actual values from any data source like JSON, database, file, and so on, and finally transform the template into a dynamic HTML file that can be rendered by the client. This approach helps in keeping HTML pages simple without losing data content.

# Working of template engines

Template engines behind the scenes use a template file similar to an HTML file with special tags or syntax, and a data object which is used for binding values and generating dynamic content. The template engine then parses the HTML template file, replaces all the placeholders with data fetched from the JavaScript request, and the final HTML output is sent to the browser for rendering. template engines can be used on the server side as well, where we can generate HTML output before the final content is sent to the client for rendering, or we can send raw content to the client side, where the HTML output is generated and rendered in the browser using JavaScript.

The following diagram explains how the template engine works in Node.js.

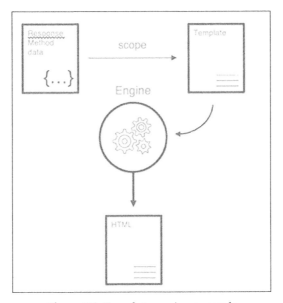

**Figure 7.1**: *Template engine example*

Here, we can see that any request made by the client is processed by Node.js express server and template engines used as middleware which processes all the static HTML pages and updates its content by binding data into templates and finally returns the HTML file to the client browser.

The following popular template engines used for Node.js:

- Jade
- Vash
- EJS

- Mustache
- Dust.js
- Nunjucks
- Handlebars
- atpl
- haml

# Advantages of template engines

The following are some of the key advantages of using the template engines inside Node.js.

- Improves developer productivity
- Improves readability and maintainability
- Faster performance
- Maximizes client-side processing
- One template for multiple pages
- Templates are accessible from a Content Delivery Network (CDN)

# Disadvantages of template engines

The following are some of the key advantages of using the template engines inside Node.js:

- Embedding HTML and JS code becomes hard to maintain over time.
- When building large applications, we can't use template engines efficiently to render all the web pages as completed to any JavaScript library like Angular/React.
- Template engines add extra complexity and abstraction, which can make debugging and testing difficult.
- This requires you to learn new syntax and rules that may not be compatible with other tools or languages.
- Depending on the size and complexity of the models and data, there may be performance issues and limitations when developing real-time applications.
- Template engines may not support all the features that are needed for building web pages, something as interactivity, state management, or routing.

# Key components of template engines

The following are key components that should be included in the template engines:

- It should be compiled and run stand-alone (without an additional web server).
- It should be able to generate all kinds of output, including text data, json, xml, and so on.
- It is meant to be simple, small, lightweight, and easy to use for developing real-time applications without much complexity.
- Its template syntax should be very clear and straightforward.
- It should have good syntax error checking and good error reporting that can help writing and debugging templates a lot easier.
- Some of the additional features of template engines include:
  - placeholders/string replacement
  - conditional
  - loops
  - macros (with parameters)
  - limited "embedded expressions" (formatting, arithmetic, and so on)

# HTML rendering with templates

When we build any server-side application that has support for a template engine, the template engine replaces all the variables inside the template file with actual values and makes the final HTML content, which is then rendered by the client. This makes it a lot easier for any backend developer to quickly build our application with less effort and complexity.

Let's add the following code to the **server.js** file in the root directory.

```
const express = require('express');

const app = express();

const path = require('path');

const PORT = 3000;
```

```
// setting the templating engine on the app.
app.set('view engine', 'ejs');

// views location
app.set('views', path.join(__dirname, '/views'));

app.get('/', (req, res) => {

  res.render('home.ejs', { msg: "Hello World !!" });

});

app.listen(PORT, () => console.log('listening on port ' + PORT));
```

Now we will create a new file named **views/home.ejs** inside our views folder. This will contain some of the content related to the home page.

```
<!DOCTYPE html>
<html lang="en">

<head>
  <meta charset="UTF-8">
  <meta name="viewport" content="width=device-width,
initial-scale=1.0">
  <title>Home</title>
</head>

<body>
  <h1>The Home Page</h1>
  <h1>Weclome Message: <%= msg %> </h1>
</body>
</html>
```

In this example, we have tried to showcase how we can write a html using ejs templating engine. As you can see, we are setting the welcome message and updating the home page html content to show the message on the html page.

**Building**:

```
PROBLEMS    OUTPUT    DEBUG CONSOLE    TERMINAL

● PS D:\Book\Building-Real-Time-application-using-Node_fork.js\chap_07> npm i

  up to date, audited 107 packages in 960ms

  13 packages are looking for funding
    run `npm fund` for details

  3 moderate severity vulnerabilities

  To address all issues (including breaking changes), run:
    npm audit fix --force

  Run `npm audit` for details.
○ PS D:\Book\Building-Real-Time-application-using-Node_fork.js\chap_07> []
```

*Figure 7.2*: *Building Node Application*

**Running**:

    PS      D:\Book\Building-Real-Time-application-using-Node_fork.js\
    chap_07> node server.js

**Output**:

**The Home Page**

**Weclome Message: Hello World !!**

*Figure 7.3*: *Output of Ejs template.*

# Exploring the EJS template engine

EJS is much more similar to HTML than Pug is, retaining the usual method of opening and closing tags as well as specifying attributes. Variables are declared using angle brackets and the percent sign in this manner: `<%= name %>`.

We can use EJS tags in the following different ways:

- **<%= %>**

    This is used to embed code that should return the result of an expression/calculation at runtime and output it to a view (page).

- **<%- %>** :

    This is used to output the provided value without escaping. It is advised you escape all HTML variables before rendering to prevent cross-site scripting (XSS) attacks.

- **<% %>**

    This is used to embed JavaScript code that returns output, control flow, conditions, variable declarations, include statements, and so on.

- **<%# %>**

    This is used to include comments in the files.

**When to use EJS?**

We use EJS in most situations whenever you need to generate output HTML with a lot of JavaScript if you're dealing with creating web applications where dynamic content is produced or involves real-time updates to HTML content.

Let's understand with an example.

Suppose we want to generate a list of employees for our web page.

**Case 1:**

We can use a legacy way of developing web pages that can loop through an array of employees and generate HTML content by concating results.

```
var html = "<h1>"+ "employeeObj.description" + </h1>";
html += "<ul>";
for(var i=0; i< employees.length; i++)
{
    html +="<li><a href='employees/" + employees[i] + "'>"
    html += employees[i]+"</a></li>"
}
html += "</ul>"
```

So here we can see that syntax is very hard to understand and takes lots of effort to write this code.

**Case 2**:

Something we can easily do using the EJS templating engine.

```
<h1><%=title%></h1>
<ul>
    <%for (var i=0;i<employees.length; i++){%>
      <li>
          <a href='employees/<%= employees[i] %>'></a>
          <%=employees[i]%>
      </li>
    <%}%>
</ul>
```

Here we can notice, a couple of lines of code look so clear and easy-to-understand logic.

# Creating dynamic content using EJS

The following steps will be used to create a Node.js web application to understand how to use ExpressJS and EJS template engines. Here we will see how to render a user's data on the web page.

**Step 1**: Installing dependencies of express and the **ejs** template engine

```
npm install express ejs –save-dev
```

**Step 2**: Setting up the view engine

```
const express = require('express');

const app = express();

const path = require('path');

const PORT = 3000;
```

```
// setting the templating engine on the app.
app.set('view engine', 'ejs');

// views location
app.set('views', path.join(__dirname, '/views'));

app.listen(PORT, () => console.log('listening on port ' + PORT));
```

We created our express application. The application listens on port **3000**.

**Step 3**: Setting the template engine

The following line of code tells the express server that we want to use EJS as our template engine.

```
app.set('view engine', 'ejs');
```

**Step 4**: Setting up the view folder

Let's create a folder called **views**. The view folder will contain all of our templates.

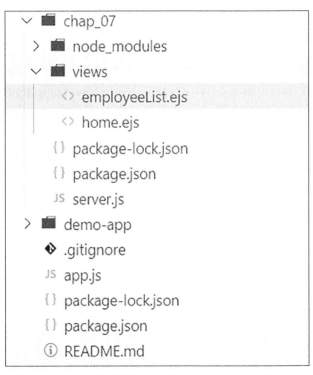

**Figure 7.4**: *View the folder inside the express application*

Here we have added a new file called **employeeList.ejs**, which will generate our HTML page to show a list of employees.

```
<!DOCTYPE html>
<html lang="en">
<head>
  <meta charset="UTF-8">
  <meta name="viewport" content="width=device-width,
initial-scale=1.0">
  <title>List of Employees!</title>
</head>
<body>
  <h1>List of all Employees!</h1>
  <ul>
    <% for (let emp of employees) { %>
      <li> <%=emp.name %> </li>
    <% } %>
  </ul>
</body>
</html>
```

The second template is **home.ejs**, which will be used to show welcome messages on the home page.

```
<!DOCTYPE html>
<html lang="en">
<head>
  <meta charset="UTF-8">
  <meta name="viewport" content="width=device-width, ini-
tial-scale=1.0">
  <title>Home</title>
</head>
<body>
  <h1>The Home Page</h1>
  <h1>Weclome Message: <%= msg %> </h1>
```

```
</body>
</html>
```

**Step 5**: Setting up the routes

We will create the routes for our homepage and employee list page.

```
// home route
app.get('/', (req, res) => {
    res.render('home.ejs', {
        msg: "Hello World !!"
    });
});


// employees route
app.get('/employees', (req, res) => {
    const employees = [{
            name: "test",
            salary: 20000,
            age: 30,
            doj: "12-12-2000"
        },
        {
            name: "test",
            salary: 20000,
            age: 30,
            doj: "12-12-2000"
        }
    ];
    res.render('employeesList.ejs', {
        employees
    });
});
```

As we have seen, the default route "\", when accessed, displays or renders the `home.ejs` page. Meanwhile, the "\`employees`" renders the `employessList.ejs` page.

We passed the `employees` object to the rendered object to pass the employee properties to the web page and render it.

**Step 6**: Templating our view files

Here we can pass employee data from the server backend, we just need to display it on our webpage using template engine syntax.

In our code of HTML, we will use <%%> syntax to add dynamic content like loops, conditions, etc., and generate HTML out of that as a response.

```
<ul>
    <% for (let emp of employees) { %>
      <li> <%=emp.name %> </li>
    <% } %>
  </ul>
```

**Step 7**: Running the application

After running the application, you will get the following output that can be accessed using given URLs.

**Home Page**

http://localhost:3000/home

Once you open the preceding URL in the browser, you will land on the following home page shown in *Figure 7.5*.

*Figure 7.5*: *Output of home view*

**List of Employee page**

http://localhost:3000/employees

Once you open the preceding URL in the browser, you will land on the following list of employees page shown in *Figure 7.6*.

*Figure 7.6*: *Output of Employees list view*

# Conclusion

In this chapter, we have covered some of the core concepts of template engines and how we can use them to build web applications that are easy to develop in a short time. We also learned about one of the popular template engines EJS and explored some of the basic syntax of creating dynamic content using EJS syntax.

In the next chapter, we will learn about Middlewares Functions and explore some of the commonly used functions in Node.js applications.

# Further readings

You can use the following online resources to gain more understanding of template engine concepts used in Node.js.

- https://expressjs.com/en/resources/template-engines.html
- https://blog.logrocket.com/top-express-js-template-engines-for-dynamic-html-pages/
- https://thesassway.com/how-to-create-a-template-engine-in-node-js/
- https://ejs.co/
- https://www.youtube.com/watch?v=AIPG2UJTRQg
- https://www.youtube.com/watch?v=wEqMxTJl-TE
- https://handlebarsjs.com/

CHAPTER 8

# Middleware Functions

## Introduction

In this chapter, we will learn about Middleware Functions which are used to transform request and response objects during the application request-response cycle. We will also try to use some of the Middleware Functions which are widely used for building any Node.js web applications.

## Structure

In this chapter, we will cover some of the following topics related to templating engines used in Node.JS:

- Introduction to Middleware
- Importance of Middleware
- Advantage of Using Middleware
- Using Inbuilt Middleware with Express
- Creating our First Custom Middleware
- Middleware Chaining

## Introduction to Middleware

Middlewares are defined as JavaScript functions that can be used to access, modify or transform client requests and responses. Each middleware function contains three different parts which include the `req` `(request object)`, `res` `(response object)`, and the next() function in the application's request-response loop. The `next()` function is used to call another middleware function once the current middleware function is executed.

Middleware functions can perform the following tasks:

- Run any code
- Modify the request and response objects
- Terminate the request-response cycle
- Call the next stack middleware

# Importance of Middleware

Middleware functions is important in building any kind of Node.js web application. The following are the key reasons for using middleware functions:

- Middleware helps to process requests and responses for the client.
- It controls how different application components work together.
- This is a cost-effective way of handling multi-cloud resources.
- It plays an important role in request balancing, concurrent processing, and auth management.
- With middleware, we can securely call backend assets such as capacity, databases, and more.
- It improves rendering execution for the client side significantly.
- By utilizing middleware, we can manipulate HTTP headers effectively.

# Advantages of Using Middleware

Following are some of the key advantages of using middleware in Node.js applications:

- Middleware helps Node.js applications transform request and response objects to save server time.
- Middleware can be utilized to include logging and verification functionality.
- Middleware increases client-side rendering performance.
- Middleware is used for setting HTTP headers for both request and response like auth, token, content type, and more.
- Middleware brings a huge difference in optimization and superior execution of requests.

# Key Components of Middleware

Every Middleware function is written following three defined parameters:

- **req**: This is used to define HTTP request arguments.
- **res**: This is used to define HTTP response arguments.
- **next**: This is used to define a callback argument.

```
/**
 * @param {Object} request - Express request object (commonly
named `req`)
 * @param {Object} response - Express response object (commonly
named `res`)
 * @param {Function} next - Express `next()` function
 */
function middlewareFunction(request, response, next) {
    // execute something
}
```

*Figure* 8.1 explains the process of defining middleware and the different key components used while working with middleware.

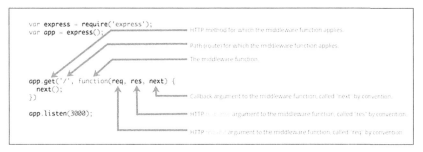

**Figure 8.1**: *Middleware usage*

Here, we have defined an express route ('/') GET method which has the first parameter as a url path that is used to access the root path of the application and second parameter is a middleware function with req, res and next arguments.

# Understanding the Next( ) Function

The **Next()** function plays an important part in the application's request and response cycle. It is a middleware function that runs the following middleware function once it is invoked. In other words, the `Next()` function is executed if the current middleware function doesn't complete the request and response cycle. It is important to note that middleware execution never hangs within the request queue.

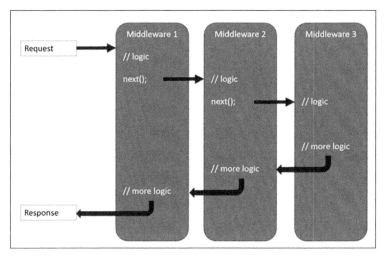

***Figure 8.2***: *Middleware execution steps*

In the preceding diagram, we have added multiple middleware functions, which are used to perform specific logic. After performing logic, control is moved to the next middleware using `Next()` function.

# Using Inbuilt Middleware with Express

Middleware functions have become an important part of an application built with the Express applications. They get to the HTTP ask and reaction objects and can either end the HTTP ask or forward it for assistance preparing to another middleware function. Middleware capacities are connected to one or more course handlers in an Express application and execute in grouping from the time an HTTP ask is gotten by the application till an HTTP reaction is sent back to the caller.

Every HTTP request and the response in Express can be effectively used by the middleware. Indeed, the middleware can terminate HTTP demands autonomously or can exchange the request to another middleware function. With the assistance of express middleware, we can construct versatile single-page, half-breed, and multi-page web applications seamlessly.

# Types of Express Middleware

Following are the different types of middleware used in Express:

- Application-level middleware `app.use`
- Router-level middleware `router.use`
- Built-in middleware `express.static`, `express.json`, `express.urlencoded`
- Error handling middleware `app.use(err,req,res,next)`
- Third-Party middleware `body-parser`, `cookie-parser`

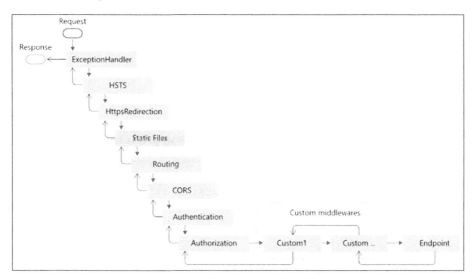

**Figure 8.3**: *Different types of Middleware*

In the preceding diagram, we can see how different steps are executed before calling the middleware function inside the request-response process.

In the following section, we will try to cover some of the most popular middleware in detail.

# Application-level Middleware

The following syntax is used for adding general application-level middleware:

```
app.use(function)
```

In application-level middleware, we can use multiple middleware functions, which can help us to transform or validate requests and responses.

For example, we can create an application route like '**/response**', which returns a response along with request time that is captured using the middleware function **requestTime().**

```
var express = require('express')
var app = express()

var requestTime = function (req, res, next) {
    req.requestTime = Date.now()
    next()
}

app.use(requestTime)

app.get('/response', function (req, res) {
    var responseText = 'Hello World!<br>'
    responseText += '<small>Requested at: ' + req.requestTime +
'</small>'
    res.send(responseText)
})

app.listen(3000, (req, res) => {
    console.log('server started running on 3000')
})
```

In the preceding code, it is mandatory that the **getEmployees()** router should be verified by the backend using **authUser** middleware, and if authenticated successfully, the rest of the operations are executed by **Next()** function. In case the user is not verified, it will throw an error with an HTTP code of 401(Unauthorized) request.

# Router-level Middleware

The following syntax is used for adding router-level middleware:

```
router.use((req, res, next) => {
   // operations
    next()
})
```

Router-level middleware is very similar to application-level middleware and works almost the same way, but it can be created and constrained to an instance of **express.Router ()**.

```
const router = express.Router()
```

Express permits you to form **Router** objects. They permit you to scope middleware to a particular set of routes. If you need the same middleware to run for numerous routes, but not for all routes in your application, they can be exceptionally valuable.

We can make use of the **router.use()** and **router.METHOD()** functions for loading router-level middleware.

```
const express = require('express');
const app = express();
const router = express.Router()

router.use((req, res, next) => {
   // operations
    next()
})

router.get("/employees", (req, res, next) => {
   // operations
    next()
}, (req, res, next) => {
```

```
    // operations
     next()

}, (req, res) => {
    res.json({
        status: true,
        id: req.params.id
    })
})


app.use('/', router)


app.listen(3000, (req, res) => {
    console.log('server started running on 3000')
})
```

# Built-in Middleware

The following syntax is used for adding built-in middleware:

```
app.use({
    urlencoded: false
});


app.use(bodyParser.urlencoded({
    extended: false
}))


app.use(bodyParser.json())
```

This built-in middleware does not depend on the 'Connect' work, and unlike the previous version of middleware, the adaptation Express 4.X now acts as a module.

In general, beneath the Express sorts of middleware, you can utilize the following three built-in middleware functions as follows:

- **static**: This works as static resources to the application (HTML records, pictures, and more).
- **json**: This works by computing the approaching request by joining hands with the JSON payloads.
- **Express.urlencoded**: This is used to combine the request body in the form of URL-encoded.

```
const express = require('express');


const bodyParser = require('body-parser');
const { error } = require('console');


const app = express();


app.use({
    urlencoded: false
});


app.use(bodyParser.urlencoded({
    extended: false
}))


app.use(bodyParser.json())


app.listen(5000, (req, res) => {
    console.log('server started running on port')
})
```

# Error Handling with Middleware

The following syntax is used for adding error-handling middleware:

```
app.use((err, req, res, next) => {
    console.log(err);
});
```

Express.js is competent at dealing with any sort of errors that might occur while running an express application. Express has the propensity of the default error handler, which takes care of all the error-handling capacities and is similar to any other type of middleware functions.

We can notice from the following code that the only difference between error handler and other middleware is that error-handling middleware has **four** arguments unlike **three** for any other middleware:

```
const express = require('express');
const bodyParser = require('body-parser');
const { error } = require('console');

const app = express();

app.get('/error', (req, res, next) => {
    next(new Error('error!'));
});

app.use((err, req, res, next) => {
    console.log(err);
    if (!res.headersSent) {
        res.status(500).send(err.message);
    }
});

app.listen(5000, (req, res) => {
    console.log('server started running on port')
})
```

# Third-party Middleware

The following syntax is used for adding third-party middleware:

```
const bodyParser = require('body-parser');
app.use(bodyParser.urlencoded({
    extended: false
}))
```

There can be many different cases where we might have to include some extra features within the backend operations. In such cases, we need to install a third-party package, which can be applied in **express** apps either at the application level or router level.

```
const express = require('express');
const bodyParser = require('body-parser');
const { error } = require('console');

const app = express();

app.use(bodyParser.urlencoded({
    extended: false
}))

app.use({
    urlencoded: false
})

app.use(bodyParser.json())

function authUser(req, res, next) {
    if(isUserVerified){
        next();
```

```
        }else{
            throw error("User not Authorized");
        }
    }


    app.post('/employees', authUser, (req, res) => {
        var list = [{
            name: 'wrewr',
            salary: '3423'
        }];
        res.json({
            "status": true,
            "data": list
        });
    });


    app.listen(3000, (req, res) => {
        console.log('server running on port')
    })
```

In the preceding code, all specified middleware like bodyParser.urlencoded and bodyParser.json() will fill the '**req.body**' property together with the parsed body along with the '**content-type**' request handler.

# List of Third-party Middleware

*Table 8.1* shows a list of commonly used Third-party middleware within express applications:

| Name | Description | Syntax |
|------|-------------|--------|
| body-parser | Parse HTTP request body. See also body, co-body, and raw-body | express.bodyParser |
| compression | Compress HTTP responses | express.compress |
| connect-rid | Generate a unique request ID | NA |

| cookie-parser | Parse cookie header and populate req. cookies. See also cookies and keygrip | `express.cookieParser` |
|---|---|---|
| cookie-session | Establish cookie-based sessions | `express.cookieSession` |
| cors | Enable cross-origin resource sharing (CORS) with various options | `NA` |
| errorhandler | Development error handling/debugging | `express.errorHandler` |
| method-override | Override HTTP methods using header | `express.methodOverride` |
| morgan | HTTP request logger | `express.logger` |
| multer | Handle multi-part form data | `express.bodyParser` |
| response-time | Record HTTP response time | `express.responseTime` |
| serve-favicon | Serve a favicon | `express.favicon` |
| serve-index | Serve directory listing for a given path | `express.directory` |
| serve-static | Serve static files | `express.static` |
| session | Establish server-based sessions (development only) | `express.session` |
| timeout | Set a timeout period for HTTP request processing | `express.timeout` |
| vhost | Create virtual domains | `express.vhost` |

***Table 8.1**: List of Third-Party Middleware*

# Creating our First Custom Middleware

We have seen the working of different types of middleware in Node.js applications since the beginning of this chapter. Now, let us see how to create our own custom Node.js Middleware from scratch for a better understanding.

With Node.js Middleware, we will be able to run any kind of code, adjust the request and response objects, stop any ongoing request-response cycle, and consequently call the next middleware within the stack when one middleware is completed.

```
function myCustomMiddleware(req, res, next) {
    // custom middleware here...
}
```

Let's try to create a custom middleware, which will be used to authenticate users before the processing of the request happens.

Here, we have created a separate code for getting user details from the user request header:

```
// getToken would be based on your authentication strategy


const user = require("../getUsers");
```

In the **setCurrentUser()** function, we will get a token from the request using the authorization request header and pass that to the **getUser** function to retrieve user details. Once user detail is fetched, we will again assign it to the request payload, and the **next()** function is used to process other middleware until a response is returned.

```
module.exports = function setCurrentUser(req, res, next) {

    // grab authentication token from req header

    const token = req.header("authorization");

    // look up the user based on the token

    const user = getUser(token).then(user => {

        // append the user object the request object

        req.user = user;

        // call next middleware in the stack

        next();

    });

};
```

To test the preceding code, let's create a **server.js** file and add the following code:

```
const express = require("express");

const setCurrentUser = require("./middleware/setCurrentUser.js");

const isLoggedIn = require("./middleware/isLoggedIn.js");

const app = express();

app.use(setCurrentUser);

app.get("/users", isLoggedIn, function(req, res) {

  // get users...

});
```

Here, the first thing we do is set the current user context inside the express application request pipeline and use the same information to check if the user is logged in or not before processing any route method like '**/users**'.

# Middleware Chaining

Middleware can be chained. We can use more than one middleware in an Express application, which means we can use more than one middleware in **app.use()** or **app.METHOD()** and can use a comma (,) to separate them.

The following syntax is used for middleware chaining:

```
app.get(path, (req, res, next) => {}, (req, res) => {})
```

In the following code, we have different kinds of middleware for handling different logics like authentication, logging, and transformations like **middleware1**, **middleware2**, **middleware3**, and more. All these middlewares can be chained one after another and are called in the same sequence in which they are defined with a given route:

```
const middleware1 = (req, res, next)=>{
    //execute some code
    next()  // pass execution to the next middleware
}

const middleware2 = (req, res, next)=>{
    //execute some code
}

const middleware3 = (req, res, next)=>{
    //execute some code
}

app.get("/", middleware1, middleware2, middleware3 );

  // OR
app.get("/", function(req, res, next){
    // first middleware
    next()  //Pass execution to the next middleware
},
function(){
    // second middleware
})
```

The following diagram from the official source provides a clear explanation.

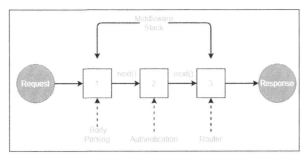

**Figure 8.4**: *Middleware chaining*

Here, the client request is being processed by the express server, and while processing the request couple of additional middleware functions are executed like body-parser, authentication, and more, before returning the response by the router.

# Conclusion

In brief, Node.JS middleware disentangles information administration through the request-response lifecycle. It allows us to run any codes with this middleware and seamlessly oversee the ask and reaction objects. Additionally, we can terminate the request-response lifecycle and conjure the following work to execute subsequent middleware work. By and large, Node.JS middleware moves forward the network between application components, gadgets, and databases.

In the next chapter, we will learn about authentication and authorization in Node.js applications.

# Further Readings

The following links can help understand more about Middleware in depth:

- https://www.oreilly.com/library/view/nodejs-the/9781838826864/video25_23.html

- https://aws.amazon.com/blogs/developer/middleware-stack-modular-aws-sdk-js/

- https://commercetools.github.io/nodejs/sdk/Middlewares.html#example

- https://simonplend.com/how-does-middleware-work-in-express/

- https://www.youtube.com/watch?v=_GJKAs7A0_4

- https://www.youtube.com/watch?v=y18ubz7gOsQ

# CHAPTER 9

# Authentication and Authorization

## Introduction

In this chapter, we will learn about the concept of Authentication and Authorization used for securing our Node.js web application. We will also learn about different techniques that are used for implementing authentication and authorization inside any kind of Node.js enterprise application.

## Structure

This chapter will cover the following topics related to Authentication and Authorization in Node.js:

- Introduction to Authentication and Authorization
- Authentication Types
- Popular Authentication Techniques
- Brief about Authorization
- Authorization Techniques
- Difference between Authentication and Authorization
- Securing RESTAPI

## Introduction to Authentication and Authorization

The authentication process is typically used to verify clients' details such as usernames, emails, credentials, and more. In contrast, authorization is used to confirm what operations they can perform based on certain roles.

Companies use authentication and authorization solutions to identify users based on their identities, such as email or username, and provide access to use applications and IT systems. Authentication is the **process of confirming a user's identity**. One of the most popular ways of authentication is the use of usernames and passwords.

Authorization refers to the process of permitting a user to access certain resources or functions after verifying their identity. For example, a system administrator may be granted the superuser access to any resource, while a standard user is barred from accessing the same resource. Most identity and access management (IAM) solutions provide both authentication and authorization functions used to secure on-premise and cloud-based applications, services, and IT infrastructure. IAM solutions help ensure that every user has a set of defined roles and responsibilities and can access the desired resources.

# Brief about Authentication

Authentication is the process of identifying an individual by verifying a person's identity, who they claim to be, to access a given system. The server uses authentication to know who is going to access the secure data. Server authentication is mostly used in combination with a username and password. Various other ways can also be used for server authentication, such as cards, retina scans, voice recognition, and fingerprints.

Authentication alone does not guarantee what kinds of operations logged-in persons will perform, including what files or data they can view or update.

Following are the different categories of information required to process user Authentication:

- **What you do know**: Password is the most commonly used way to identify any user who can access one session or transaction.
- **What you have**: This can be done using a mobile device or app, a security code, or a digital ID card.
- **What you are**: This has now become a popular way to identify anyone using biometric information such as a fingerprint, retina scan, or facial recognition.

Let's understand the authentication process through the following diagram.

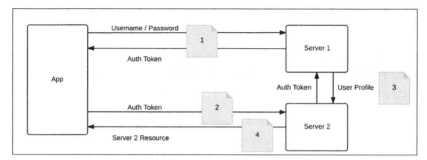

*Figure 9.1*: *Example of Authentication process*

Here, the client first opens a webpage on his client browser. On the login page, the user enters the username and password that they might have created while registering themselves with the system for the first time. Once the server confirms the identity of the user, a valid token is returned to the client, which is used to set up a secure request/response cycle until an active session is maintained between the client and the server.

After the client either logs out of the system or remains idle for some time, the token expires and no one else can access the system.

# Importance of Authentication

Following are some key benefits of using Authentication in building web applications:

- Server authentication is mostly used when the server needs to know exactly who is trying to access data or a website hosted on that server.

- Client authentication is required when the client makes sure that it is the correct server that they are trying to access.

- To establish a secure connection between the two systems, the user must verify their identity with both the server and the client.

- The client verification process typically involves the server providing the client with a certificate that verifies that the server belongs to the given company.

- Authentication helps to protect data and information that are stored digitally on servers.

# Authentication Types

Depending on the security level and type of application, there are different authentication factors or techniques as follows:

- **Single-factor Authentication**

  Single-factor or one-step authentication is the easiest and most commonly used way to authenticate a server. This method only needs the user to apply a username and password for accessing the system.

- **Two-factor authentication**

  Two-factor authentication requires two-step verification to authenticate any user. This not only requires a username and password combination to verify identity but also needs to verify some unique information that is only answered by the user including some security questions, such as the first name of a school, maid name, and more, or an OTP.

- **Multi-factor authentication**

  This is the most secure, advanced, and modern authorization technique used in securing most client and server associations. It uses two or more levels of different and independent authentication factors. This type of verification is commonly used by financial institutions, banks, and law enforcement agencies. This kind of authentication eliminates security issues caused by identity theft, password compromises, and more.

# Popular Authentication Techniques

Now we will discuss some of the popular authentication techniques used in securing modern web applications built using Node.js or any other tech stack.

# Password-based Authentication

This is one of the easiest and oldest ways to authenticate any user trying to access the system. For this kind of authentication, a password against a specific username is used to verify. If the password and username provided by the user are matched against the system database, the user is successfully authenticated.

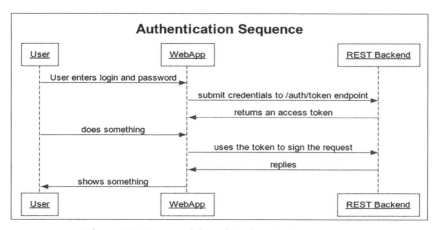

**Figure 9.2**: *Password-based Authentication process*

# Passwordless Authentication

With this technique, the user does not need to provide a password along with the username. So, instead of using a password, they receive an OTP (One Time Password) on their registered mobile number after the OTP is verified against the system. If an OTP match is found, the user is granted access to the system; otherwise, they are asked to re-verify themselves.

# 2FA/MFA

2-factor authentication/multi-factor authentication is a combination of other authentication techniques we have explored before. This authentication process can be set up on any system where, in the first step, the user can enter their regular credentials like username and password. After they have been successfully verified, the system asks them to verify some other details like an OTP, PIN, or any security questions. This kind of additional information is used to make sure that user credentials are not compromised over the internet and to provide additional security against illegal access.

# Single Sign-On (SSO)

SSO is a way of authentication used to allow access to multiple applications with a single set of credentials. For example, within a company, all users are created on the active directory, which is used for authentication and providing access to all the applications that are under that company domain. It allows the user to log in once and be automatically logged into all other systems from the same centralized active directory.

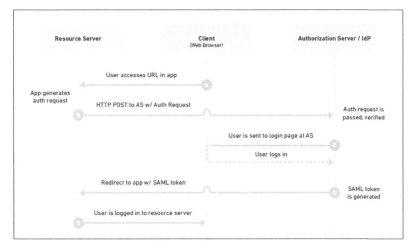

**Figure 9.3**: *SSO-based Authentication Process*

Let's understand how Microsoft SSO works behind the scenes.

When a user tries to access any of the Microsoft product suites, they will be redirected to log in using  https://outlook.live.com/. Once the user is verified using MFA, that is, by providing a username and password along with OTP, they can now access all other applications hosted under the Microsoft domain.

# Social Authentication

This type of authentication technique does not require the user to enter their credential like a username or password when they try to access an external system. Instead, these users are validated using their social network logins, such as Gmail, Facebook, Microsoft, Apple, and more, with their existing credentials.

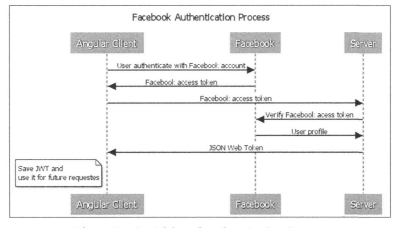

**Figure 9.4**: *Social-based Authentication Process*

# Brief about Authorization

Authorization is the process of giving someone permission based on some roles to do a specific task. In other words, authorization gives us the ability to check whether a user has the right to access a resource such as files, images, or data. It determines what data the user can access. Authorization usually works along with authentication so that the system allows users based on their credentials. Once they are inside the system, they can access specific data.

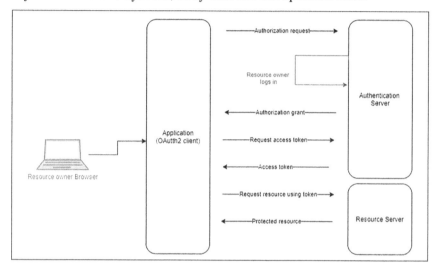

***Figure 9.5***: *Example of the Authorization process*

The authorization process starts with the client requesting the browser, and the user verifies their credentials with the system. Once verification is successful, the system will grant an authorization token, which is used for further accessing the web application.

For example, consider a customer on an e-commerce application trying to access their orders. They first log into the platform using their email and password combination. As per their authorization roles, customers will be able to access some of the pages. However, certain modules like admin or staff can't be seen by end users.

# Importance of Authorization

The following are the key benefits of using Authorization:

- Authorization is the process by which a server determines whether a client can access a resource file or data.

- Authorization is usually combined with authentication so that the server has some idea of who the client requesting access is.

- The type of authentication required for authorization may vary; in some cases, passwords may be required, while in others, they may not.

-  In some cases, there is no permission; any user can access a resource or file simply by requesting it. Most websites on the Internet do not require authentication or authorization.

# Authorization Techniques

In this section, we will learn some of the different techniques used for performing Authorization in Node.js.

# Role-based Access Control

Role-based access control (RBAC) restricts access to a system or networks of multiple systems based on a person's role and profile in an organization. This has become one of the primary methods of advanced access control systems and is being implemented by most organizations.

Employees may only use information that is necessary for the effective performance of their duties. Acceptance can be based on several factors, such as competence, responsibility, and job qualifications. In addition, access to computer resources can be limited to certain tasks, such as viewing, creating, or editing a file. Therefore, lower-level employees generally do not have access to sensitive information unless they need it to perform their duties. This is especially useful if you have a large number of employees and use third parties and contractors that makes it difficult to accurately monitor network access. Using RBAC helps protect your company's sensitive data and critical applications.

# JSON Web Token

The JSON Web Token is a widely used JSON (JavaScript Object Notation) format with some additional structure.

From the official documentation:

JSON Web Token (JWT) is an open standard (RFC 7519) that defines a compact and self-contained way for securely transmitting information between parties as a JSON object. This information can be verified and trusted because it is digitally signed. JWTs can be signed using a secret (with the HMAC algorithm) or a public/private key pair using RSA or ECDSA.

Example of JWT Token:

```
{
    "name": "John Doe",
    "email": "john@johndoe.com",
    "admin": true
}
```

The following are the key benefits of using JWT:

- They are light and easy to use in client applications, for example, mobile applications.
- They are self-contained, meaning that the Liberty JVM server can consume the token directly and use whatever the token requires as the identity to execute the request.
- They can be signed symmetrically with a shared secret using the HMAC algorithm or asymmetrically using a private key.
- They have a built-in expiration mechanism. They can be extended to cover custom requirements.

# SAML

SAML stands for Security Assertion Markup Language. It is an open standard that provides authorization information to service providers. These credentials are exchanged using digitally signed XML documents.

# OpenID Authorization

It helps clients verify the identity of end users based on authentication.

# OAuth

OAuth is an authorization protocol that allows an API to authenticate and access requested resources.

# Difference between Authentication and Authorization

*Table* 9.1 outlines the difference between authentication and authorization.

| Authentication | Authorization |
|---|---|
| Authentication is the process of identifying a user to provide access to a system | Authorization is the process of permitting to access the resources |
| In this process, both the user or client and server are verified | In this process, it is verified whether the user is allowed through the defined policies and rules |
| It is usually performed before the authorization | It is usually done once the user is successfully authenticated |
| It requires the login details of the user, such as username, password, and more | It requires the user's privilege or security level |
| Data is provided through the Token IDs | Data is provided through the access tokens |
| Example: Entering Login details is necessary for the employees to authenticate themselves to access the organizational emails or software | Example: After employees successfully authenticate themselves, they can access and work on certain functions only as per their roles and profiles |
| Authentication credentials can be partially changed by the user as per the requirement | Authorization permissions cannot be changed by the user. The permissions are given to a user by the owner/manager of the system, and he can only change it |

***Table 9.1***: *Difference between Authentication and Authorization*

# Securing Real-World APIs

Let's build a sample application where we can learn how to apply authentication and Authorization to secure our backend application.

Add the following code in **server.js**, which will be used to initialize and run our backend server application:

```
const express = require("express");

const cors = require("cors");

const app = express();

const Connection = require("./connection");


require("./app/routes/product-routes")(app);

require("./app/routes/user-routes")(app);


var corsOptions = {
  origin: "http://localhost:5000"
};


app.use(cors(corsOptions));

app.use(express.json());

app.use(express.urlencoded({
  extended: true
}));


app.get("/", (req, res) => {
  res.json({
    message: "Applying authentication in node.js application"
  });
});


const PORT = process.env.PORT || 8080;


app.listen(PORT, () => {
  Connection();
  console.log("Running on port ", PORT);
});
```

## Installing dependencies

Run the following command to install all the dependencies:

```
PS D:\Book\Building-Real-Time-application-using-Node_fork.js\
chap_09\webApp> npm i
```

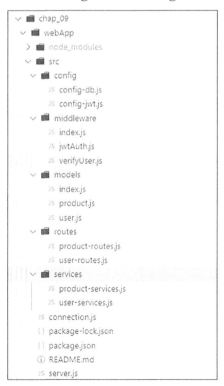

**Figure 9.6**: *Output installing dependencies*

## Understanding applications in depth

We will create our application using the following folder structure:

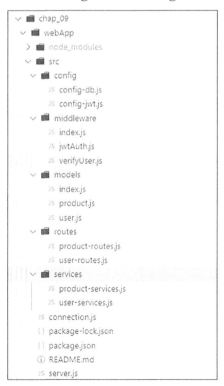

**Figure 9.7**: *Folder structure of application*

We will create our user and product models using Mongoose for persisting all the client data.

```
let mongoose = require('mongoose');
const {
  Schema
} = mongoose;

const userSchema = new Schema({
  // String is shorthand for {type: String}
  username: String,
  email: String,
  password: String
});

// Creating a Model
let user = mongoose.model('User', userSchema);

// Exporting the created module
module.exports = user;

let mongoose = require('mongoose');
const {
  Schema
} = mongoose;

const productSchema = new Schema({
  // String is shorthand for {type: String}
  name: String,
  price: String,
  isDeleted: Boolean
});
```

```
// Creating a Model
let product = mongoose.model('Product', productSchema);


// Exporting the created module
module.exports = product;
```

The next step is handling client requests through routing, and for this, we will add a couple of routes related to product and user modules.

Create a file named **product-routes.js** inside the '**src/routes**' folder and add the following code:

```
const { jwtAuth } = require("../middleware");
const productServices = require("../services/product-services.
js");


module.exports = function(app) {
  app.use(function(req, res, next) {
     res.header("Access-Control-Allow-Headers", "Authorization",
"Origin, Content-Type, Accept");
     next();
  });


  // add a product
  app.post("/api/v1/products/addproduct", [jwtAuth.verifyToken],
productServices.create);


  // find all product
  app.get("/api/v1/products/getproducts", [jwtAuth.verifyToken],
productServices.findAll);


  // find product by product id
  app.post("/api/v1/products/getproductbyid", [jwtAuth.verifyTo-
ken], productServices.findOne);
```

```
    // update product by product id
    app.post("/api/v1/products/update", [jwtAuth.verifyToken],
productServices.update);


    // delete productby product id
    app.post("/api/v1/products/delete", [jwtAuth.verifyToken],
productServices.delete);


};
```

Create another file named **user-routes.js** inside the **src/routes** folder and add the following code:

```
const { verifyUser } = require("../middleware");
const userServices = require("../services/user-services.js");


module.exports = function(app) {
  app.use(function(req, res, next) {
    res.header("Access-Control-Allow-Headers", "Authorization",
"Origin, Content-Type, Accept");
    next();
  });


  //user registration
  app.post("/api/v1/signup", [verifyUser.checkExistingUsername],
[verifyUser.checkExistingEmail], userServices.signup);


  //user login
  app.post("/api/v1/signin", userServices.signin);
};
```

To communicate between the client request and the database, we will create services like **ProductService** and **UserService**.

Create a services folder and add the file **product-service.js** inside the 'src/services' folder, and then add the following code:

```
const db = require("../models");
const Product = db.product;
// const Op = db.Sequelize.Op;


// Add new product
exports.create = (req, res) => {
  console.log("Request : ", req.body)
  validateRequest(req);

  const product = {
    name: req.body.name,
    price: req.body.price,
    isDeleted: req.body.isDeleted ? req.body.isDeleted : false
  };

  Product.create(product)
    .then(data => {
      res.send(data);
    })
    .catch(err => {
      res.status(500).send({
        message:
          err.message || "Error when add a product!"
      });
    });
};

// Find all products
exports.findAll = (req, res) => {
  Product.findAll({ where: {isDeleted: false} })
```

```javascript
    .then(data => {
      res.send(data);
    })
    .catch(err => {
      res.status(500).send({
        message:
          err.message || "Error when get all product!"
      });
    });
};

// Find product by product id
exports.findOne = (req, res) => {
  console.log("Request : ", req.body)
  validateRequest(req);

  const id = req.body.id;
  Product.findByPk(id)
    .then(data => {
      if (data) {
        res.send(data);
      } else {
        res.status(404).send({
          message: "Product not found!"
        });
      }
    })
    .catch(err => {
      res.status(500).send({
        message: "Error when get product by product id : " + id
      });
    });
};
```

```
// Update product by product id
exports.update = (req, res) => {
  console.log("Request : ", req.body)
  validateRequest(req);

  const id = req.body.id;
  Product.update(req.body, {
    where: { id: id }
  })
    .then(num => {
      if (num == 1) {
        res.send({
          message: "Product successfully updated."
        });
      } else {
        res.send({
          message: "Update process was failed"
        });
      }
    })
    .catch(err => {
      res.status(500).send({
        message: "Error updating product with product id : " + id
      });
    });
};

// Delete product by product id
exports.delete = (req, res) => {
  console.log("Request : ", req.body)
  validateRequest(req);
```

```
const id = req.body.id;
Product.destroy({
  where: { id: id }
})
  .then(num => {
    if (num == 1) {
      res.send({
        message: "Product successfully deleted."
      });
    } else {
      res.send({
        message: "Delete process was failed!"
      });
    }
  })
  .catch(err => {
    res.status(500).send({
      message: "Couldn't delete product with product id : " + id
    });
  });
};

function validateRequest(req){
  if (!req.body) {
    res.status(400).send({
      message: "Request is empty!"
    });
    return;
  }
}
```

Create another service file named **user-service.js** inside the '**src/services**' folder and add the following code:

```
const database = require("../models");
const configuration = require("../config/config-jwt.js");
const User = database.user;

var jwt = require("jsonwebtoken");
var bcrypt = require("bcryptjs");

exports.signup = (req, res) => {
  console.log("Request : ", req.body)
  validateRequest(req);

  User.create({
    username: req.body.username,
    email: req.body.email,
    password: bcrypt.hashSync(req.body.password, 8)
  })
  .then(res.send({ message: "User successfully registered" }))
  .catch(exception => {
    res.status(500).send({ message: exception.message });
  });
};

exports.signin = (req, res) => {
  validateRequest(req);

  User.findOne({
    where: {
      username: req.body.username
    }
  })
```

```
    .then(user => {
      if (!user) {
        return res.status(404).send({
            message: "User not found" });
      }


        var passwordIsValid = bcrypt.compareSync(req.body.password,
    user.password);
        if (!passwordIsValid) {
            return res.status(401).send({
                accessToken: null,
                message: "Invalid password!"
            });
        }


        // Set expired token in 10 minutes
        var token = jwt.sign({ id: user.id }, configuration.secret, {
          expiresIn: 86400
        });


        user.then(
          res.status(200).send({
            id: user.id,
            username: user.username,
            email: user.email,
            accessToken: token
          }))
        })
        .catch(err => {
          res.status(500).send({ message: err.message });
        });
    };
```

```
function validateRequest(req){
  if (!req.body) {
    res.status(400).send({
      message: "Request can't be empty!"
    });
    return;
  }
}
```

We have used a couple of middleware helper functions and components such as the JWT configuration file, token verification, user verification, and more.

Create a middlewares folder and add the file **jwt-auth.js** inside the 'src/ middlewares' folder, and then add the following code:

```
const jwt = require("jsonwebtoken");
const configuration = require("../config/config-jwt.js");
const database = require("../models");
const User = database.user;

verifyToken = (req, res, next) => {
    const bearer = req.headers['authorization'];
    let token = bearer.split(" ")[1];

    if (!token) {
        return res.status(403).send({
            message: "Error when get token!"
        });
    }

    jwt.verify(token, configuration.secret, (err, decoded) => {
        if (err) {
            return res.status(401).send({
                message: "User unauthorized!"
```

```
                });
            }
            req.userId = decoded.id;
            next();
        });
    };


    const jwtAuth = {
      verifyToken: verifyToken
    };


    module.exports = jwtAuth;
```

Create another file named **verify-user.js** inside the 'src/middlewares' folder and add the following code:

```
    const database = require("../models");
    const User = database.user;

    checkExistingUsername = (req, res, next) => {
      User.findOne({
        where: {
          username: req.body.username
        }
      })
      .then(user => {
        if (user) {
          res.status(400).send({
            message: "Username already used!"
          });
          return;
        }
        next();
```

```
    });
  };


  checkExistingEmail = (req, res, next) => {
    User.findOne({
      where: {
        email: req.body.email
      }
    }).then(user => {
      if (user) {
        res.status(400).send({
          message: "Email already used!"
        });
        return;
      }
      next();
    });
  };


  const verifyUser = {
    checkExistingUsername: checkExistingUsername,
    checkExistingEmail : checkExistingEmail
  };


  module.exports = verifyUser;
```

Now, the final step is to add the database connection details that we can use to connect to the local MongoDB server:

```
let mongoose = require('mongoose');


// Replace with your DB server
const server = '127.0.0.1:27017';
```

```
// Replace with your DB name
const database = 'mycartdb';

const Connection = () => {
  mongoose.connect(`mongodb://${server}/${database}`)
    .then(() => {
      console.log('Database connection successful')
    })
    .catch(err => {
      console.error('Database connection error')
    })
}

module.exports = Connection;
```

# Running Application

To start the application, run the following command in the terminal:

```
PS D:\Demo\webApp> node server.js
```

**Output:**

```
Running on port  8080
Database connection successful
```

We will notice that inside our MongoDB Compass, the application has successfully created database **mycartdb**, which has two collections:

- products
- users

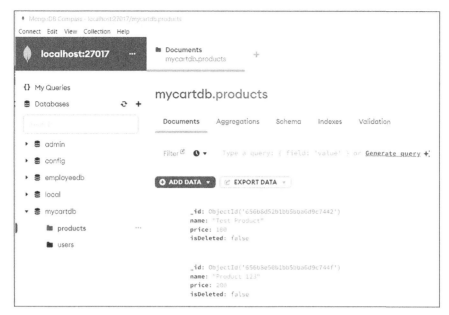

**Figure 0.8**: *mycartdb database created successfully*

Now, we will try to get the list of products by calling the following products API:

http://localhost:8080/api/v1/products/getproducts

In response, we will get an Unauthorized error due to an invalid token.

**Figure 9.9**: *Unable to get the list of Products with error*

After we have provided correct authorization header JWT token value, we will get data back from API.

**Figure 9.10**: *Getting List of Products*

# Conclusion

In brief, we can say that authentication is used to confirm the identity of the user, while authorization is mostly used to confirm the access and access rights of the user based on their roles. If the user cannot prove their identity, they will not be able to access the system. On the other hand, if your authentication proves your real identity, but you don't have permission to do a certain action, you can't use it. However, both these protection methods are often used together.

In the next chapter, we will learn about Socket.IO, which is used to create real-time applications like chat using socket programming.

# Further Readings

The following links can help understand more about the Authentication and Authorization process in depth:

- https://www.techtarget.com/searchsecurity/definition/authentication-authorization-and-accounting
- https://www.youtube.com/watch?v=u6-sUkoAQ9w
- https://www.youtube.com/watch?v=fUWkVxCv4IQ
- https://www.codementor.io/@manashkumarchakrobortty/authentication-and-authorization-in-node-js-19brdvhsyw
- https://www.udemy.com/course/nodejssecurity/

# CHAPTER 10

# Socket.IO

## Introduction

In this chapter, we will learn about some core concepts of WebSocket Programming and Socket.IO, which are used to build real-time applications. We will create one simple real-time web-based application using Socket.IO.

## Structure

This chapter will cover the following topics related to Socket.IO in Node.JS:

- Exploring WebSocket Programming
- Using Socket.IO with Express
- Communication between Client and Server
- Creating a Simple Chat Application

## Exploring WebSocket programming

In this section, we will cover some of the core concepts of WebSocket programming and understand what WebSocket really means, and how it's different from HTTP protocol. Here we will explain some of the advantages and disadvantages of using the WebSocket protocol.

## Introducing WebSocket

WebSocket is a protocol similar to HTTP that provides two-way communication channels over a single TCP connection. This allows Internet devices to communicate with each other, one acting as a client and the other as a server, and both can initiate communication. WebSocket protocol is used for creating real-time applications between the client and server over a single TCP socket connection.

We use the WebSocket protocol for two purposes:

- To open a handshake and assist in data transmission: when a server receives a handshake request sent by a client.
- Once the server establishes a WebSocket connection, they can optionally send data to each other with minimal overhead.

WebSocket communication occurs over a single TCP socket using either the WS (port 80) or WSS (port 443) protocol.

Let's understand the WebSocket workflow with the help of *Figure 10.1*:

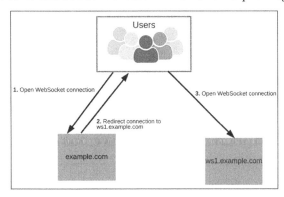

*Figure 10.1*: *WebSocket Programming example*

There are one or more users who can connect with each other through a common chat application hosted on **example.com**. The first user sends a request to the server to open a WebSocket connection to create a real-time channel that will be used for one-to-one communication. The server in return redirects that connection to **ws1.example.com**, which will be used for further communication between two users. Once all the communication is complete, the WebSockets are closed until a new connection is established.

# Usage of WebSockets

The WebSocket protocol is mostly used in building a solution that requires real-time communication between different partners. WebSockets establish a TCP socket connection between multiple devices or processes.

Following are some of the use cases of using WebSockets:

- Chat programs
- Stock price updates
- Real-time location tracking on the map

- Live interaction with the audience
- Online auctions
- Updates for IoT devices
- Online collaboration tools like Google Docs, Jira, Confluence, and so on.

## Advantages of WebSocket

Following are some of the key benefits of using WebSockets:

- We can easily build real-time applications using WebSockets.
- Channels created using WebSockets are more secure as compared to the HTTP protocol.
- WebSocket is ideal for use cases that require frequent two-way communication with low latency.
- Applications that need to communicate frequently or on a large scale.

## Disadvantages of WebSocket

Following are some of the key disadvantages of using WebSockets:

- WebSocket should be used everywhere as compared to popular HTTP protocols.
- WebSocket implementation can easily overcomplicate your application architecture, especially on the server side.

## WebSocket versus HTTP

Both HTTP and WebSocket are widely used for building communication applications. Let's compare both and understand the major differences:

| WebSocket | HTTP |
|---|---|
| WebSocket is a framed and bidirectional protocol | HTTP is a one-way protocol that works on top of TCP |
| A WebSocket protocol can support continuous data transmission | HTTP is stateless |
| They are mainly used in real-time application development | HTTP is used to develop RESTful and SOAP applications |

| All communication happens at both ends, making it a faster protocol | In HTTP, the connection is established at the other end, which makes it slightly slower than WebSocket |
|---|---|
| WebSocket uses a single TCP connection and requires a single party to terminate the connection | HTTP must create a separate connection for separate requests |
| The connection remains active until this happens | Once the request is completed, the connection is automatically disconnected |

*Table 10.1: Difference between WebSocket and HTTP protocols*

# Establishing WebSocket Connections

WebSockets do not use the **http://** or **https://** protocol. Instead, WebSocket URIs use the new **ws** or **wss** (for secure WebSocket). The rest of the URI follows the same pattern, which has an HTTP URI:  host, port, path, and any request parameters.

> "ws:" "//" host [ ":" port ] path [ "?" inquiry]

> "wss:" "//" host [ ":" port ] path [ "?" inquiry]

WebSocket connections can only be made with URIs that follow the preceding pattern. This means that when you see a URI with the pattern ws:// (or wss://), both the client and the server **MUST** follow the WebSocket connection protocol to comply with the WebSocket specification.

This model assumes that servers and clients follow the standard WebSocket connection protocol. Establishing a WebSocket connection starts with an HTTP update request, which has a number of headers, such as Connection: Update, Update: WebSocket, Sec-WebSocket-Key, and so on.

WebSocket connections are established by updating an HTTP request/response pair.

A client that supports WebSockets and wants to establish a connection sends an HTTP request that includes the following mandatory headers:

- **Connection**

    The connection header specifies whether the network connection remains open after the transaction ends. The common value of this header is keep-alive to ensure the connection's persistence so that subsequent requests can be made to the same server. During the WebSocket open handshake, we set the Upgrade header to indicate that we want to keep the connection and use it for non-HTTP requests.

- **Update**

  Clients use the Update header to establish a WebSocket connection with the server.

- **Sec-WebSocket-Key**

  Sec-WebSocket-Key is a 16-byte base64 encoded random value generated by the client.

- **Sec-WebSocket Version**

  This specifies the default version of the WebSocket protocol being accepted, and currently, version 13 is being accepted.

The following is an example of a WebSocket request made by the client to the server:

```
GET ws://example.com:8181/ HTTP/1.1
Host: localhost:8181
Connection: Refresh
Rule: No cache
Cache Management: No cache
Update: Online crack
Sec-WebSocket Version: 13
Sec-WebSocket-Key: r53kcU32uC66gDdTuKASOvm
```

When the client sends the first request to open a WebSocket connection, it waits for a response from the server. The response must contain an HTTP 101 exchange protocol response code. An HTTP 101 protocol switch response indicates that the server is switching to the protocol requested by the client in the update request header. In addition, the server must have HTTP headers that confirm a successful connection update:

```
HTTP/1.1 101 exchange protocol
Update: websocket
Connection: update
Sec-WebSocket-Accept: fA9dggdnMPU791JgAE3W4TRnyDM=
```

- **Connection: Update**

  Confirm that the connection has been updated.

- **Update: WebSocket**

  Confirm that the connection has been updated.

- **Sec-WebSocket-Accept: ab4dghdnMid7KgJVAEDSVMEDSabdec**

  Sec-WebSocket-Accept is a hash value based on base64-encoded using SHA-1 algorithm. This complex algorithm is used to identify both the client and server that support WebSocket protocol. There can be some security issues if both parties interpret WebSocket data as an HTTP request.

When the client receives a response from the server, the WebSocket connection is opened to begin sending data.

# WebSocket Protocol

The WebSocket protocol is a type of framework protocol that includes various components. It also applies the type of frame type, data part, and the length of the payload to ensure proper operation. To understand the WebSocket protocol in detail, knowing its building block is crucial.

The main parts are as follows:

- Fin Bit is the core of WebSocket. It is created automatically when you connect.
- RSV1, RSV2, and RSV3 Bits are reserved bits for additional options.
- An opcode is part of each frame and explains the process of interpreting the useful data of a particular frame. Some common opcode values are 0x00, 0x0, 0x02, 0x0a, 0x08, and many others.

| Opcode value | Description |
| --- | --- |
| 0x00 | This frame continues the payload of the previous frame |
| 0x01 | Means a text frame. The server decodes text frames into UTF-8 encoding |
| 0x02 | Means binary. The server transmits the binary frames unmodified |
| 0x03-0x07 | Reserved for future use |

| 0x08 | Indicates that the client wants to disconnect |
|------|-----------------------------------------------|
| 0x09 | Ping frame. Acts as a heartbeat mechanism to ensure that the connection is still alive. The recipient must respond with a pong |
| 0x0a | Pog frame. This frame ensures that the connection is alive and always returns a response to a Ping frame |
| 0x0b-0x0f | Reserved for future use |

**Table 10.2**: *List of OpCode*

- A mask bit is activated when one bit is 1. WebSocket requires the use of a client-selected random key for all payload data. The mask key along with the payload helps to split the payload data in the XOR operation. This is very important for application API security, as obfuscation prevents cache misinterpretation or cache poisoning from afar.

Now, let's understand its main parts in detail:

**Payload length**

It is used to encode the total data length of the WebSocket payload. The payload length is displayed when the encoded data length is less than 126 bytes. If the payload length exceeds 126 bytes, additional fields are used to describe the payload length.

**Mask key**

Each frame that the client sends to the server is masked with a 32-bit value. The mask key is displayed when the mask bit is 1. When the mask bit is 0, the mask key is zero.

**Useful data**

Any arbitrary application data and extension data is called user data. This information is used by the client and servers to negotiate and is used in early WebSocket handshakes.

# Using Socket.IO with Express

The following steps will be used to create an Express server using Socket.IO.

You will need to create a new server-side JavaScript file called server.js. It will contain all of your server instantiations and handle your Socket.IO messaging.

Let's create **Server.js** file and add the following code:

```
var express = require('express'),
  app = express(),
  http = require('http'),
  socketIO = require('socket.io'),
  server, io;

app.get('/', function (req, res) {
  res.sendFile(__dirname + '/index.html');
});

server = http.Server(app);
server.listen(5000);

io = socketIO(server);

io.on('connection', function (socket) {
  socket.emit('greeting-from-server', {
    greeting: 'Hello Client'
  });
  socket.on('greeting-from-client', function (message) {
    console.log(message);
  });
});
```

The server will serve a static HTML file called **index.html** when the user navigates to the root directory of the server. The HTML file will handle the client-side Socket.IO messaging.

Let's create an index.html file and add the following code:

```
<!DOCTYPE html>
<html>
<head>
</head>
```

```
<body>
    <script src="/socket.io/socket.io.js"></script>
    <script>
        var socket = io('http://localhost:5000');
        socket.on('ping-from-server', function (message) {
            document.body.appendChild(
                document.createTextNode(message.greeting)
            );
            socket.emit('ping-from-client', {
                greeting: 'My first socket programming'
            });
        });
    </script>
</body>
</html>
```

Running application:

```
PS D:\Demo\web-app> node server.js
```

Now check the browser http://localhost:5000 for output:

**Figure 10.2**: *Output of First socket application*

Firstly, here we have created a new **Express** server:

```
var express = require('express')
```

Next, we set up our **HTTP** server, which will handle all the requests between the client and server:

```
http = require('http'),
server = http.Server(app);
server.listen(5000);
```

We imported the Socket.IO module and passed the HTTP server directly to the `Socket.IO` constructor method to create the server instance to listen for new socket connections:

```
socketIO = require('socket.io'),
io = socketIO(server);
io.on('connection', function (socket) {
  socket.emit('ping-from-server', {
    greeting: 'My first Socket programming'
  });
  socket.on('ping-from-client', function (message) {
    console.log(message);
  });
});
```

Finally, we created our front-end application, which will send the request to our WebSocket server created initially.

# Communication between Client and Server

Socket.IO is mainly used for creating real-time applications based on direct communication channels created between client and server.

Socket.IO can send an event to a specific browser client. It can also send events from the server to multiple browsers. Socket.IO is capable of using many transfer mechanisms. This is the key to support all web browsers. Supported transmissions are WebSockets, Flash, Ajax long polling, Ajax multipart streaming, Forever Iframe, and JSONP polling. Allowed transports and the order in which they are tried can be customized. You can change the "transports" option to an array of transport names.

## Reasons to Choose Node.js and Socket.IO

Node.js and Socket.IO offer several advantages, as follows:

- **Real-time functionality**: Socket.IO is a JavaScript library that supports real-time two-way communication between clients and servers, making it an ideal choice for designing real-time chat applications. Socket.IO uses WebSocket under the hood, which enables real-time data transfer with low latency.

- **Scalability**: Node.js is designed to be highly scalable, meaning it can handle many simultaneous connections without lag or responsiveness, making it the right choice for building live chat applications that support thousands or even millions of users.

- **Cross-Platform Compatibility**: Node.js as a programming language is compatible with several operating systems including Windows, Linux, and macOS. This means engineers can code once and deploy across multiple platforms, making it easier and faster to develop and maintain live chat applications across devices and environments.

# Creating a Simple Chat Application

We will create our backend server application using Node.js and then connect with the front-end, which will be developed using React.js.

We will design our application using the basic structure, as shown in *Figure 10.3*:

**Figure 10.3**: *Project Structure*

Let's create a **server/router.js** file and add the following code:

```
const express = require('express');
const router = express.Router();
```

```
    router.get('/', (req, res) => {
        res.send('server is up and running');
});


    module.exports = router;
```

Let's create a **server/client.js** file and add the following code:

```
    const clients = [];


    const addClient = ({ id, name, room }) => {
        const existingClient = clients.find((client) => client.room
=== room.ToLowerCase() && client.name === name.ToLowerCase());


        if(existingPerson ) {
            return { error: 'Client name is taken'};
        }


        const client= { id, name, room };


        clients.push(client);


        return { client};
    }


    const removeClient = (id) => {
        const index = clients.findIndex((client) => client.id === id);


        if(index !== -1) {
            return clients.splice(index, 1)[0]
        }
    }
```

```
const getClient = (id) => clients.find((client) => client.id ===
id);


const getClientInRoom = (room) => clients.filter((client) => cli-
ent.room === room);


module.exports = { addClient, removeClient, getClient, getClien-
tsInRoom };
```

Let's create a **server/index.js** file and add the following code:

```
const http = require('http');

const express = require('express');

const socketio = require('socket.io');

const cors = require('cors');


const { addClient, removeClient, getClient, getClientsInRoom } =
require('./clients');


const router = require('./router');


const app = express();

const server = http.createServer(app);

const io = socketio(server);


app.use(cors());

app.use(router);


io.on('connect', (socket) => {
  socket.on('join', ({ name, room }, callback) => {
    const { error, client} = addClient({ id: socket.id, name,
room });


    if(error) return callback(error);
```

```
    socket.join(client.room);

    socket.emit('message', { client: 'admin', text: `${client.
name}, welcome to room ${client.room}.`});
    socket.broadcast.to(client.room).emit('message', { client:
'admin', text: `${client.name} has joined!` });

    io.to(client.room).emit('roomData', { room: client.room, cli-
ents: getClientsInRoom(client.room) });

    callback();
  });

  socket.on('sendMessage', (message, callback) => {
    const client = getClient(socket.id);

    io.to(client.room).emit('message', { client: client.name,
text: message });

    callback();
  });

  socket.on('disconnect', () => {
    const client= removeClient(socket.id);

    if(client) {
      io.to(client.room).emit('message', { client: 'Admin', text:
`${client.name} has left.` });
      io.to(client.room).emit('roomData', { room: client.room,
clients: getClientsInRoom(client.room)});
    }
  })
});
```

```
server.listen(process.env.PORT || 5000, () => console.log(`Server
has started.`));
```

Let's create a **server/package.json** file and add the following code:

```
{
  "name": "app-server",
  "version": "1.0.0",
  "description": "",
  "main": "index.js",
  "scripts": {
    "start": "nodemon index.js",
    "test": "echo \"Error: no test specified\" && exit 1"
  },
  "keywords": [],
  "author": "",
  "license": "",
  "dependencies": {
    "cors": "^2.8.5",
    "express": "^4.17.1",
    "nodemon": "^2.0.5",
    "socket.io": "^2.3.0"
  }
}
```

Next, we are going to build our frontend application using React library.

For those who are not aware of React, they can learn more about this popular frontend library at https://react.dev/learn

Let's create a **clientApp/package.json** file and add the following code:

```
{
  "name": "my-chat-app",
  "version": "1.0.0",
```

```
    "private": true,
    "dependencies": {
      "@testing-library/jest-dom": "^4.2.4",
      "@testing-library/react": "^9.5.0",
      "@testing-library/user-event": "^7.2.1",
      "query-string": "^6.13.5",
      "react": "^16.14.0",
      "react-dom": "^16.14.0",
      "react-emoji": "^0.5.0",
      "react-router": "^5.2.0",
      "react-router-dom": "^5.2.0",
      "react-scripts": "3.4.1",
      "react-scroll-to-bottom": "^4.0.0",
      "socket.io-client": "^2.3.1"
    },
    "scripts": {
      "start": "react-scripts start",
      "build": "react-scripts build",
      "test": "react-scripts test",
      "eject": "react-scripts eject"
    },
    "eslintConfig": {
      "extends": "react-app"
    },
    "browserslist": {
      "production": [
        ">0.2%",
        "not dead",
        "not op_mini all"
      ],
      "development": [
        "last 1 chrome version",
        "last 1 firefox version",
```

```
        "last 1 safari version"
    ]
  }
}
```

Let's create a **clientApp/src/index.js** file and add the following code:

```
import React from 'react'
import ReactDOM from 'react-dom';,o
import App from './App';
ReactDOM.render(<App />, document.querySelector('#root'));
```

Let's create a **clientApp/src/App.js** file and add the following code:

```
import React from 'react';
import { BrowserRouter as Router, Route } from
'react-router-dom';
import Join from './components/Join/Join';
import Chat from './components/Chat/Chat';

const App = () => (
    <Router>
        <Route path="/" exact component={Join} />
        <Route path="/chat" component={Chat} />
    </Router>
);
export default App;
```

Let's create a **clientApp/src/components/Chat/Chat.js** file and add the following code:

```
import React from "react"
import Messages from "../Messages/Messages";
```

```
import { useState, useEffect } from "react"

import io from "socket.io-client";


import "./Chat.css";

import queryString from "query-string";

let socket;

export default function Chat({ location }) {

    const [name, setName] = useState('');
    const [room, setRoom] = useState('');
    const [message, setMessage] = useState('');
    const [messages, setMessages] = useState([]);
    const [users, setUsers] = useState('');

    const ENDPOINT = 'localhost:5000';

    useEffect(() => {
        const { name, room } = queryString.parse(location.search);

        socket = io(ENDPOINT);
        setName(name);
        setRoom(room);

        socket.emit('join', { name, room }, (error) => {
            if(error) {
                alert(error);
            }
        });
```

```
    }, [ENDPOINT, location.search]);

    useEffect(() => {
        socket.on('message', (message) => {
            setMessages(messages => [...messages, message]);
        });

        socket.on('roomData', ({ users }) => {
            setUsers(users);
        });
    }, []);

    const sendMessage = (event) => {
        event.preventDefault();

        if(message){
         socket.emit('sendMessage', message, () => setMessage(''));
        }
    }

     return (
        <div className="outerContainer">
            <div className="container">
            <div className="infoBar">
                <div className="leftInnerContainer">
                    <img className="onlineIcon" src={onlineIcon}
alt="online"/>
                    <h3>{ room }</h3>
                </div>
                <div className="rightInnerContainer">
                    <a href="/"><img src={closeIcon} alt="close"
                    /></a>
                </div>
```

```
                    </div>
                        <Messages messages={messages} name={name}/>
                        <form className="form">
                            <input
                            className="input"
                            type="text"
                            placeholder="Type a message..."
                            value={message}
                            onChange={(event) => setMessage(event.target.
                            value)}
                            onKeyPress={event => event.key === 'Enter' ?
sendMessage(event) : null}
                            />
                            <button className="sendButton" on-
Click={(event) => sendMessage(event)}>Send</button>
                        </form>
                </div>
            </div>
        );
    }
```

Let's create a **clientApp/src/components/Home/Home.js** file and add the following code:

```
import React from 'react';
import { useState } from 'react';
import { Link } from 'react-router-dom';
import './Home.css';

function Home() {
    const [name, setName] = useState('');
    const [room, setRoom] = useState('');

    function handleNameEvent(event) {
```

```
                setName(event.target.value);
        }
        function handleRoomEvent(event) {
            setRoom(event.target.value);
        }


        return (
            <div className="homeOuterContainer">
                <div className="header">

                </div>
                <div className="homeInnerContainer">
                    <h1 className="heading">Chat App</h1>
                        <div><input placeholder="Name" className="homeIn-
put" type="text" onChange={handleNameEvent} required /></div>
                        <div><input placeholder="Room" className="homeIn-
put mt-20" type="text" onChange={handleRoomEvent} /></div>


                        <Link onClick={event => (!name || !room) ? event.
preventDefault() : null} to={`/chat?name=${name}&room=${room}`}>
                            <button className="button mt-20" type="sub-
mit">Start Chat</button>
                        </Link>
                </div>
            </div>
        )
}


export default Home
```

Let's create a **clientApp/src/components/Message/Message.js** file and add the following code:

```
import React, { useState } from 'react'
```

```
import './Message.css';

function Message({ message: { text, user }, name }) {

    let isSentByCurrentUser = false;

    const trimmedName = name.trim().toLowerCase();

    if(user === trimmedName) {
        isSentByCurrentUser = true;
    }

    return (
        isSentByCurrentUser
        ? (
            <div className="messageContainer justifyEnd">
                <div className="">
                    <p className="sentText pr-10">{trimmedName}</p>
                    <div className="messageBox backgroundBlue">
                        <p className="messageText
colorWhite">{ReactEmoji.emojify(text)}</p>
                    </div>
                </div>
            </div>
        )
        : (
            <div className="messageContainer justifyStart">
                <div className="">
                    <p className="sentText pl-10">{user}</p>
                    <div className="messageBox backgroundLight">
                        <p className="messageText
colorDark">{ReactEmoji.emojify(text)}</p>
                    </div>
                </div>
```

```
                    </div>
               )
          );
     }


     export default Message;
```

**Running Backend Application:**

```
     PS D:\Book\chap_10\web-app\server> node index.js
```

**Output:**

```
     Server has started at http://localhost:5000.
```

**Running Client Application:**

```
     PS D:\Book\chap_10\web-app\clientApp> npm start
```

**Output:**

```
     Compiled successfully!
     You can now view my-chat-app in the browser.
       Local:            http://localhost:3000
       On Your Network:  http://192.168.1.106:3000


     Note that the development build is not optimized.
     To create a production build, use npm run build.
     webpack compiled successfully
```

After the frontend application is started successfully, navigate to http://localhost:3000 using the Chrome Browser.

As soon as the application is launched, we will land on the home page where the user will get the option to start their chat using **Name** and **Room** details.

*Figure 10.4: Chat Home page*

After entering the Username and room details, when clicking on the `Start Chat` button, the user enters the chat room.

*Figure 10.5: John started chatting in the Friends chat room*

Open another browser like **Firefox or Edge** to simulate another user, where different users will start chatting using their Username and room details.

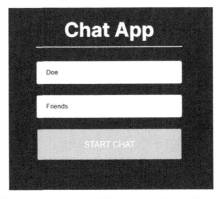

*Figure 10.6: Doe started talking in the Friends chat room*

On the Edge browser, you will see the screen where **Doe** has started chatting.

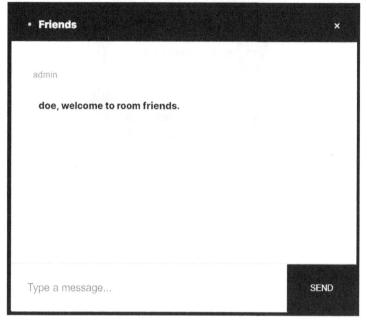

**Figure 10.7**: *Doe joined the Friends chat room*

Whereas, on the Chrome browser where **John** had already started talking, you will see a different message about **Doe** joining the room just now.

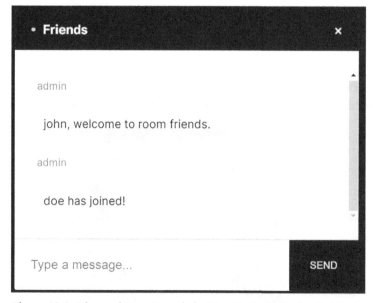

**Figure 10.8**: *John and Doe started chatting in the Friends chat room*

Once both users have joined the chat room, they can start a discussion.

*Figure 10.9*: *John and Doe's discussion in the Friends chat room*

After the completion of all the discussions between both users, **Doe** will end the chat session and **John** will receive a notification about exiting from the room.

*Figure 10.10*: *Doe's leaving Friends chat room*

# Conclusion

WebSocket enables a two-way interactive communication session between client and server without requesting a response from the server. It offers both speed improvements and real-world features compared to other protocols. However, as with any application, using WebSocket requires careful programming practices as well as runtime protection against unique threats. We explored further into Socket.IO, which provides an easy ready-made API for creating real-time web applications using the Node.js platform.

In the next chapter, we will learn about different ways of error handling and logging in Node.js applications.

# Further Readings

The following links can be helpful in understanding more about Middleware in depth:

- https://www.developer.com/web-services/intro-web-sockets/
- https://www.youtube.com/watch?v=8ARodQ4Wlf4
- https://socket.io/docs/v4/
- https://www.geeksforgeeks.org/introduction-to-sockets-io-in-node-js/
- https://medium.com/@ipenywis/node-js-socket-io-introduction-and-getting-started-01-fecfcd60b9b7
- https://www.crowdbotics.com/blog/build-chat-app-with-nodejs-socket-io
- https://www.section.io/engineering-education/understanding-socket/

# CHAPTER 11

# Handling and Logging Errors

## Introduction

In this chapter, we will learn about some of the core concepts around errors in JavaScript and how we can handle them gracefully. We will also explain about different types of errors in Node.js applications and what can cause them to happen. This chapter will focus on how to handle errors inside the Node.js application using various techniques available inside the framework. At the end of this chapter, we will explain logging errors in Node.js applications using one of the most popular Winston packages.

## Structure

This chapter will cover the following topics related to Handling and Logging Errors in Node.JS:

- Defining Errors in JavaScript
- Type of Errors
- Defining Error Handling in JavaScript
- Understanding Error Handling in Depth
- Handling Errors Using Middleware Functions
- Custom Error Handling
- Building Express Application Using Error Handling
- Logging Errors in Node.js Application
- Logging Errors Using the Winston

# Defining Errors in JavaScript

Errors are statements that can prevent a program from working properly. There are main two types of errors that can occur when writing a JavaScript program which include syntax and runtime errors. The most common type of error found in JavaScript code belongs to syntax or compile-time errors, which occur when something goes wrong with the syntax of the program code itself. Syntax errors are also called parsing errors.

# Types of Errors

Three types of errors can occur when executing JavaScript code:

- Compile time error
- Runtime error

Let's try to understand each of them in more detail.

**Compile time error**

Syntax or compile-time errors appear when the user makes a mistake in the predefined syntax of the JavaScript language. The interpreter cannot interpret these compile-time errors. In NodeJS, the interpreter can find these syntax errors at compile time.

These errors are mostly typos (spelling mistakes) or sometimes ignore important characters, such as using a semicolon to end a sentence. In some programming languages, like Ruby, incorrect indentation or formatting can cause syntax errors. Most importantly, these errors prevent the program from running until the error is corrected.

As shown in *Figure 11.1*, we get a syntax error when **port11** is mistakenly written in place of using **port:**

```
const express = require('express')


const app = express()
const port = 3000


app.listen(port, () => {
```

```
    console.log(`Example app listening at
http://localhost:${port11}`)
})
```

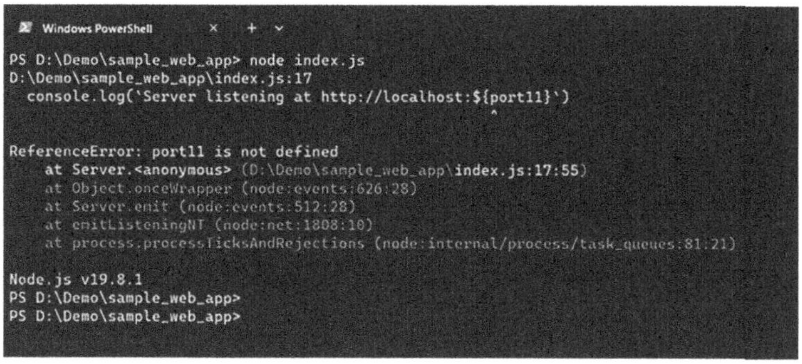

**Figure 11.1**: *Syntax Error in JavaScript*

## Runtime error

A runtime error occurs during the execution of the program and is detected only when the program starts its execution. Sometimes, they are also known as runtime errors, and these errors can suddenly crash the program or terminate running applications in the middle of executions. One example is getting **RangeError** when accessing the 5th array element, which is not defined in the array.

In this kind of situation, we use exception handling, which allows us to maintain the normal flow of the program without any execution failures.

Here are some of the scenarios where these types of errors could occur as these scenarios are very limited.

- When there is division by zero and integer overflow.
- Segmentation faults, such as accesses outside the array, can also cause runtime errors.

As a developer, you are responsible for handling these types of errors. In the following example, we are trying to access the length property of Array; it's throwing an error because **tempArr** is initiated with a null value:

```
const tempArr = null;
if(tempArr.length > 0){
    console.log(`Length of array - ${tempArr.length}`);
}
```

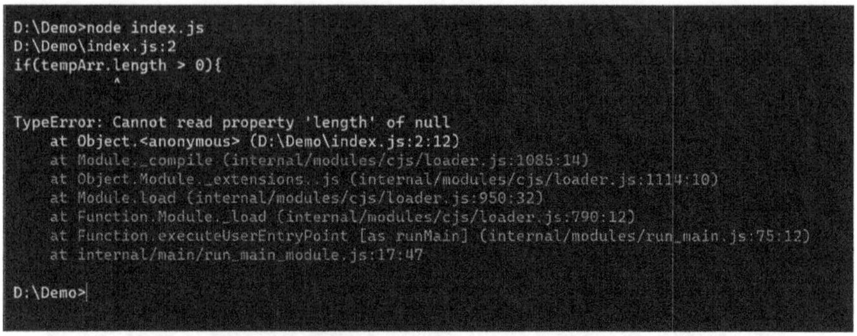

*Figure 11.2: Runtime Error in JavaScript*

# Defining Error Handling in JavaScript

JavaScript exception handling is one of the most powerful features that helps to prevent our programs and applications from unexpected crashes. In addition, it also helps developers to write and maintain the normal flow of our programs.

**Exception** is known as an unexpected or abnormal condition that occurs during the execution of a program. The word **handling** refers to how we deal with these unusual situations.

JavaScript exception handling is the process of handling abnormal statements that occur during program execution. These exception techniques also provide proper error tracking mechanisms, which means that the exception explains itself with all the details of why an error occurred, along with its location in the code.

We use the **try-catch** block, a default feature of the JavaScript language and widely used for handling errors and exceptions in our application:

```
try {
    console.log("Code executed after timeout")
    throw new Error("throw Error!")
} catch (error) {
    next(error)  // call middleware handler to pass error
}
```

We will try to understand how we can use a **try-catch** block to handle our errors and throw meaningful messages to the end user. In this example, we have created a **sum()** function, which will add two numbers and alert the result to the user:

```
function sumNbr(a, b) {
    try {
        console.log(`Value of variable a & b is : ${a}, ${b}`);
        alertdd(`Sum - ${a+b}`)
    } catch (e) {
        console.log("Error: " + e.description);
        throw new Error(e);
    }
}
sumNbr(5, 5);
```

When we execute the preceding code, we will get an exception, since we have mistakenly typed **alert** as **alertdd**.

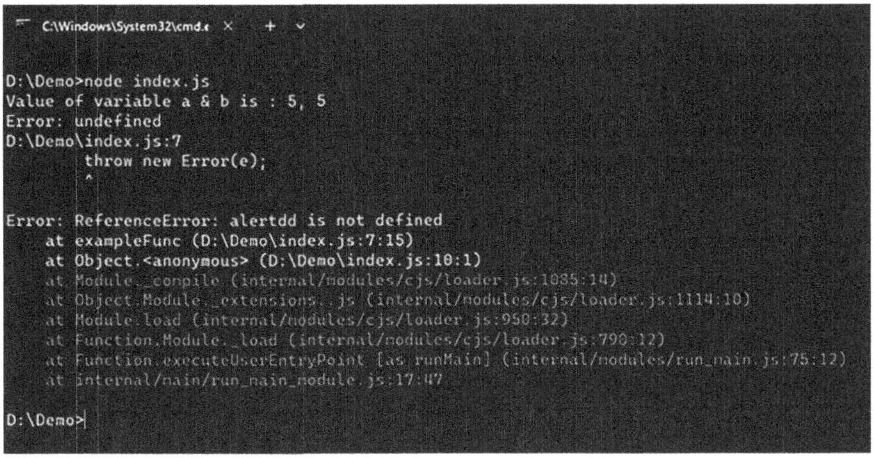

**Figure 11.3**: *Error handling in JavaScript*

# Factors Causing Errors in Node.js

System errors or application exceptions can occur in many different ways. One such example includes referring to an undefined variable or passing an argument of the wrong type.

Some of the common Node.js errors include:

- **EvalError**: These errors occur when the global function **eval()** gets executed:

```
try {
    throw new EvalError("Hello", "exampleFile.js", 10);
} catch (e) {
    console.log(e instanceof EvalError); // true
    console.log(e.message); // "Hello"
    console.log(e.name); // "EvalError"
    console.log(e.fileName); // "exampleFile.js"
    console.log(e.lineNumber); // 10
    console.log(e.columnNumber); // 0
}
```

- **RangeError**: These errors occur when you try to access a variable outside its range, such as trying to retrieve the fourth element of an array that only contains three elements:

```
var verifyNumber = function (num) {
    if (num < MIN || num > MAX) {
        throw new RangeError('Parameter range must be between
' + MIN + ' and ' + MAX);
    }
};

try {
    verifyNumber(50);
} catch (e) {
    if (e instanceof RangeError) {
        // Handle range error
    }
}
```

- **ReferenceError**: These errors occur when you try to access a variable that does not exist inside the JavaScript scope:

```
function sumOfNumbers() {
    let val1 = 2;
    let val2 = 3;
    return val1 + val2;
}


sumOfNumbers();


console.log(val1);
```

- **SyntaxError**: These errors occur when developers write incorrect code, such as using a string in place of an integer value:

```
function check(x, y){
    if((x === 10) && (y ===5){    // Missing closing parenthesis;
return true
    } else {
      return false
    }
}
```

- **TypeError**: These errors occur when you try to access a variable that is not a valid type:

```
let a = 1
console.log(a())


//output
Uncaught TypeError: a is not a function
```

- **URIError**: These errors occur whenever invalid parameters are passed to the **encodeURI** or **decodeURI** parameters:

```
// Error here
decodeURIComponent('%E0%B4%A');
```

# Types of Errors in Node.js

Various types of errors can happen while running Node.js backend server applications. These errors have been defined in a couple of different ways, as follows:

## Functional Errors

These errors are mostly expected during the execution of a Node.js program and should be handled appropriately. These kinds of errors don't mean that the program itself has any bugs, so we need proper ways to handle these errors.

Following are some of the common reasons for causing functional errors:

- These errors can be caused if a connection to the server cannot be established.
- These errors can be caused if server details are not found.
- These errors can happen due to invalid user input.
- These errors can happen when the server returns some invalid response like 400 or 500 responses.
- Sometimes applications throw errors when the system itself is running out of memory.

## Programming Errors

These errors are called bugs because of some problems in the code itself, which are introduced during the development of functionality. For example, these are common errors in the Node.js function when applications are trying to read a property of an undefined object.

Following are list of some usage cases of Programming errors:

- When an asynchronous function is called without a callback function.
- Sometimes programmers forget to resolve the promise at the end of functions.

- In most instances, we pass incompatible variables as function parameters, such as passing a string when an object was expected, and vice-versa.

- In some places, we might see that the wrong number of parameters are passed in the function.

# Understanding Error Handling in Depth

Error handling is the most ignored piece of the puzzle in building a software application and is not addressed properly in almost every case. Most of the developer's focus lies on writing code that defines routing, route handlers, application logic, database queries, and more. Sometimes teams that follow good practices and standard processes of developing software put more effort into organizing code quality, maintaining software, and improving performance.

As a result, error handling takes a back seat until and unless the software starts behaving differently due to errors and exceptions occurring while running the applications. Putting lots of effort into developing applications with standard practices, adding the most optimized code, and releasing good quality products are good things. However, it's also very important to remember that an application error will negatively impact the user, and all previous hard work will go in vain.

In this world of competition among different large and small software companies, it becomes very important to ensure that our application can handle all possible errors and exceptions. If errors are not addressed before shipping the product into the market, they can directly affect the company's business. At the same time, we need to make sure that errors provide only meaningful information about errors to end users so that they can understand what has happened while running the application. Therefore, it is important to be very thoughtful and smart when it comes to dealing with bugs in our program.

# Error Handling Inside Express

Express.js is one of the most popular server-side frameworks based on the JavaScript language. One very important aspect of Express.js is its ability to automatically detect any kind of errors and allow them to be fixed by writing minimal additional code. This in-built error handling mechanism reduces complexity and provides better application support that can scale without the need to worry about tracking errors. Most error handling in express functionality is achieved through middleware functions.

Middleware functions are triggered as soon as the server receives a request and are executed before returning a response to the client. Since they have access to both the request and response objects, they can be used to transform any data along with calling the `next()` middleware function.

Two important aspects of middleware functions make it easy to implement error handling in Node.js applications:

- The middleware runs when a request arrives at the route and is completed when the response is returned to the client.
- There are several native and third-party middleware that are publicly available, such as session management, authentication, login, redirection, and more.

# Express.js Default Error Handling

Express provides default error detection to prevent your application from crashing while handling errors. Regardless of whether we are writing synchronous or asynchronous code, we need to ensure proper error handling, which can make applications robust.

Let's try to understand how error handling can be used in Express applications, especially in synchronous and asynchronous code execution.

### Synchronous code

When JavaScript code is executed sequentially, and one at a time, we say the code has run synchronously. Express automatically catches when an error occurs in synchronous code.

We can demonstrate this situation by throwing an error:

```
app.get('/', (req, res) => {
    throw new Error("Hello Error!")
})
```

When we run the preceding code, Express detects this error with proper details, including the error status code, message, and even stack traces in some situations. These are handled by Express's default built-in error handler middleware function, which helps to save you from large try-and-catch blocks, as shown in the following code:

```
app.get('/', (req, res, next) => {
    try {
        throw new Error("Error!")
    } catch (error) {
        next(error)
    }
})
```

## Asynchronous code

When developing backend applications, we mostly use asynchronous JavaScript logic to handle all the requests, which can be used to read and write files, query databases, and make external HTTP API requests. As we have seen, Express auto-detect all errors using a built-in error handler when executing synchronous code. However, in the case of asynchronous code, our server application ends because of an error.

```
app.get('/', (req, res) => {
    setTimeout(() => {
        console.log("Code executed after timeout")
        throw new Error("Error thrown!")
    }, 1000)
})
```

Let's try to handle this error when executing asynchronous code:

```
const express = require('express')
const app = express()

app.get('/', (req, res) => {
    setTimeout(() => {
```

```
        try {
            console.log("Code executed after timeout")
            throw new Error("throw Error!")
        } catch (error) {
            next(error) // pass on error to next middleware handler
        }
    }, 1000)
})


app.listen(3000, () => {
    console.log(`Server listening at http://localhost:3000`);
})
```

The preceding code is executed successfully without any errors or exceptions that could crash our server.

*Figure* 11.4 shows the error that occurs after the execution of asynchronous code:

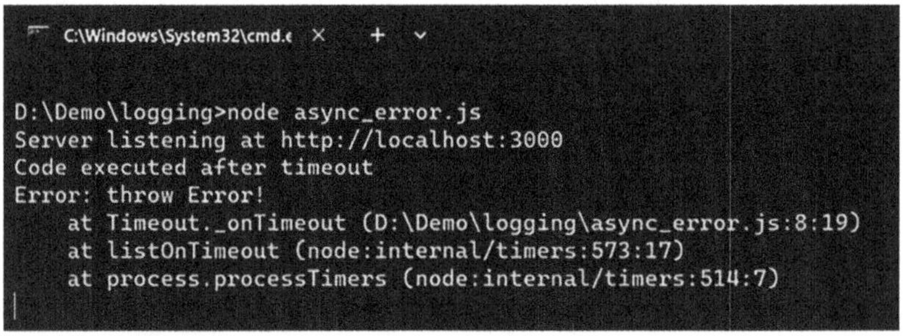

**Figure 11.4**: *Error happening after async code executed*

And *Figure* 11.5 shows the browser error shown after the asynchronous code is executed:

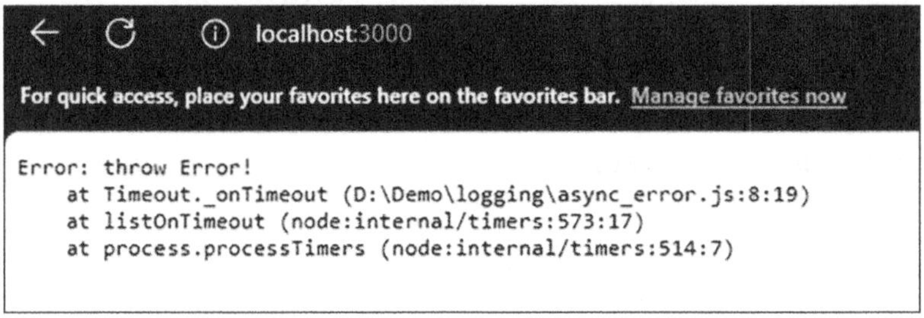

**Figure 11.5**: *Browser error shown after async code executed*

# Custom Error Handling

The default error-handling middleware of Express is very useful in dealing with unexpected, unhandled errors in most scenarios. However, this default error handling is not sufficient to cater to all the requirements for building robust server applications using Node.js. Most application developers prefer to handle errors in their way.

For example, errors can be logged to the database, file, and more, for further analysis, debugging, and reporting purposes.

In the following example, we will try to handle the error in the route itself. Depending on the success or failure of the operation, we will either return the error or redirect the user to some custom error page:

```
const express = require('express')
const app = express()

app.get('/page1', (req, res) => {
    try {
        // do some operation like reading file or database call
        return res.send("Page one returned")
    } catch (error) {
        console.error(err)
        res.status('500').send(err) // return error to user
    }
})

app.get('/page2', (req, res) => {
    try {
        // do some operation like reading file or api call
        return res.send("Page two data")
    } catch (error) {
        console.error(err)
        res.redirect('/error') // redirect to error page
    }
```

```
})

app.get('/error', (req, res) => {
    res.send("Error page.")
})

app.listen(3000, () => {
    console.log(`Server listening at http://localhost:3000`);
})
```

We have defined two separate routes that can perform different operations, such as reading files or connecting to databases. This approach will work in small applications where we have only a couple of routes, but as soon as we keep on adding more and more routes, our error-handling logic gets duplicated and will become a nightmare to maintain over a long time.

After running the application, the following output will be observed when navigating through different pages:

1. http://localhost:3000/

*Figure 11.6: Error on navigating to the home page*

2. http://localhost:3000/page1

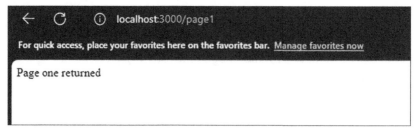

*Figure 11.7: Display output on navigating to page1*

3.  http://localhost:3000/page2

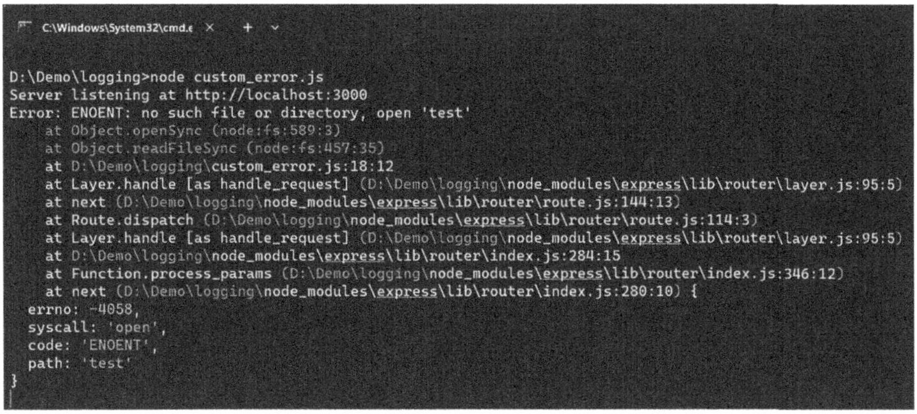

*Figure 11.8: Throwing error on navigating to page 2*

# Handling Errors Using Middleware Functions

As demonstrated in the preceding example, we can handle different kinds of errors with the help of a try-catch block inside our Express application. This works perfectly fine and allows us to run our applications without crashing them at runtime. However, the major disadvantage of this approach is that if we have 100 routes, then it becomes difficult to define common logic for each route.

Using Express middleware functions is a better solution to implement error handling in Node.js applications. As per our requirements. We can write multiple middleware functions to handle different kinds of errors in our application. All routes can benefit from these functions by making a **next()** function call.

Middleware functions are much easier to work as they can automatically access the error, request, and response objects and can be called in a specific order using only the **next()** function.

**In the following code example, we will replace the require with req.**

For example:

```
app.use((error, req, res, next) => {
    console.log("Log error",error)
    next() // use to call next set of middleware
})
```

**Note:** *The most important thing is the order in which middleware functions are defined and called subsequently. The error handler must define the middleware functions after the route handlers so that subsequent (error) calls are directed to them.*

```
const express = require('express')
const promises = require('fs').promises
const app = express()

app.get('/page1, (req, res, next) => {
  promises.readFile('./page1.txt')
    .then(data => res.send(data))
    .catch(err => next(err));
})
app.get('/page2, (req, res, next) => {
  promises.readFile('./page2.txt')
    .then(data => res.send(data))
    .catch(err => {
        err.type = 'redirect';
        next(err);
    })
})

app.get('/error', (req, res) => {
  res.send("Custom error landing page.")
})

app.use((error, req, res, next) => {
  console.log("Error Handling Middleware called")
  console.log('Path: ', req.path)
  console.error('Error: ', error)
```

```
    if (error.type == 'redirect')
        res.redirect('/error')
      else
        res.status(500).send(error)
})
app.listen(5000, () => {
    console.log(`Example app listening at http://local-
host:${5000}`)
})
```

Here, we put all our logic for error handling in the middleware functions, so that we can write our logic for customized error handling depending on the type of error that occurs in the application.

This approach allows code reusability and also has become more efficient. As soon as an error occurs, Express will collect all the errors using the middleware function and send a customized response to the client.

When we run the preceding code, we will get the following output after browsing localhost:3000/page1:

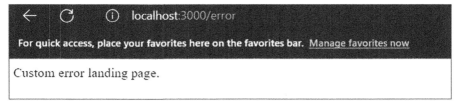

*Figure 11.9*: *Error middleware function in Express*

We will get a custom error page if any such errors occur that are not handled properly when browsing localhost:3000/page2:

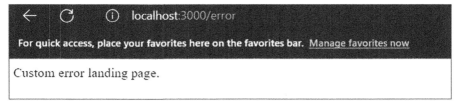

*Figure 11.10*: *Custom error page using middleware function in Express*

# Adding Multiple Middleware Handlers

Till now, we have seen only one middleware to handle all errors. However, in real applications, there can be one or multiple middleware functions typically used to handle different errors and return transformed responses. For example, one middleware can be used for error logging, while another for transforming client response. So, we can add as many different middleware functions as needed to make modular applications.

The following code is written to implement multiple middleware functions:

```
const express = require('express')
const promises = require('fs').promises
const app = express()

app.get('/page1', (req, res, next) => {
    promises.readFile('./page1.txt')
        .then(data => res.send(data))
        .catch(err => next(err))
})
app.get('/page1', (req, res, next) => {
    promises.readFile('./page1.txt')
        .then(data => res.send(data))
        .catch(err => {
            err.type = 'redirect'
            next(err)
        })
})

app.get('/error', (req, res) => {
    res.send("Custom error landing page.")
})

function errorLogHandler(error, req, res, next) {
    console.error(error)
```

```
        next(error)
    }

    function errorHandler(error, req, res, next) {
        if (error.type == 'redirect') {
            res.redirect('/error')
        } else {
            next(error)
        }
    }

    app.use(errorLogHandler)
    app.use(errorHandler)

    app.listen(3000, () => {
        console.log(`Server listening at http://localhost:${3000}`)
    })
```

Here, we have implemented the same code but in a more modular way that can scale better as more routes are added to the application, allowing us to define as many different error-handling situations.

**Important Note:** We just need to make sure that all middleware functions are defined in proper sequence so that they either return a response or call the next set of middleware functions. If we don't follow the same, the request might keep on waiting without returning any response or error to the client.

# Building Express Applications with Error Handling

We will create a sample application to understand how we can implement some of the different error-handling techniques inside a Node.js application based on Express.

## Setting up the project

Let's create a new project inside our root folder:

```
PS D:\demo\sample_web_app> npm init
This utility will walk you through creating a package.json file.
It only covers the most common items, and tries to guess sensible
defaults.

See `npm help json` for definitive documentation on these fields
and exactly what they do.

Use `npm install <pkg>` afterwards to install a package and
save it as a dependency in the package.json file.

Press ^C at any time to quit.
package name: (webapp) sample_web_app
version: (1.0.0)
description:
entry point: (index.js)
test command:
git repository:
keywords:
author:
license: (ISC)
About to write to D:\demo\sample_web_app\package.json:

{
  "name": "sample_web_app",
  "version": "1.0.0",
  "description": "",
  "main": "index.js",
  "scripts": {
    "test": "echo \"Error: no test specified\" && exit 1"
```

```
    },
    "author": "",
    "license": "ISC"
}


Is this OK? (yes) yes
PS D:\demo\sample_web_app>
```

## Installing dependencies

Now, we can install all the required dependencies for our project, which includes Express.js:

```
PS D:\demo\sample_web_app>  npm i --save express


added 58 packages, and audited 59 packages in 909ms


8 packages are looking for funding
  run `npm fund` for details


found 0 vulnerabilities
```

## Creating Express server

We will add a couple of basic modules to our application, such as routes, middleware, and more, which can be used to test different kinds of scenarios.

Create an **index.js** file and add the following code that can be used to run our core Express server:

```
// index.js
const express = require('express')
const app = express()
const port = 5000;


// We will add other server-related code
```

```
app.listen(port, () => {
    console.log(`Server listening at http://localhost:${port}`)
})
```

Now, we can run our server to test if everything is working as expected before moving to the next section:

*Figure 11.11: Output express application running*

### Adding some routes

We will add sample routes in the **routes.js** file, which will be used to handle user requests. To check if the routes are working as expected, let's add some of the mock data that will be returned as a response:

```
const express = require('express');
const router = express.Router();
// Home page
router.get('/', (req, res) => {
    res.send("Home Page.....");
})


// Get the list of todos
router.get('/todos', (req, res, next) => {
    fetch('https://jsonplaceholder.typicode.com/todos')
        .then(res => res.json())
        .then(todos => {
            res.header("Content-Type", 'application/json');
            res.send(JSON.stringify(todos, null, 4));
        })
```

```
          .catch(err => next(err))
    })

    router.get('/error', (req, res) => {
        res.send("The URL you are trying to reach does not exist.");
    })

    module.exports = router;
```

To make this route available to the user, we need to hook to the Express pipeline:

```
    // index.js
    const express = require('express')
    const routes = require('./routes')
    const app = express()
    const port = 5000

    // Routes
    app.use(routes)

    app.listen(port, () => {
      console.log(`Server listening at http://localhost:${port}`)
    })
```

After running the application, we will navigate to get the list of **todos** pages:

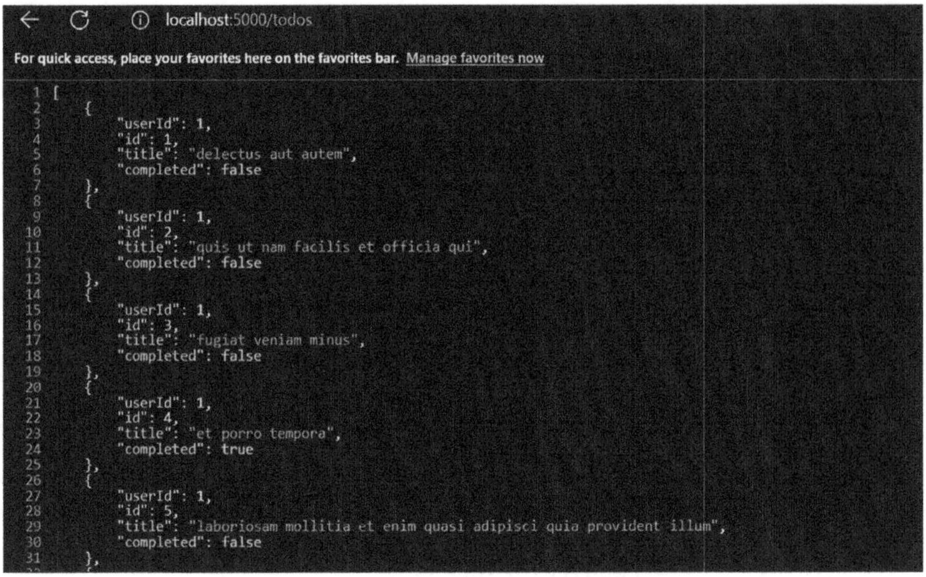

*Figure 11.12*: *Output getting a list of todos*

## Handling some custom errors

We can add some fundamental error handling, such as **todos not found**, by defining some custom classes as follows:

Let's create an **errors.js** file and add the following code snippet:

```js
// errors.js
class TodoIdNullError extends Error {
    constructor(todo_id, content) {
        super();
        this.name = this.constructor.name;

        this.message = `Invalid Todo id provided - ${todo_id})`;
        this.statusCode = 500;
    }
}


class TodoNotFoundError extends Error {
    constructor(todo_id, content) {
```

```
            super();
            this.name = this.constructor.name;

            this.message = `Todo not found - ${todo_id})`;
            this.statusCode = 500;
        }
    }


module.exports = {
    TodoIdNullError,
    TodoNotFoundError
}
```

Once we have defined a custom error handling class, let's allow routes to throw these custom errors inside our Express application:

```
// routes.js
const express = require('express');
const router = express.Router();
const {
    TodoIdNullError,
    TodoNotFoundError
} =  require("./errors");

// Home page
router.get('/', (req, res) => {
    res.send("Home Page.....");
})

// Get the list of todos
router.get('/todos', (req, res, next) => {
    fetch('https://jsonplaceholder.typicode.com/todos')
        .then(res => res.json())
```

```
        .then(todos => {
            res.header("Content-Type", 'application/json');
            res.send(JSON.stringify(todos, null, 4));
        })
        .catch(err => next(err))
})


// Get the list of todos
router.get('/todos/:id', (req, res, next) => {
    if(req.params.id){
        throw new TodoIdNullError();
    }


    fetch('https://jsonplaceholder.typicode.com/todos/' + req.
params.id)
        .then(res => res.json())
        .then(todos => {
            res.header("Content-Type", 'application/json');
            res.send(JSON.stringify(todos, null, 4));
        })
        .catch(err => {
            throw new TodoNotFoundError();
            next(err);
        })
})


router.get('/error', (req, res) => {
    res.send("The URL you are trying to reach does not exist.");
})


module.exports = router;
```

Now try to run the application and navigate the following URL, which has an invalid ID provided:

http://localhost:5000/todos/null

**Output:**

**Figure 11.13**: *Output custom error for passing null id value*

As shown in *Figure 11.14*, when we use valid **id = 1**, we will get a response successfully:

http://localhost:5000/todos/1

**Figure 11.14**: *Output getting details of todo using id*

**Handling errors using Middlewares**

We have seen how to handle any error using a custom error-handling technique, which works fine in many small applications. However, as soon as we add more routes, it requires the repetition of similar code, which is not easily maintainable.

To avoid such mesh and improve efficiency, we can use middleware functions along with routes, so that all the errors get handled in one place and we have more control over different implementation logic at the application level.

Let's create a file named **middleware_error.js** and add the following code:

```
// middleware_error_handler.js
const errorLogHandler = (err, req, res, next) => {
  console.error('\x1b[31m', err)
  next(err)
}


const errorHandler = (err, req, res, next) => {
  res.header("Content-Type", 'application/json')
  res.status(err.statusCode).send(JSON.stringify(err, null, 4))
}
const invalidPathHandler = (req, res, next) => {
  res.redirect('/error')
}


module.exports = {
  errorLogHandler,
  errorHandler,
  invalidPathHandler
}
```

Update our core server logic inside **index.js** to add support for middlewares, which we have created earlier:

```
// index.js
const express = require('express');
const routes = require('./routes');
const { errorLogHandler, errorHandler, invalidPathHandler } = re-
quire('./middleware')
```

```
const app = express();
const port = 5000;

app.use(routes);

// middleware
app.use(errorLogHandler)
app.use(errorHandler)
app.use(invalidPathHandler)

app.listen(port, () => {
  console.log(`Server listening at http://localhost:${port}`)
})
```

Now, let's run the application and try to browse some of the application URLs to see what error we get:

http://localhost:5000/todosss

**Figure 11.15**: *Output custom error page*

# Logging Errors in Node.js Application

In most applications, logs are primarily used for debugging and troubleshooting purposes. However, there are certain areas in which logs can be used for many other things, including studying application behavior, improving certain code logic, performing analysis on products through data mining, and more.

Following is a list of areas where logs can be used:

- **Requests/Response**:

  This is one of the most widely used areas, where we log all the requests made by the client that can be used for debugging and resolving issues with minimum effort. These request logs can be used for analytics and data mining user activities on websites.

- **Availability**:

  We can add certain logs, such as info and debug, which helps us to track application workflows and improve overall system design. Additionally, we can log errors and exceptions, which help us to identify issues within the system and use them to make the application more stable.

- **Threats**:

  Sometimes we use logs to analyze what kind of data is being transferred and to easily track any vulnerability in our system, such as exposed passwords, API keys, client secrets, and user personal information.

- **Events/Changes**:

  When we develop a distributed system based on microservice architecture, we must log different information, including request payloads, status, and errors, that might be happening across multiple systems.

Let's take a simple example of writing logs to the console inside a Node.js application:

```
const express = require("express");
const app = express();

app.get("/", (req, res, next) => {
    console.log("This is landing page");
    res.status(200).send("My landing page..");
});

app.get("/event", (req, res, next) => {
    try {
        throw new Error("Error thrown while calling event!");
    } catch (error) {
        console.error("Events Error logging");
        res.status(500).send("Error!");
    }
```

```
    });

    app.listen(3000, () => {
        console.log("Server Listening On Port 3000");
    });
```

We can use console logs mostly for debugging purposes, and once our code is fixed, we normally remove these logs. To permanently persist logs, we might need to use better tools that can help us log this information into files or databases. One of the popular tools is Winston logger, which we will explore in the next section.

# Using Winston Logger

Winston is one of the most popular logging tools designed as a simple and generic logging library that supports multiple transports. A transport is mostly defined as a backup storage device like files or databases. Each Winston logger can have multiple transports configured at different logging levels provided in Winston. For example, we may want to store error logs in a database or file for the production environment, but for local debugging, all logs are printed to the console or dumped into the file system.

Logging levels in Winston conform to the severity ordering specified by RFC5424: severity of all levels is assumed to be numerically ascending from most important to least important.

The list of logging levels defined in Winston is as follows:
- error: 0
- warn: 1
- info: 2
- http: 3
- verbose: 4
- debug: 5
- silly: 6

Create a folder called **logger.js** and add the following code:

```
const winston = require("winston");
const logger = winston.createLogger({
```

```
    level: "debug",
    format: winston.format.json(),
    transports: [new winston.transports.Console()],
});


module.exports = logger;
```

Create a folder called **error_logger_winston.js** and add the following code:

```
const express = require("express");
const logger = require("./logger");
const app = express();

app.get("/", (req, res, next) => {
  logger.debug("The is landing page");
  res.status(200).send("Welcome Landing page.");
});

app.get("/mypage", (req, res, next) => {
  try {
    throw new Error("Error thrown!");
  } catch (error) {
    logger.error("Log error using winston logger");
    res.status(500).send("Error!");
  }
});

app.listen(5000, () => {
  logger.info("Server Listening On Port 3000");
});
```

We get the following output after running application:

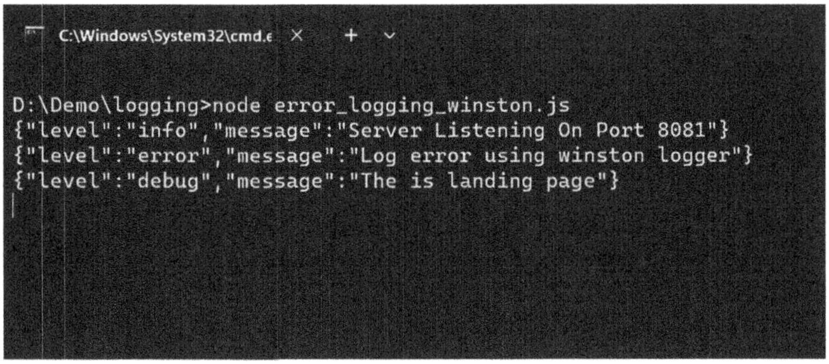

*Figure 11.16*: Output of Logging using Winston Logger

# Conclusion

Proper error handling is imperative for writing good code and delivering reliable software. In this chapter, we have discussed errors and the importance of handling them in Node.js. We have also learned how to create custom error handlers and middleware functions to handle errors gracefully.

In addition, we have shown how to handle errors inside a real Node.js application.

In the next chapter, we will cover more about Test Driven Development (TDD) with Mocha and Chai.

# Further Readings

The following links can help understand more about Middleware in depth:

- https://www.oreilly.com/library/view/nodejs-the/9781838826864/video25_23.html
- https://aws.amazon.com/blogs/developer/middleware-stack-modular-aws-sdk-js/
- https://commercetools.github.io/nodejs/sdk/Middlewares.html#example
- https://simonplend.com/how-does-middleware-work-in-express/
- https://www.youtube.com/watch?v=_GJKAs7A0_4
- https://www.youtube.com/watch?v=y18ubz7gOsQ

# CHAPTER 12

# TDD with Mocha and Chai

## Introduction

In this chapter, we will learn about Test-Driven Development (TDD) using tools like Mocha and Chai. The main focus of this chapter will be developing a solid foundation of different concepts of unit testing and exploring some of the frameworks available in the market, like Mocha and chai. At the end of the chapter, we will try to see some examples of how to write unit tests using key concepts like spy, stub, mock, and so on.

## Structure

This chapter will cover the following topics related to TDD with Mocha used in Node.JS:

- Node.js Unit Testing concepts
- Test-driven development principles
- Testing frameworks types
- Setting up the first test using Mocha
- Running and debugging tests
- Generating reports in HTML and text

## Node.js Unit Testing Concepts

Unit testing is one of the key types of automated testing used for validating code by developers. The main focus of writing unit test cases is on verifying the code in isolation, which means the system under test cannot interact with any external dependencies such as databases, file systems, or any kind of HTTP services.

To make this possible, we fake all the required dependencies with dummy implementations by using techniques like mocks or stubs.

The main goal of unit tests is to be written easily and run without much configuration, as they often tend to perform just a single function call. Apart from this, unit test results are easy to collect and display. It is important to write unit tests in a way that tests every possible outcome of a given code. In every unit test, the return value of the unit must be equal to the expected value, or the test should fail.

# Importance of Unit Testing

Node.js unit testing helps to improve code quality and the overall stability of the product. Assume a user is trying to perform registration after launching a new application. The user tries to submit the application form, but due to some issues, the application returns an error message, and the user is not able to register successfully. From this example, we can understand the importance of testing our API logic and making sure it works as expected. The easiest way to achieve this is by unit testing our core business logic at the smallest units of code in our application.

Apart from improved code quality, unit tests can be used to create our regression suite. A **regression suite** is the name given to a collection of unit test cases that are used to either manually test applications or through automated applications. A comprehensive and structured set of unit tests case execution inside our CI/CD pipelines helps developers identify any issues in the early phases of development.

# Test-Driven Development Fundamentals

Test-driven development is a methodology that defines how we can perform both development and testing to improve product quality. In the past, before we followed TDD, we used to write our code logic first and then write a unit test to validate the piece of code, whereas test-driven development requires us to write the test first and then make changes in the code until our code logic passes the test already written.

Using the TDD method, the code we produce is cleaner, more stable, and less prone to breaking in the long run and causing any issues. When we are writing a unit test in TDD, it should simply test a small piece of logic, such as an algorithm or business problem, and pass or fail after validating logic. Unit tests should always be deterministic, which means that they should always give either pass or fail results.

# Test-Driven Development Workflows

There are the following five steps that define TDD workflows:

1. **Reading, understanding, and processing a feature or bug request**

   This is the first step in the process of TDD, where we define our unit test cases for required features or bugs.

2. **Translate the requirement by writing a unit test**

   As we have defined our desired goal for a feature or bug, we start designing our unit test case according to the business logic.

3. **Write and develop compliant code**

   Now we start writing our unit test cases according to a feature or bug defined with proper acceptance criteria.

4. **Run all the tests and repeat this step until it passes**

   We run all the unit test cases again and again until all of them pass and we have developed all the desired code logic.

5. **Clean up the code by refactoring. Rinse, lather, and repeat**

   The final step in this process is to re-think logic and perform the required code refactoring to ensure we follow the correct design principle and our code is free of known bugs.

# Key Principles of Test-Driven Development

Since the beginning of software development, the developer's main focus has been on writing code first and then performing manual testing to identify any bugs or issues related to business logic. After some time, we realized the need to automate the testing of bugs and started to write unit tests to make sure we identified issues at the time when developers wrote the code itself and reduced bugs post-development. Now TDD demands developers to first write a unit test, run the test, and then make additional code changes to fix the failed unit test.

The following are three key principles of TDD:

- **First test fail**

  This is the first step towards following the TDD approach, where we start with writing enough code logic, which will cause our first test to fail with minimum implementation.

  As shown in *Figure 12.1*, the RED step is the start of our TDD process, where the idea is that when we test our simple logic, which passes all the basic code, then we can assume that our code is production-ready.

- **Code updates and testing**

  Once our unit test either passes or fails, we need to update our code logic depending on the test result. Now we need to make a small change in the code (refactoring) and run the test again. Once our test passes (GREEN state), we can keep adding more code and switching from a green test to another green test. As soon as all tests are green, we should select the very next failed test after doing some code refactoring.

- **Code refactoring and testing**

  In this step, we do some code refactoring to improve our code quality and consider all the test scenarios to pass. This step is a constant cycle of writing a failed test, fixing code to pass it, and keep moving to the next failed test, and then changing the code to pass this test. From *Figure 12.1*, we can tell that every code refactoring is done, the test case fails (RED state) and we need to make some changes to make it pass (GREEN state).

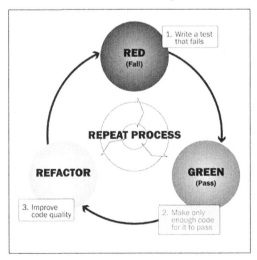

*Figure 12.1*: *Steps of Test Driver Development Process*

The most important point to note is that TDD does not specify how to write precise test cases. However, we always need to determine scenarios or use cases of how the developed system is expected to perform. This helps create our understanding of how each functionality works and makes sure that we have written our business code and tested it accordingly.

As developers, our main goal should be to write and run continuous tests to discover new defects, whether functional or non-functional and to verify that the changes or improvements caused defects or bugs.

# Different Types of Testing Frameworks

Following are some of the most popular testing frameworks available:

### Mocha

It is the most popular JavaScript testing framework because of its flexibility. With Mocha, developers have more freedom to write test cases. There are many third-party tools available that provide much of the required testing functionality, like assertions, mocking, and so on. Using Mocha (a testing framework) with Chai (an assertion library) has become a very popular combination.

### AVA

AVA is a small, lightweight testing tool that is highly arbitrary and helps to execute tests simultaneously, which results in better performance. AVA does not support the use of global values similar to Mocha and uses a clear syntax to help focus on the most important information that we need to test.

### Tape

This is another very small framework. Like AVA, it does not support global values. It has a quick installation, and you don't need to configure much.

### Jasmine

Jasmine is again one of the very popular JavaScript testing frameworks used in TDD or BDD JavaScript applications. It provides multiple utilities which can be used to easily automate tests for both synchronous and asynchronous code. Jasmine has been widely adopted in frontend work, where developers use this framework to test Angular/React/Vue applications.

### Jest

Jest is also a popular framework developed by Facebook. Built on top of Jasmine, it was specifically designed for unit testing, primarily React and React Native applications, but after gaining popularity, it began to be used to test other applications. The main focus of Jest is to provide support and simplicity for testing heavy web applications.

In addition to unit testing, Jest is mostly used for performing component testing (that is, testing different components of an application in isolation). Jest is independent of third-party applications and software, making it the most widely used JavaScript automation testing framework. It is considered one of the best unit testing frameworks.

# Unit Testing key concepts

Following are some of the key concepts that are widely used in writing unit test cases:

- **Mocking**

  Mocking is mainly used for testing code in isolation by simulating the behavior of real objects and replacing the real object with a mocked object or function. We can use a mocked lookup object to make a function call that throws an unwanted error to check the expected behavior of the function to handle any kind of error.

- **Snooping**

  Snooping helps to eavesdrop on function calls, which later on can be used to verify that the object was called with the correct arguments. The spy which is defined on any function does not change the behavior of the function.

- **Stumping**

  Stumps are very similar to spies. Instead of screwing up a function definition, we can control the behavior of the function using a stub. When we are unit testing a function that is making an external service call, we would like to mock that dependency to return some predefined result which can help us to unit test our logic.

# Advantages of Unit Testing in Node.js

Here are some benefits of unit testing we should consider while testing:

- **Improve code quality**

  Unit testing helps to improve the quality of your code. This gives more guarantee that the business logic we have written is correct and that unexpected behavior cannot occur. Unit testing also helps us find bugs and defects in our code that might have been introduced while refactoring.

- **Coding errors identification**

   Testing helps you find bugs early in the software development life cycle. Unit testing is particularly useful for finding errors in business logic. If you find bugs earlier in the software development cycle, you can fix problems earlier so they don't affect other parts of the code later.

- **Better design and code structure**

   When we write tests, we validate the design of our system and check that every piece of code fits into the entire application code base. Writing testable code helps us make better design decisions accordingly.

- **Better quality product**

   Unit testing helps to improve the overall quality of our application, resulting in better products and increasing user satisfaction. Good-quality software will help our customers have more confidence in the platform and force them to use it without any complaints.

- **Code coverage reports for visualization**

   Code coverage measures the amount of code that is executed by unit tests and includes details like what lines, branches, or methods were converted during execution. Once all the tests are executed, our report plugin generates reports in different formats like JSON, HTML, text, and so on.

# Node.js Unit Test Anatomy

Following are the key steps (also known as **AAA**) that are required to be performed inside each test:

1. **Arrange**

This is the first step that is used to set up the correct state, mock dependencies, or add spy to objects. This initial set of objects that we use forms a baseline for running tests.

2. **Act**

This step is known as the *Action* phase, we call the actual function or piece of code that we are looking to test.

## 3. **Assert**

This step is also called as *Assertion* phase, where we verify that our code logic produces the expected result. Apart from this, we can also determine whether the given functions have been called with the correct arguments.

```
1    // test/server.js
2
3    var expect = require("chai").expect;
4    var request = require("request");
5
6    describe("Color Converter API", function () {
7
8        describe("Convert RGB to Hex", function () {
9
10           var url = "http://localhost:5100/convert/rgb-hex?red=255&green=255&blue=255";
11
12           it("returns status 200", function (done) {
13               // Arrange
14               const expectedResult = 200;
15
16               // Act
17               request(url, function (error, response, body) {
18
19                   // Assert
20                   expect(response.statusCode).to.equal(expectedResult);
21                   done(),
22               });
23           });
24
25           it("returns the color in hex", function (done) {
26               request(url, function (error, response, body) {
27                   expect(body).to.equal("ffffff");
28                   done();
29               });
30           });
31
32       });
```

*Figure 12.2: Example of AAA*

# Advantages of using Mocha and Chai

Some major advantages of using Mocha and Chai are as follows:

- **Asynchronous Testing Support**: Node.js applications often contain asynchronous operations such as web requests or database interactions. Mocha handles asynchronous tests gracefully, so you can write tests containing asynchronous code without additional libraries or complex configurations.

- **Readable and expressive statements**: Chai integrates seamlessly with Mocha, providing many statement styles and expressive syntax options. It offers several statement styles, including commonly used words such as '*elect*', '*assert*', and '*should*', so you can choose a style that suits your preferences and readability needs.

- **Community Support**: Mocha and Chai have gained significant popularity in the Node.js community due to their large user base and thriving ecosystem, so you'll find plenty of resources, tutorials, and community support when using these frameworks.

# Practical tips for writing unit tests

Consider the following four helpful tips as you write your first unit tests:

- Always define a small set of statements within a given unit test. When we add a larger number of assertions, it means we might not be testing the smallest unit of code independently. It suddenly makes sense to split a unit test into multiple test definitions whenever testing complex behavior or scenario.

- Make sure to avoid repeating the same assertions. When a particular test case verifies a null value for a given property, let's try to avoid asserting null values of the same property in another test. Too many assertions make it very difficult to determine which important scenarios are tested on a priority basis.

- Everyone should follow strict organization, operation, and protection principles for writing test cases for applications. This makes our tests more readable, easier to organize, and more maintainable in the long run.

- We should always avoid using unproven tests. When we are writing our test cases, we need to make sure they are valid and always test something positive. Sometimes we write a test without assertions with only the arrange and act phase of testing.

## Methods to write unit tests

There are two main methods of writing unit tests:

- `describe()`: This is a series of test scripts that call a global function with two parameters: a string and a function.

```
// start a test suite of one or more tests
describe('#sum()', function () {

    // ...add some tests

})
```

- **it()**: This is the smallest single test case written for execution. **it()** calls a global function with two parameters, that is, a string and a function. You can write multiple **it()** statements in the **describe()** method. The third method used in unit testing is based on the developer's choice. Each **it()** statement has one of the following functions that takes a value and expects to return it in its actual form:

```
// begin a test suite of one or more tests
describe('#sum()', function () {
    // test a functionality
    it('should add numbers', function () {
        // add an assertion
        expect(sum(1, 2, 3, 4, 5)).to.equal(15);
    })


    // ...some more tests
})
```

- **expect()**: This is a BDD-style library. Natural language arguments are chained here. It is mainly used for non-descriptive topics such as logical values or numbers.

```
// begin a test suite of one or more tests
describe('#sum()', function () {
    // test a functionality
    it('should add numbers', function () {
        // add an assertion
        expect(sum(1, 2, 3, 4, 5)).to.equal(15);
    })
})
```

- **should()**: This is a BDD-style library. The natural language statements are also chained in this case. However, it extends each object with the should property to start the string.

- **assert()**: This is a TDD-style library. It offers additional tests and is cross-browser compatible.

# Introduction to Behavior-Driven Development (BDD)

Behavior-driven development (BDD) is an agile software methodology that fully aims to reduce cross-team communication gaps among team members. This method has proved more effective in developing understanding and increasing collaboration, improving the quality of development. It encourages teams to express requirements clearly and share a common understanding of how the product should work. This framework came into existence after developers got used to writing TDD, where tests are written before code, and passing tests is a critical strength in software development.

## BDD and Unit Testing

Behavior-driven development philosophy helps developers to focus more on customer requirements and perform unit testing and acceptance testing so that we can improve our product quality and help customers gain more confidence in us.

Unit tests should be written in the same order as the behavior of the component under test, and we can verify all the requirements given by the business or stakeholders. By clearly specifying all requirements, we make sure that requirements are not misunderstood by any team members.

A user story might be written in the following format:

- As a [role]
- I want [feature]
- So that [benefit]

For example, we can write a use case of a user getting a list of products on an e-commerce site.

- **As a** user
- **I want** to get a list of products
- **So that** I can check the price of each product

We can write our BDD tests as follows:

- **Given** the user has logged into the system
- **When** the user enters text in the search
- **And** click on **enter** key
- **Then** user views the list of items

Cucumber is one of the popular frameworks for writing BDD tests that allows every team member to review tests and collaborate to gain a common understanding of the features being developed.

In the following diagram, we can see a live example of writing a cucumber feature file, which is used to verify menu option functionality available in our application.

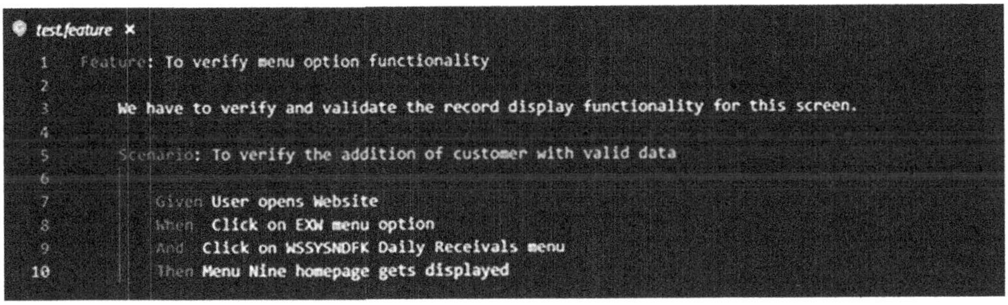

**Figure 12.3:** *Example of BDD test using Cucumber framework*

# Key Benefits of BDD

The following are the key benefits of using BDD in our development process:

- Improve collaboration between cross-functional teams that include stakeholders, testers, and developers.
- It is an external operation, meaning that the unit implementing the program unit being constructed provides control of the *desired behavior*.
- Test cases more clearly express which feature we are trying to develop and test.
- This forces critical analysis and design because the developer must fully understand the desired output and how it will be tested before developing production code.
- This helps in reducing or overcoming all the bottlenecks that might come in the future due to wrong design implementations.

# Installation of Mocha and Chai

The following steps are used for the installation of Mocha and Chai:

1. **Project Setup**

Let's create a new folder for your project with the following command:

```
PS D:\Demo> mkdir unit_test
```

2. **Project Init**

Navigate to the above test directory and run the command:

```
PS D:\Demo\unit_test>  npm init -y
```

3. **Install mocha and chai**

Let's run the following commands to install mocha and chai both locally and globally:

```
//To install Mocha globally
npm install Mocha -g

//To install the Mocha project:
npm install Mocha -- save - dev

//To Install the chai locally:

npm install Chai -- save - dev
```

**Output:**

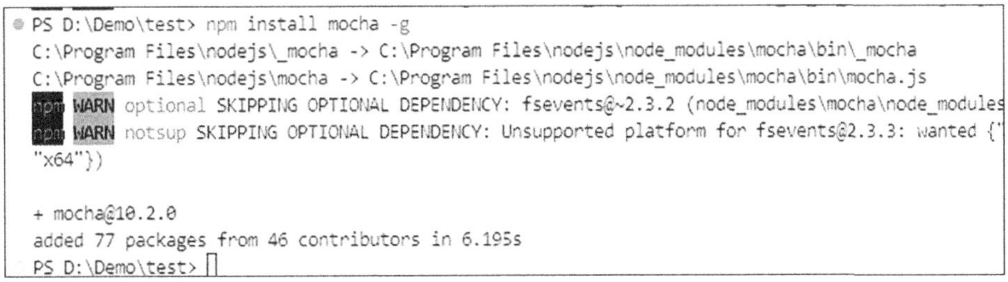

```
PS D:\Demo\test> npm install mocha -g
C:\Program Files\nodejs\_mocha -> C:\Program Files\nodejs\node_modules\mocha\bin\_mocha
C:\Program Files\nodejs\mocha -> C:\Program Files\nodejs\node_modules\mocha\bin\mocha.js
npm WARN optional SKIPPING OPTIONAL DEPENDENCY: fsevents@~2.3.2 (node_modules\mocha\node_modules
npm WARN notsup SKIPPING OPTIONAL DEPENDENCY: Unsupported platform for fsevents@2.3.3: wanted {
"x64"})

+ mocha@10.2.0
added 77 packages from 46 contributors in 6.195s
PS D:\Demo\test> []
```

***Figure 12.4***: *Output of npm install mocha*

Once we have installed mocha and chai, our **package.json** will be updated as follows:

```json
{
  "name": "unit_test_demo",
  "version": "1.0.0",
  "description": "",
  "main": "index.js",
  "directories": {
    "test": "test"
  },
  "scripts": {
    "test": "echo \"Error: no test specified\" && exit 1"
  },
  "keywords": [],
  "author": "",
  "license": "ISC",
  "devDependencies": {
    "chai": "^4.3.10",
    "mocha": "^10.2.0"
  }
}
```

Here we will notice that *mocha* and *chai* are added as **devDependencies** because these frameworks are only required in our locally for executing test cases. These dependencies are not required in production to run our application.

**Adding Source code and Test**

Create two folders named **src** and **test**, and place them inside our working directory. We will use the **src** folder to store the main file and the test directory to store the test cases for unit testing.

Let's create a simple Node.js application that we can use to write our code and test cases. We will use the following folder structure to create our application which is used for performing color conversion from RGB to HEX and vice versa.

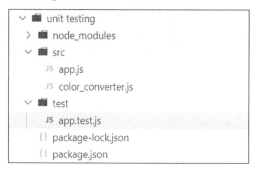

**Figure 12.5**: *Folder structure of Sample application*

**src/app.js**

```js
var express = require("express");
var app = express();
var converter = require("./color_converter");


app.get("/", function (req, res) {
    res.send("Hello world");
});


app.get("/convert/rgb-hex", function (req, res) {

    var red = parseInt(req.query.red, 10);
    var green = parseInt(req.query.green, 10);
```

```
            var blue = parseInt(req.query.blue, 10);
            var hex = converter.convertRgbToHex(red, green, blue);
            res.send(hex);


    });


    app.get("/convert/hex-rgb", function (req, res) {


            var hex = req.query.hex;
            var rgb = converter.convertHexToRgb(hex);
            res.send(JSON.stringify(rgb));


    });


    app.listen(5100, () => {
        try {
            console.log(`Server listening at http://localhost:5100`)
        } catch (error) {


        }
    })
```

## src/color_converter.js

```
    exports.convertHexToRgb = function (hex) {


      var red = parseInt(hex.substring(0, 2), 16);
      var green = parseInt(hex.substring(2, 4), 16);
      var blue = parseInt(hex.substring(4, 6), 16);


      return [red, green, blue];


    };
```

```
exports.convertRgbToHex = function (red, green, blue) {

  var redHex = red.toString(16);
  var greenHex = green.toString(16);
  var blueHex = blue.toString(16);

  return pad(redHex) + pad(greenHex) + pad(blueHex);

};

function pad(hex) {
  return (hex.length === 1 ? "0" + hex : hex);
}
```

## test/app.test.js

```
// test/server.js

var expect = require("chai").expect;
var request = require("request");

describe("Color Converter API", function () {

    describe("Convert RGB to Hex", function () {

        var url = "http://localhost:5100/convert/rgb-
hex?red=255&green=255&blue=255";

        it("returns status 200", function (done) {
            request(url, function (error, response, body) {
                expect(response.statusCode).to.equal(200);
                done();
```

```
            });
        });

        it(“returns the color in hex”, function (done) {
            request(url, function (error, response, body) {
                expect(body).to.equal(“fffff”);
                done();
            });
        });

    });


    describe(“Convert Hex to RGB”, function () {
        var url = “http://localhost:5100/convert/hex-rgb?
hex=00ff00”;

        it(“returns status 200”, function (done) {
            request(url, function (error, response, body) {
                expect(response.statusCode).to.equal(200);
                done();
            });
        });

        it(“returns the color in RGB”, function (done) {
            request(url, function (error, response, body) {
                expect(body).to.equal(“[0,255,0]”);
                done();
            });
        });
    });
});
```

```
PS D:\Demo\unit testing> npm install request --save-dev


PS D:\Demo\unit testing> npm install express --save-dev
```

**Running Unit tests:**

```
● PS D:\Demo\unit testing> npm run test

> unit_test_demo@1.0.0 test D:\Demo\unit testing
> mocha --reporter spec



  Color Converter API
    Convert RGB to Hex
      ✓ returns status 200
      ✓ returns the color in hex
    Convert Hex to RGB
      ✓ returns status 200
      ✓ returns the color in RGB


  4 passing (51ms)

PS D:\Demo\unit testing> []
```

**Figure 12.6**: *Output of running unit tests*

# Hooks used in writing Unit Tests

We have several Mocha hooks that are used in writing unit tests. Some of these hooks are either for setting up some of the pre-conditions or performing some clean-up activities after running tests.

## BeforeEach

The **beforeEach** method is a function (or hook) of the test libraries that allows to set of some pre-conditions defined against each test case to get executed. This particular code block runs before each test in your test package. For example, in the following code **beforeEach** method is executed twice in a sequence of two tests defined in the following test suite. Each execution occurs immediately before the execution of the actual test function.

The following code written in mocha uses **beforeEach()**:

```
describe("Tests with beforeEach", function () {
    beforeEach(function () {
        console.log("Initialising...");
```

```
    });

    it("Test1", function () {
        //write test logic here
    });

    it("Test2", function () {
        //write test logic here
    });
});
```

Run cmd: `npm run test`

*Figure* 12.7 shows the output of running the preceding test scenario for using `beforeEach` in mocha tests.

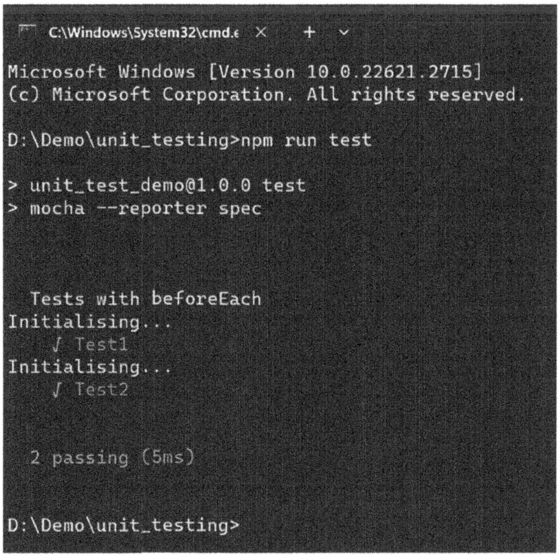

**Figure 12.7**: *Using beforeEach inside unit tests*

# AfterEach

The `afterEach` method is a function (or hook) of the test libraries that allows developers to perform clean-up activities after each test case is executed. This particular code block runs after each test in your test package. For example, in the following code `afterEach` method is executed twice in a sequence of two tests defined in the following test suite. Each execution occurs immediately after the execution of the actual test function.

```
describe("Tests with afterEach", function () {

    it("Test1", function () {
        //write test logic here
    });

    it("Test2", function () {
        //write test logic here
    });

    afterEach(function () {
        console.log("cleanup activities...");
    });
});
```

**Output**:

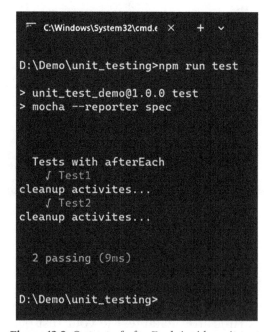

**Figure 12.8**: *Output of afterEach inside unit tests*

# Spices

Spies are functions that store information about their usage, including arguments passed to them and return values. They are an essential part of the unit testing framework because they allow you to verify that a function was called as expected and to check the arguments passed to it.

In the following example, we are going to implement adding a new user to the system and call **save()** function defined in the database object to persist user information.

**src/database.js**

```
const Database = {
    save(newUser, callback){
        // some database operation......
    }
}


module.exports = Database;
```

**src/newUser.js**

```
const Database = require('./database');


function addNewUser(info, callback) {
    var user = {
        name: info.name,
        nameLowercase: info.name.toLowerCase()
    };


    try {
        Database.save(user, callback);
    } catch (err) {
        callback(err);
    }
```

```
        }


        module.exports = addNewUser
```

Now to test the preceding code, we need to create a spy on **save** function defined inside the database object. This will help us to isolate any external call and test only logic which is to call **addNewUser** functionality.

**test/newUser.test.js**

```
        const Database = require('../src/database');
        const sinon = require("sinon");
        const addNewUser = require('../src/newUser');


        describe("Spy example", () => {
            it('should pass user object to save', function () {
                var save = sinon.spy(Database, 'save');
                var info = {
                    name: 'test'
                };
                var expectedUser = {
                    name: info.name,
                    nameLowercase: info.name.toLowerCase()
                };


                addNewUser(info, function () {});


                save.restore();
                sinon.assert.calledWith(save, expectedUser);
            });


        });
```

**Output:**

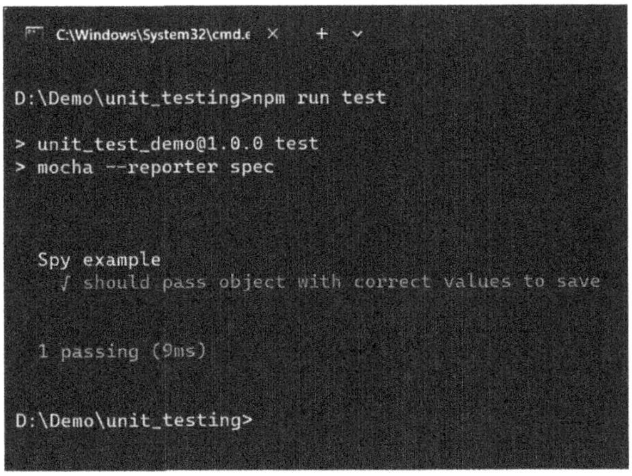

**Figure 12.9**: *Output of using spy inside unit tests*

# Stubs

Stubs are functions that replace the behavior of another function with predefined values. They can be used to control the output of a function or to avoid interacting with external dependencies.

We will create an implementation of the product service that we are going to test.

```
const request = require("request");


async function getAllProducts() {
  return request.get("https://example.com/products");
}


module.exports = { getAllProducts };
```

Let's create a test file named **product.service.test.js** and add the following code.

```
const expect = require("chai").expect;
const sinon = require("sinon");
const request = require("request");
```

```
const service = require(".../src/product.service");

describe("Product Service", () => {
  afterEach(() => {
    sinon.restore();
  });

  it("should return all the products", async () => {
    const products = [{ id: "1", name: "Product123" }];
    sinon.stub(request, "get").returns(products);

    const serviceProducts = await service.getAllProducts();

    expect(serviceProducts).equal(products);
  });
});
```

Here we have tried to replace the behavior of the GET method of the request and returned our own mocked response as product list. In this way, we are not going to make any actual API calls to the backend server but just test our code in isolation.

**Output:**

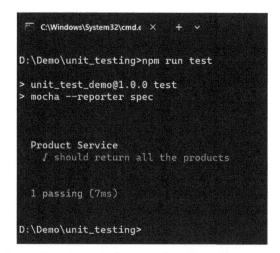

**Figure 12.10**: *Output after use of Stubs inside unit tests*

## Mocks

Mocks are a combination of spies and stubs and are often used to ensure that a function has been called a certain number of times with certain arguments and returns the expected value.

Here, we are trying to update an order using a patch request in the following code

```
const request = require("request");


async function updateOrder(orderId) {
  const url = "https://example.com/orders/";


  const order= await request.get(url + orderId);
  if (!order) return;


  await request.patch(url + orderId);
}


module.exports = { updateOrder};
```

Let's create our **order.service.test.js** file and add the following code to test order service functionality.

```
const expect = require("chai").expect;
const sinon = require("sinon");
const request = require("request");


const service = require("../src/order.service");


describe("Order Service", () => {
  afterEach(() => {
    sinon.restore();
  });
```

```
it("should not update the order", async () => {
  const mockReq = sinon.mock(request);
  const getOrder = mockReq.expects("get").returns(null);
  const updateOrder = mockReq.expects("patch").returns({});

  await service.updateOrder("abc");

  expect(getOrder.callCount).equal(1);
  expect(updateOrder.callCount).equal(0);
});

it("should update the Order", async () => {
  const mockReq = sinon.mock(request);
  const getOrder = mockReq.expects("get").returns({});
  const updateOrder = mockReq.expects("patch").returns({});

  await service.updateOrder("abc");

  expect(getOrder.callCount).equal(1);
  expect(updateOrder.callCount).equal(1);
});
});
```

In this test, we have created our implementation of the mock request and returned different mock values from our get and update methods of order APIs without calling them.

**Output:**

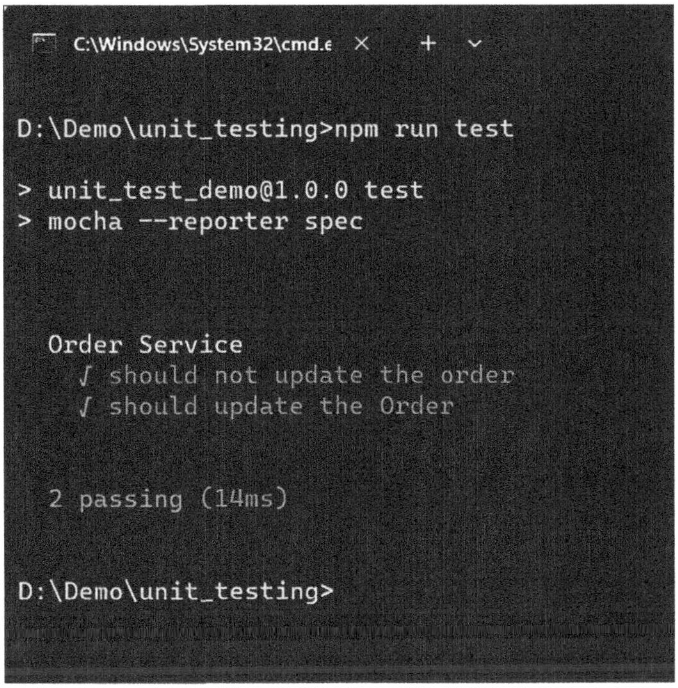

**Figure 12.11**: *Output after use of Mocks inside unit tests*

## Async code

We can test async code very easily using inbuilt support of the same inside the Mocha library.

Let's create a file **async.js** and add the following code which will call an external url.

```
const axios = require('axios');

function get(url, cb) {
  return axios.get(url);
}
```

Now we can write our test to validate the preceding code.

```
describe('get()', function() {
  it('works', async function() {
    const res = await get('http://example.com/responses');
    assert.equal(res.data.args.answer, 42);
```

```
    });
});
```

## Callback and Promise

We can test any of async calls using default functionality provided in Mocha using callbacks and promises. The only thing we need to do is to pass the done function at the end of the callback chain to make sure it gets executed after the last assertion.

Let's create a file called **http_request.js** which will be used to make RESTful API calls using http modules.

```
const http = require('http');

var httpRequest = {
  get: url => {
    return (new Promise(function(resolve, reject) {
      http.get(url, res => {
        resolve(res);
      });
    }));
  }
};

module.exports = httpRequest;
```

Create a new file called **async.test.js**

```
const req = require('../src/http_request');
const http = require('http');
const expect = require("chai").expect;

describe('sample tests for async code', function () {
    it('callback', function (done) {
```

```
        http.get('http://www.example.com', function (res) {
            expect(res.statusCode).equal(200);
            done();
        });
    });

    it('promise', function (done) {
        req.get('http://www.example.com/').then(function (res) {
            expect(res.statusCode).equal(200);
            done();
        })
    });
});
```

**Output**:

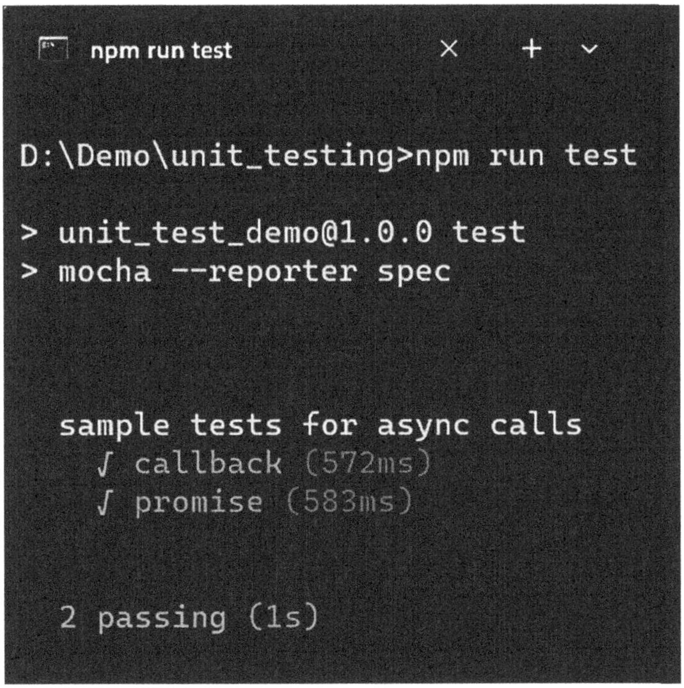

*Figure 12.12*: *Output callback and promise in unit tests*

# Conclusion

Unit testing is the easiest way to ensure the quality of code and the overall stability of Node.js applications. Unit testing also helps you find bugs and errors in your code that might not be identified while writing the code itself. In addition, early detection of coding errors reduces overall development costs and also helps to improve system design, with multiple code refactoring to fix test cases. Mocha and chai is one of the popular libraries that we have explored to test our Node.js application.

In the next chapter, we will cover more about debugging our Node.js application and identify issues easily.

# Further Readings

The following links can help understand more about Unit testing in-depth:

- https://blog.logrocket.com/testing-node-js-mocha-chai/
- https://brightsec.com/blog/unit-testing-in-nodejs/
- https://www.lambdatest.com/learning-hub/nodejs-unit-testing
- https://www.youtube.com/watch?v=Bs68k6xfR3E
- https://www.youtube.com/watch?v=M44umyYPiuo
- https://mochajs.org/

# CHAPTER 13

# Debugging

## Introduction

In this chapter, we will learn more about overall debugging concepts and explore some of the tools and debugging techniques available to any developers who can use them to find issues and make sure their applications are working as per the expected design. We will also learn about how and when different debugging techniques might be used. At the end of this chapter, we will go through a live example of debugging express applications inside the VS code editor.

## Structure

This chapter will cover some of the following topics related to debugging tools and techniques used in Node.js:

- Introduction to debugging
- Importance of debugging
- Debugging strategies
- Debugging techniques
- Debugging an express application

## Introduction to Debugging

Debugging is a technique that allows us to investigate the issues and bugs inside our application. This allows us to find exactly how our code works in the local system or production live environment. With the help of debugging tools, we can also test different conditions and business logic that need to behave as expected or give some errors. Debugging is one of the key areas which are normally underestimated by developers. Debugging helps individuals to understand the code more accurately and they can improve development skills to write a clear code very efficiently.

# Importance of Debugging

The following are the key benefits of using debugging:

- Debugging is an important part of determining the cause of any application failure.

- Debugging helps to find code smells and bugs that might be added due to bad coding practices.

- Debugging may sometimes cause a process for finding issues and then writing the program itself.

- Debugging helps software components to fine-tune them so that they can perform as per expectation.

# Debugging Strategies

There are different kinds of debugging strategies that developers can follow in order to debug their code and find any issues and deviations.

- **Source code analyzer**

  Source code analyzer strategies include various security, common code analyzers, and complexity analyzers can be useful for debugging.

- **Complexity analyzer**

  The complexity analyzer can find complex modules that are difficult to understand and test.

- **Static analysis**

  A programmer examines the code without running the program. Print debugging (also called tracing). The programmer monitors real-time or recorded output and tracks progress.

- **Remote debugging**

  The developer debugger runs on a different system than the program being debugged.

- **Postmortem debugging**

  A programmer stops debugging a program only when it encounters fatal exceptions.

# Debugging Techniques

Following are the key techniques that we can use to debug any Node.js application.

## Using Console.log

In most JavaScript-based systems, `console.log()` commands are the easiest and most common ways to implement debugging in Node.js. We can do many advanced things with Console.log, but this has become a favorite technique for any developer to quickly use and get the desired result.

From *Figure 13.1*, we can see that we have added our first console.log statement which we have used to log our query params and test what users are sending when they are `calling /employees?name=Ajay` route.

```
console.log(query)
```

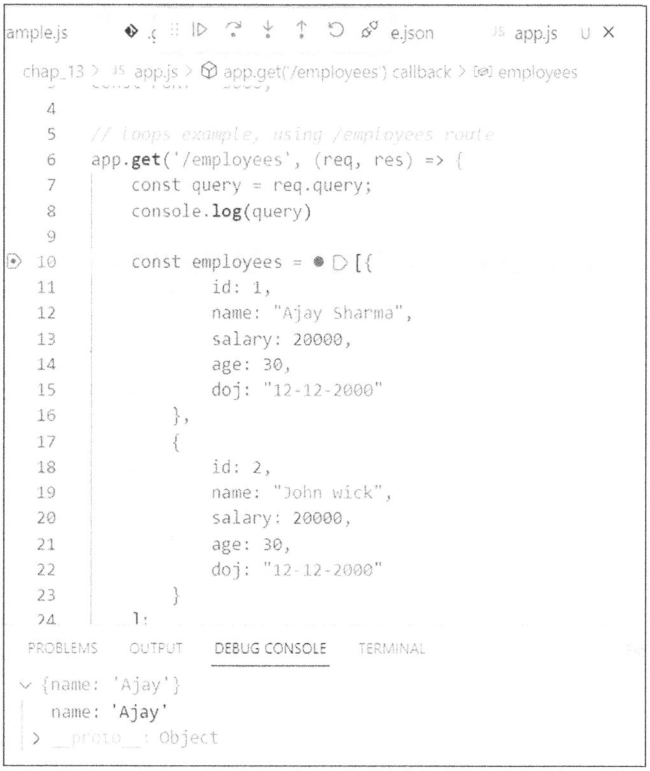

**Figure 13.1**: *Using console.log for debugging*

# Using Node Inspector

Node Inspector is a native debugging tool that easily integrates with Chrome DevTools and allows one to set any breakpoints, inspect variables, and step through Node.js code very similar to debugging a JavaScript application in a web browser.

The first step is to install the Node Inspector package globally using the following commands.

```
npm install -g node-inspect
```

The next step is to start our Node.js application in debug mode by running the following command.

We can open Chrome DevTools by navigating to chrome://inspect and we can find the following output when opening our application in the browser.

localhost:3000/employees?name=Ajay

*Figure 13.2*: *Output of debug log using Node Inspector*

Finally, we can attach any debug breakpoints inside the DevTools and after the page refresh, we will notice that code execution has stopped at the breakpoint.

```
 app.js ×
  1    const express = require('express');
  2    const app = express();
  3    const PORT = 3000;
  4
  5    // loops example, using /employees route
  6    app.get('/employees', (req, res) => {   req = IncomingMessage {_readableState: ReadableState, _events: {…}, _
  7        const query = req.query;   query = {name: 'Ajay'}
  8        console.log(query)
  9
 10        const employees = [{
 11            id: 1,
 12            name: "Ajay Sharma",
 13            salary: 20000,
 14            age: 30,
 15            doj: "12-12-2000"
 16        },
 17        {
 18            id: 2,
 19            name: "John wick",
 20            salary: 20000,
 21            age: 30,
 22            doj: "12-12-2000"
 23        }
 24        ];
 25        let filtered = [];
 26
 27        if (query) {
 28            if (query.name) {
 29                filtered = employees.filter(item => item.name.indexOf(query.name) >= 0);
 30            } else if (query.id) {
 31                filtered = employees.filter(item => item.id == query.id);
 32            } else {
 33                filtered = employees
```

**Figure 13.3**: *Attaching debugger inside Chrome DevTools*

We can also check all local and global variables as well as call stack similar to any frontend application built using JavaScript.

**Figure 13.4**: *Call stack and other details inside Chrome DevTools*

## Using Node.js debug module

We can also use the debug module package, which is widely used for adding debugging information for the entire application. This package has several configurations which we can use to control the behavior of our debugging.

```
var debug = require('debug')('http')
  , http = require('http')
  , name = 'My Demo App';


  debug('Starting %o', name);


http.createServer(function(req, res){
  debug(req.method + ' ' + req.url);
  res.end('hello world\n');
}).listen(5000, function(){
  debug('listening');
});
```

Here we have imported the debug module using the required method and stored the reference in the debug local variable. Once the debug reference is available, we can add as many debug lines inside our applications.

# Debugging an Express Application

We will be using the following steps to learn how we can debug any Node.js application.

## Creating a Node.js application

We will create a simple Node.js application with a list of products that can be filtered by providing different inputs using query parameters.

Now let's create an **app.js** file which we will use to write our core application logic.

```javascript
const express = require('express');
const app = express();
const PORT = 3000;

// loops example, using /employees route
app.get('/employees', (req, res) => {
    const query = req.params.query;

    const employees = [{
            id: 1,
            name: "Ajay Sharma",
            salary: 20000,
            age: 30,
            doj: "12-12-2000"
        },
        {
            id: 2,
            name: "John wick",
            salary: 20000,
            age: 30,
            doj: "12-12-2000"
        }
    ];
    let filtered = [];

    if (query) {
        if (query.name) {
            filtered = employees.filter(item =>
    item.name.contains(query.name));
        } else if (query.id) {
```

```
            filtered = employees.filter(item => item.id == query.id);
        } else {
            filtered = employees
        }
    }

    res.json({
        filtered
    });
});


app.listen(PORT, () => console.log('listening on port ' + PORT));
```

In this application, we are simply taking a list of predefined employees and will run some query parameters to return the expected result.

As part of this exercise, we will try to learn how to efficiently debug a Node.js application to identify issues and resolve them by making some code changes.

To get all employees- http://localhost:3000/employees

Filter employees by their name - http://localhost:3000/employees?name=john

The next step in the Node.js debugging procedure will be to use the Nodemon package to enable debugging.

# Installing the Node.js debugger using "Nodemon"

The Nodemon is a debugging tool that is used to debug any Node JS application in the local system. We can install Nodemon globally using the following command:

```
npm install -g nodemon
```

Once Nodemon is installed globally, we will use the following command to serve the node.js application with the **Nodemon** command-line tool.

```
nodemon -L - Check app.js
```

Running this command forwards your application to a specific port, in this case, 3000, so that the application is available at http://localhost:3000.

Now we are able to run the application, the next thing is to enable the debugging option inside the VS Code.

# Start debugging in VS Code

We can start debugging by simply pressing on Window *Ctrl Shift p* or *Cmd Shift p* on MacOS to open the code command palette. After you have typed "Debug" to get the list of options and one of them is "**Attach: Add Node Process**", you will get to see the following *Figure* 13.5.

**Figure 13.5**: *Attaching debugger to node process*

When you select the **Attach: Add Node Process** option, you will see the next screen very similar to *Figure* 13.2.

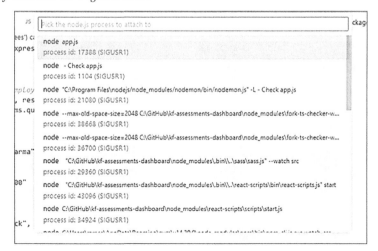

**Figure 13.6**: *Selecting an application that needs to be debugged*

We can see a list of the node processes that are running on the local system. In order to start debugging we will select the first option, which looks like *Figure* 13.7:

**Figure 13.7**: *Started debugging in the VS code*

We have successfully attached the debugger and we can allow live debugging by setting some breakpoints which will stop execution at that given line. In the next section, we will try to debug one of the express routes which is used to fetch all the employees.

# Run the debugger with Breakpoint

Let's start by putting a debugger in our application in line 10, where the route is executed after the debugger is activated.

Now let's navigate to our application using localhost:3000/employees

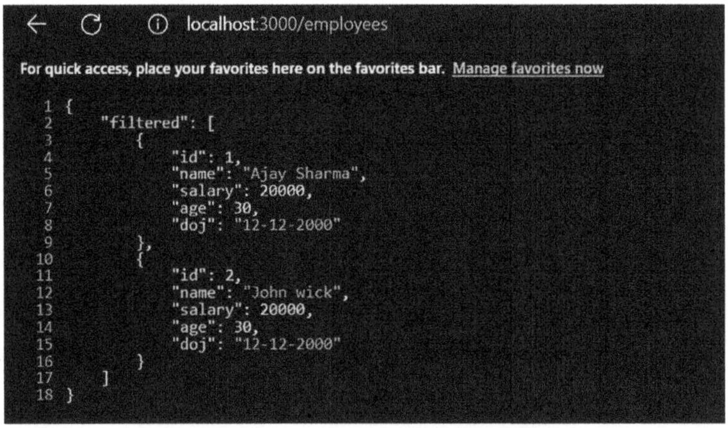

**Figure 13.8**: *Output employees API*

Now let's navigate to our application using localhost:3000/employees?name=Ajay

As soon as the preceding URL is loaded into our browser, we will notice the following output, which shows a list of employees filtered by the name '**Ajay**'.

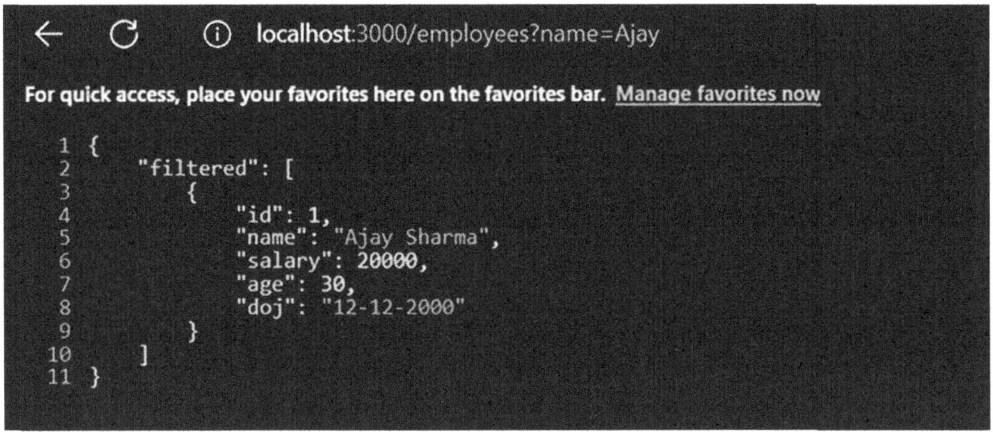

*Figure 13.9*: *Output of applying filters*

In order to debug, we will add our debug point at line no 10 and reload the application to hit the debugger breakpoint, as shown in *Figure 13.10*.

*Figure 13.10*: *Applying debug point in line no 10*

# Conclusion

Debugging Node.js applications can be a difficult task, but with the right tools and techniques, it can become a more efficient and streamlined process. By following the steps outlined in this blog, you can ensure that you are well-equipped to deal with any issues that may arise during development. Be sure to start with extensive logging and error handling, use Node.js' built-in debugging features, and use third-party tools like VS Code and NDB. With these tools and techniques at your disposal, you can reliably and efficiently debug your Node.js applications. In the next chapter, we will explore the core concept of Build and Deployment.

# Further Readings

The following links can be helpful in understanding more about Middleware in depth.

- https://code.visualstudio.com/docs/nodejs/nodejs-debugging
- https://www.knowledgehut.com/blog/web-development/debugging-in-node-js#the-debug-module%C2%A0
- https://www.youtube.com/watch?v=2oFKNL7vYV8
- https://www.youtube.com/watch?v=llPW0b1dQms
- https://www.youtube.com/watch?v=XbB5_fHHxRc
- https://nodejs.org/en/docs/guides/debugging-getting-started
- https://stackify.com/node-js-debugging-tips/

# CHAPTER 14

# Build and Deployments

## Introduction

In this chapter, we will learn about the core concept of Build and Deployment. We are going to explore how we can create our npm package and publish the same to the NPM registry. In the later section, we will cover more about CI/CD and have a detailed discussion on various aspects of DevOps and different tools used to make deployments. At the end, we will create and deploy a sample Node.js application using Docker and Kubernetes.

## Structure

This chapter will cover some of the following topics related to the concept of build and deployments and how can we use them in Node.js.

- Creating NPM package
- Publishing NPM package
- Introduction to CI/CD
- Key elements of CI/CD
- Importance of CI/CD
- Building Project dependencies
- Deploying the first Node.js server

# Creating an NPM Package

Node Package Manager is the largest open-source registry available on the internet and is used by software development communities to build Node-based systems.

First, developers build components on their local system and then publish their node application packages to NPM to share with others. Using this way of creating NPM packages, most organizations can share code within themselves or with the outside world.

Let's learn how to create an NPM package and publish it to NPM so that others can download and consume it.

## Initializing Git Repository

Create a new project named **npm_publish** and run the following command to the **init** Git repository.

```
PS D:\Demo\npm_publish> git init
```

This will create an empty **Git repository** and be used to link out the codebase to the **GitHub** repository.

```
Initialized empty Git repository in D:/Demo/npm_publish/.git/
```

## Initializing NPM

The next step is to initialize our first node-based application using the following command.

```
PS D:\Demo\npm_publish> npm init
```

This command creates a **package.json** file with the following information.

- **package name**: the package name must be unique, should be lowercase, and may contain spaces.
- **version**: This is used to identify the current package version, having a default value is 1.0.0. When we update the package, we need to update the version using a semantic versioning system.

- **description**: Here you can enter a description of your package. Tell us what your package does and how to use it.
- **entry point**: The main application file used to write code and start our node server. The default value is index.js.
- **test**: This is used to run our unit test cases written for application.
- **git-repository**: We can provide a link to a remote GitHub repository.
- **keywords**: This helps others to search and find our package in the NPM registry.
- **author**: The name of the publisher of the package.
- **license**: Any specific license or patent information or use the default license (Internet Systems Consortium (ISC) license).

**Output:**

```
PS D:\Demo\npm_publish> npm init
This utility will walk you through creating a package.json file.
It only covers the most common items, and tries to guess sensible
defaults.


See `npm help init` for definitive documentation on these fields
and exactly what they do.


Use `npm install <pkg>` afterwards to install a package and
save it as a dependency in the package.json file.


Press ^C at any time to quit.
package name: (npm_publish) demo-publish-first-package
version: (1.0.0)
description: This is used to publish node application to NPM
entry point: (app.js)
test command:
git repository: https://github.com/rameshksh/demo-pub-
lish-first-package.git
```

```
keywords: NPM publish
author: Ramesh
license: (ISC)
About to write to D:\Demo\npm_publish\package.json:

{
  "name": "demo-publish-first-package",
  "version": "1.0.0",
  "description": "This is used to publish node application to
NPM",
  "main": "app.js",
  "scripts": {
    "test": "echo \"Error: no test specified\" && exit 1"
  },
  "repository": {
    "type": "git",
    "url": "git+https://github.com/rameshksh/demo-pub-
lish-first-package.git"
  },
  "keywords": [
    "NPM",
    "publish"
  ],
  "author": "Ramesh",
  "license": "ISC",
  "bugs": {
    "url": "https://github.com/rameshksh/demo-publish-first-pack-
age/issues"
  },
  "homepage": "https://github.com/rameshksh/demo-pub-
lish-first-package#readme"
}
```

```
Is this OK? (yes) yes
PS D:\Demo\npm_publish>
```

# Creating the First NPM Package

To create a basic node application, add the following code to this **my-package/ index.js** file.

```
// index.js
function CustomMessage(){
    return "Hello word my first npm package";
}


module.exports = CustomMessage;
```

We have successfully created our package and now we will test this before publishing it to the NPM registry.

We have also added a default `README.md` file with all the required information which can be used for informational purposes by the developer using this package.

```
U        ⓘ readme.md ...\test U       JS index.js ...\demo-publish-first-package U
npm_publish > my-package > ⓘ readme.md
  1
  2    #Using custom published package in test project
  3
  4    1) Create a script.js file and add following code.
  5
  6        const msg = require('demo-publish-first-package')
  7
  8        console.log(msg())
  9
 10    2) Installing dependencies
 11        npm install demo-publish-first-package com
 12
```

*Figure 14.1: Readme file with installation steps.*

# Testing the NPM Package

To test our package, we need to locate our module on the local system so that our package is available globally. This is normally done using the *npm link* command, which allows us to load a module into our application from anywhere on our computer.

**Note**: One of the important things about the npm link is that if any changes are made in packages, those get reflected immediately in our project.

`npm link` only creates two symbolic links:

- **Global symbolic link**

  When you run `npm link` in the module root, npm creates a symlink from your **global node_modules** directory to the local modules directory. The **global node_modules** folder is a special folder where all modules installed with `npm install -g` are stored.

- **Local symbolic link**

  When you run `npm link <module_name>` inside the project directory, npm creates a symbolic link from the file `./node_modules/<module_name>` that `<global_node_module>/<module_name>`

We can undo any changes made by the `npm link` by simply removing the symbols. But it has a built-in command *npm unlink* which will remove the symlink association.

Just run `npm unlink --no-save <module_name>` in your project directory to remove the local symlink and remove the global symlink by running npm unlink in the modules directory.

The following command is used to create and package that can be located and used within other modules with the help of the `npm link` command.

```
PS D:\Demo\npm_publish\my-package> npm link
```

This will create a package globally. Here is the output of npm link cmd:

```
PS D:\Demo\npm_publish\my-package> npm link
npm notice created a lockfile as package-lock.json. You should
commit this file.
up to date in 0.559s
found 0 vulnerabilities
```

```
C:\Program Files\nodejs\node_modules\demo-publish-first-package ->
D:\Demo\npm_publish\my-package

PS D:\Demo\npm_publish\my-package>
```

Let's create a test folder and create a **script.js** file.

```
// test/script.js

const msg = require('demo-publish-first-package')

console.log(msg())
```

Now we will link our previously created package to this application.

```
PS D:\Demo\npm_publish\test> npm link demo-publish-first-package
```

Once the command is successful, we will see the following output:

```
D:\Demo\npm_publish\test\node_modules\demo-publish-first-package
-> C:\Program Files\nodejs\node_modules\demo-publish-first-package
-> D:\Demo\npm_publish\my-package

PS D:\Demo\npm_publish\test>
```

*Figure 14.2*: *Linking the NPM package with a test application*

# Running test application

After we have linked the package, now we can run our application to verify if everything is working as expected.

```
PS D:\Demo\npm_publish\test> node script.js
```

**Output:**

```
PS D:\Demo\npm_publish\test> node script.js
Hello word my first npm package
PS D:\Demo\npm_publish\test>
```

# Publishing Your NPM Package

To publish our newly created package to NPM, we need to have an account at https://www.npmjs.com/

Once we have created our account, we can log in and publish our package to the **npm** registry.

```
PS D:\Demo\npm_publish\my-package> npm login
```

**Output:**

```
PS D:\Demo\npm_publish\my-package> npm login
Username: rameshksh12
Password:
Email: (this IS public)
npm notice Please check your email for a one-time password (OTP)
Enter one-time password:
Logged in as rameshksh12 on https://registry.npmjs.org/.
PS D:\Demo\npm_publish\my-package>
```

Once we are successfully logged in to the NPM registry, we can publish our package using the following cmd.

```
PS D:\Demo\npm_publish\my-package> npm publish
```

**Output:**

```
C:\Program Files\nodejs\node_modules\demo-publish-first-package -> D:\Demo\npm_publish\my-package
PS D:\Demo\npm_publish\my-package> npm publish
npm notice
npm notice package: demo-publish-first-package@1.0.0
npm notice === Tarball Contents ===
npm notice 117B index.js
npm notice 611B package.json
npm notice === Tarball Details ===
npm notice name:          demo-publish-first-package
npm notice version:       1.0.0
npm notice package size:  499 B
npm notice unpacked size: 728 B
npm notice shasum:        e03d56fa84016cbdca17f27b9a3070b086e554ac
npm notice integrity:     sha512-m/83Q23tVpLzg[...]TX9QDALDPNTKQ==
npm notice total files:   2
npm notice
+ demo-publish-first-package@1.0.0
PS D:\Demo\npm_publish\my-package> []
```

*Figure 14.3: Output of NPM publish*

We can now search for our newly published package inside the NPM registry.

**npm**    Q Search packages

**demo-publish-first-package**
1.0.0 • Public • Published 4 minutes ago

📄 Readme          📖 Code (Beta)          📦 0 Dependencies          ⚙ 0 Dependents

This package does not have a README. Add a README to your package so that users know how to get started.

**Keywords**

NPM   publish

*Figure 14.4: Searching package in NPM registry*

# Introduction to Continuous Integration and Continuous Delivery

In today's fast-paced software development company everyone is trying to automate software development workflows that can help teams to release features more often. We have a well-defined continuous and iterative process to build, test, and deploy our code avoiding bugs and compromising software quality with less time to market software.

# Defining Continuous Integration (CI)

Continuous integration is the practice of integrating code changes early and more often into the master or main branch of a shared source code repository like Git Hub, TFS, or Bitbucket. Once the code is merged, the pipeline automatically trigger all the unit test perform end-to-end testing against each change, and automatically run the build if all the tests are passed. With continuous integration, errors and security issues can be identified and corrected more easily in the early phases of the development process. Using CI, we merge changes frequently and reduce the chance of code conflicts when multiple developers are working on the same modules. Continuous Integration also helps in setting up a pipeline where common code validation processes happen with static code analysis, which ensures good code quality.

# Defining Continuous Delivery (CD)

Continuous Delivery is a software development practice that automates the process of preparing infrastructure like servers, networking, security, and releasing applications. Once the developer finishes developing the features of a product, they are tested as part of the CI process. The job of CD is to prepare the environment first and package everything that needs to be deployed in any specific environment at any time. The software on the CD is structured so that it can be produced at any time. You can then start the deployment manually or switch to continuous deployment, where deployments are also automated.

# Defining Continuous Deployment (CD)

Continuous deployment helps organizations or individuals to deploy their applications automatically onto servers without any human intervention. In continuous deployment, predetermined criteria for code release are configured by the DevOps team, and once the criteria are met and validated, the code is automatically deployed to the first lower environment, like dev, test, or stg. As soon as QA verifies the build, the same codebase is automatically promoted to production env. Using continuous deployment, organizations have become more flexible and now they can get new features easily deployed into production and made available to users faster than ever.

# Defining Continuous Testing (CT)

Continuous testing is a software testing practice where the system performs automated testing continuously once a new code is introduced via any feature into Test/STG/PROD environments. Using well setup CI/CD pipeline, continuous testing is triggered automatically, and a series of tests are run to ensure that the application still works as expected with new changes. This usually helps to identify problems early in the development process when code is merged and deployed on DEV/TEST and prevents them from getting passed to higher environments. Continuous testing also helps developers with valuable feedback on their code quality and test coverage by running tools like Sonar Cloud, helping them to identify and resolve potential bugs before they are released to a live environment.

In Continuous Testing, the following are the key testing strategies:

- Unit testing is used to verify that the unit of code works as per the expected system design.

- Integration testing checks how different modules or services of an application when coupled inside one platform work together.

- Regression tests are used to verify that any issue that was fixed earlier should not recur again after making new code changes.

# Key elements of CI/CD

CI/CD has a basic of eight key elements to help ensure maximum efficiency in our software development lifecycle. Incorporate these basics into our process to improve the entire DevOps workflow and software.

These include the following core elements:

- **Single source repository**

  Source code control (SCM), which contains all the files and scripts needed to build a build, is critical. The archive must contain everything necessary for construction. This includes source code, database structure, libraries, proprietary files, and version control. It should also contain test scripts and scripts for building applications.

- **Regular check-in**

  We should integrate code into your trunk, mainline, or master branch–that is, trunk-based development–early and often. Avoid lower branches and work only on the main branch. Use small code snippets and fork them as often as possible. Do not combine more than one change at a time.

- **Automated builds**

  The scripts should contain everything you need to build in one command. This includes web server files, database scripts, and application software. CI processes automatically package the code and compile it into a usable application. Self-test structures CI/CD require continuous testing.

- **Test scripts**

  Our test scripts must ensure that a test failure results in a failed build. Use static pre-build test scripts to verify code integrity, quality, and security compliance. Allow building only code that passes static tests.

- **Repeated repetitions**

  Multiple commits in a repository lead to fewer hiding places for conflicts. Instead of making big changes, do small repetitive repetitions. Doing so makes it easy to undo changes in the event of a problem or conflict.

- **Stable test environments**

  We should always test our code in a cloned version of the production environment like test/stage. We should never test new code in live production. Create a cloned environment as close to the real environment as possible. Use rigorous testing scripts to identify and identify bugs that have passed the initial preview testing process.

- **Maximum visibility**

  Every developer should have access to the latest executables and see all changes made to the repository. The information in the database must be visible to everyone. Use version control to manage changes so developers know what is going on in the latest version. Maximum visibility means everyone can monitor progress and identify potential issues.

- **Predictive deployments at any time**

  Deployments should be so routine and low-risk that the team is comfortable doing them at any time. CI/CD testing and verification processes must be rigorous and reliable, giving the team the confidence to deploy updates at any time. Repetitive deployments with limited changes also present lower risks and can be easily reversed.

# Importance of CI/CD

Here are some of the key benefits gained by organizations that are implementing CI/CD in their software development life cycle (SDLC).

- **Happier users and customers:**

  Fewer errors enter production, so your users and customers have a better user experience. This increases customer satisfaction, increases customer trust, and improves the image of your organization.

- **Accelerated time:**

  When you can deploy at any time, you can bring products and new features to market faster. Development costs are lower and faster progress frees up your team for other work. Customers get results faster, giving your business a competitive advantage.

- **Fewer fire drills:**

  Testing code more often, in smaller batches, and earlier in development, can significantly reduce fire drills. This leads to a smoother development cycle and less stress on the team. Results are more predictable and errors are easier to find and correct.

- **Set realistic dates:**

  By breaking stories and tasks into smaller parts, it becomes easier to manage each step on time and track progress. This approach allows enough time to monitor progress and precisely define completion dates. Small task helps in removing bottlenecks and much of the uncertainty around delivery dates.

- **Improve Productivity:**

  As our work gets automated, the team becomes more productive and helps in the successful delivery of projects. It is estimated that developers spend 35-50% of their time testing, verifying, and debugging their code. By automating some of these processes, the developers increase their productivity.

- **Fewer context switches:**

  Every developer can focus on one task when they get better feedback on code. By working in small, testable chunks of work, developers can quickly perform multi-tasking but this should be avoided to improve productivity.

- **Reduce Burnouts:**

  CI/CDs can significantly reduce distribution problems and improve team cross-functional deliveries. This improves the developer's overall happiness, and health and reduces burnout which can be caused by many manual steps and interventions.

- **Faster recovery:**

  CI/CD accelerates problem resolution and disaster recovery by identifying and solving problems easily. CI/CD helps software get more frequent updates, making it easier to spot bugs when they appear and can be quickly fixed. If the system crashes, CI/CD helps to recover it automatically.

# Deployment Service

There are many ways to do this when preparing to deploy a Node.js application. These deployment services are divided into four main groups:

- Infrastructure as a Service (IaaS)
- Backend as a Service (BaaS)
- Traditional deployment
- Platform as a Service (PaaS)

In general, deployment involves packaging a Node.js application and configuring its configuration files. Once you're done, you can confirm the process and Command Prompt will run it.

There are several deployment services available in the market, but finding a good service depends on various business needs and, most importantly whether you want free or paid services. Following are some of the deployment service providers that are used for deploying Node.js applications.

- **Heroku:**

  A free service that started as a Ruby deployment platform that later expanded to other languages such as PHP and Python.

- **Azure DevOps:**

  Azure DevOps is a software as a service (SaaS) product offered by Microsoft on their cloud platform. Azure DevOps is used to reduce human effort by automating application development, deployment, and testing. With some services from AzureDevOps, we can quickly and efficiently deploy our application to any lower or live environment. In the past, Azure DevOps was also called Microsoft's Visual Studio Team Services (VSTS) which was used as a shared resource for storing code and performing all build and deploy operations.

- **Docker:**

  Docker is an open platform for developing, deploying, and managing applications in different environments using containers. Each docker container can run independently using compiled docker images which contain everything required to run applications using a given infrastructure. Docker fast-track code delivery, testing, and deployment reducing overall time between writing code and deploying it in production. We will cover Docker in more detail in upcoming sections.

- **Kubernetes:**

  Kubernetes is a portable, extensible, and open-source platform for managing workloads and services that promotes configuration and automation of information. It is a large and fast-growing ecosystem. Kubernetes services, support, and tools are available. We will cover Kubernetes in more detail in upcoming sections.

# Deployment pipeline

A deployment pipeline is mostly used in the context of a DevOps team. It defines an automated and streamlined process that is used for facilitating CI/CD after code changes from development to production environments.

The primary goal of the deployment pipeline is to ensure that software releases are efficient, reliable, and of consistent quality. A deployment pipeline consists of automated steps that code changes must go through before production deployment. These steps typically include code building, automated testing, and deployment to different environments such as staging and production. Each step is designed to ensure code quality and functionality, and any issues discovered during the process are addressed before moving on to the next step.

# Advantages of pipeline deployment

The main benefits of a well-executed deployment pipeline are listed as follows:

- It enables faster time-to-market for new features and bug fixes by automating and speeding up the software delivery process. The pipeline enables early detection and resolution of defects, reducing the risk of commissioning errors and costly returns.

- It fosters collaboration between development, test, and operations teams, fostering a culture of shared responsibility and continuous improvement.

- Automated processes reduce manual operations, and enable faster and more frequent releases, speeding up time to market for new features and bug fixes. Testing automation at every stage ensures that bugs and problems are caught early in development, minimizing the cost and effort of fixing them.

- Pipeline ensures consistency across environments, reducing the potential for configuration errors that can cause differences between development, staging, and production environments.

- Continuous integration and automated security checks ensure that code meets security and compliance standards before deployment.

# Key components of the deployment pipeline

The following are the key components of any deployment pipeline used by the DevOps team:

- **Version Control System (VCS):**

  VCS is a repository that is used for tracking and managing code changes made by developers. This allows multiple developers and teams to collaborate and develop features that are cross-team dependent. Some popular VCS options available in the market include Git, SVN, and Mercurial.

- **Build Server:**

  These servers are responsible for automatically building and installing the code that drives changes to VCS. The first step includes pulling the code from the repository and turning it into an artifact that can be tested and distributed within the organization or outside the community. Popular tools like Jenkins, TeamCity, GitLab CI/CD, and Travis CI are commonly used to build servers.

- **Automated Testing:**

  Automated testing performs various types of testing such as hardware testing, integration testing, functional testing, and unit testing to make sure stable code-tested code is released into any environment. Automated testing helps in catching bugs early in the development process and reduces the overall cost of product development.

- **Artifact Storage:**

  Artifacts are created by the build server and represent code that is compiled and ready for release to any specific environment. An artifact repository ensures consistent and reliable delivery in environments such as UAT and production. We use this storage for backup and restoration of different versions of artifacts. In case of any critical issue found in the current build artifact, we can easily deploy the last production build.

- **Deployment Automation:**

  We should have a simple process of deploying applications into our environments. This can be easily done by setting up automated deployment scripts and configuration management tools to ensure a consistent deployment process. Organizations can reduce many manual errors and maintain a high level of delivery when they use CI/CD tools like Azure DevOps.

# Stages of Deployment Pipeline

We will explain the main stages of the deployment pipeline and their importance in the software development process.

- **Engagement stage:**

  The deployment pipeline begins with the commit phase, which is triggered by the code commit in the version control system (VCS). In this step, code changes are taken from VCS and the build server automatically compiles the code by performing the necessary pre-build steps. The code is then subjected to static code analysis to identify potential problems such as violations of coding standards or security holes. Once the code passes these initial checks, build artifacts are created that form the basis of the next steps.

- **Automatic test phase:**

  After successfully building and creating artifacts in the binding phase, the next step involves automated testing. In this phase, various tests are performed to ensure the functionality, reliability, and performance of the code. Unit tests, which validate individual code components, are performed first, followed by integration tests, which check the interaction between different components or modules. Functional tests check whether the application works as expected from the end user's point of view.

- **Stage of implementation:**

  The application is deployed in a staging environment when the code changes have passed the automated testing phase. The staging environment resembles a production environment, which allows thorough testing under conditions that simulate real use. This step provides a final check before the application is moved to production.

- **Start of production:**

  The final stage of the deployment pipeline involves deploying code to production after testing has passed all the previous stages and the team has got approval from a higher authority in the organization. To minimize risk, organizations often use deployment strategies such as Canary releases, blue-green deployments, or introduce fallbacks to manage the release process and easily rollback in case of potential problems. Continuous monitoring of the production environment is also necessary to ensure application stability and performance.

# Introduction of pipeline tools

Several popular deployment pipeline tools are available to help automate and orchestrate the software delivery process. These tools help define a continuous integration, continuous deployment, and continuous delivery pipeline, ensuring a smooth and efficient development workflow.

Here are some of the more commonly used pipeline tools.

- **Jenkins:**

  Jenkins' rich plugin ecosystem allows customization and integration with different tools, improving its adaptability to different development environments. Integrating Jenkins with BrowserStack is simple and impressive.

- **GitLab CI/CD:**

  GitLab CI/CD automates software integration, testing, and deployment on the GitLab platform, streamlining development.

- **BrowserStack**

  BrowserStack offers seamless integration with GitLab, facilitating efficient browser and device compatibility testing.

- **Travis CI:**

  Travis CI specializes in automating build, test, and deployment workflows to ensure continuous integration and delivery.

- **CircleCI:**

  It is a powerful automation tool in the field of software development. It excels at automating build, test, and deployment processes, contributing to a seamless, continuous integration and delivery environment.

- **GitHub Actions:**

  It is a powerful force for automating software workflows. Its core strength lies in automating build, test, and deployment activities, creating a seamless ecosystem for continuous integration and delivery.

- **Azure DevOps:**

  Azure DevOps is used in automating application development, deployment, and testing. With some services from AzureDevOps, we can quickly and efficiently deploy our application to any lower or live environment.

# Deploying Node.js applications Using Docker

Docker provides a platform and set of tools that we can use to package and run applications in a loosely isolated environment called a **container**. Containers are lightweight and contain everything needed to run an application, so you don't have to rely on the host operating system configuration like software dependencies. Docker has very good isolation and security that allows us to run multiple containers simultaneously inside the same host. We can share our containers to make sure that the container works the same way wherever deployed.

When we are done with coding, and testing, deploy the application to the production environment as a container or orchestration service. It works the same way across environments like on-premises data centers, a cloud provider, or a combination of the two.

### Prerequisites

The following components should be installed on your system before going ahead with the next section:

**Docker version** - 20.10.14, build a224086 (docker -v).

**Node.js -** v16.14.2.

**Npm -** v8.6.0.

## Creating a demo project

Let's create a sample project that will be used to create a Node.js application and used to host inside a Docker container.

Add the following code inside app.js:

```
var express = require('express');
var app = express();

app.get('/', function (req, res) {
   res.send('Hello, My server using Express');
});

var server = app.listen(8081, function () {
   var host = server.address().address;
   var port = server.address().port;

   console.log("Server is listening at http://%s:%s", host, port)
});
```

## Creating Dockerfile

A Dockerfile is a text document that contains instructions for building a Docker image, and these instructions are executed in the order in which they are written. The format of this file is as follows:

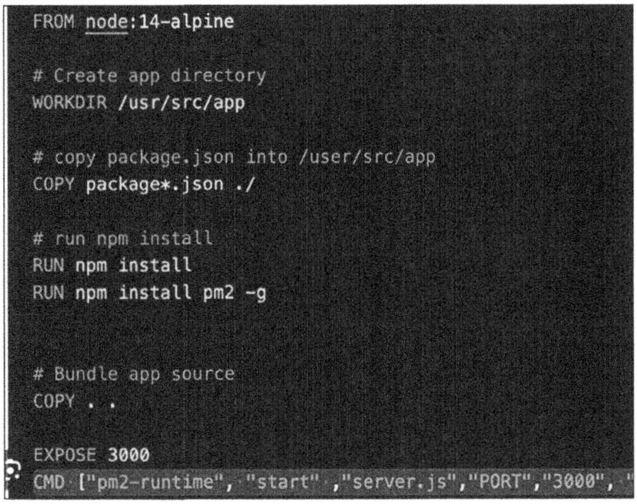

**Figure 14.5**: *Sample Docker file*

Any line starting with # is a comment (except for parser commands), while other lines must contain the specific command and its arguments. Although command names are not case-sensitive, they are often capitalized to distinguish them from arguments.

The first (uncommented) line in the docker file should specify the base image that should be used as a base for the custom image. Subsequent commands are executed on this base image, and the output of each successive command adds another layer to that image before the final image is built and its ID is printed to the console.

Create a Docker file for your application and open it in a text editor using the following command:

```
# Use Node 16 alpine as parent image
FROM node:16-alpine


# Change the working directory on the Docker image to /app
WORKDIR /app


# Copy package.json and package-lock.json to the /app directory
COPY package.json package-lock.json ./
```

```
# Install dependencies
RUN npm install

# Copy the rest of project files into this image
COPY . .

# Expose application port
EXPOSE 3000

# Start the application
CMD npm start
```

Let's understand in detail what each line means inside our DockerFile.

### FROM node:16-alpine

The first instruction in the Docker file involves selecting a base image, which is the official Node.js Alpine Linux image for v16.x.

### WORK DIRECTOR. /app

The WORKDIR command specifies the working directory of the Docker image for all subsequent RUN, CMD, ENTRYPOINT, COPY, or ADD commands on the file. This folder will be created if it does not already exist. # Copy package.json and package-lock.json to the /app folder

### COPY package.json package-lock.json ./

This COPY command copies the package.json and package-lock.json files from the machine's project directory to the container file system of the current working directory, which is /app according to the previous WORKDIR statement.

### RUN npm install

At this point, the npm install command is run from the /app directory of the Docker image file system. Since it contains the package.json and package-lock.json files, it uses the information in both files to download all dependencies from the NPM registry.

**COPY. .**

After the project and dependencies are installed, the COPY command is used again to copy the remaining project files to the /app directory on the Docker image file system.

**EXPOSE 3000**

Next, the EXPOSE command tells Docker that our application will listen at runtime on port 3000. Here you can use a TCP or UDP protocol (e.g. 3000/tcp or 3000/udp), although if no protocol is specified, the default is TCP.

**CMD npm starts**

Finally, the CMD command is used to launch the application by running the startup script defined in the package.json file. This command is executed when a container based on this Docker image is started. At this point, we have defined all the necessary instructions to create a Docker image for our project.

## Building the Dockcr imagc

The docker build command is used to create a Docker image from a Docker file.

Run the following command from the root of your project to create a Docker image:

```
PS D:\Demo> docker build . -t demoapp
```

**Output:**

```
. . .  Successfully built cd4bdd2ae572
 Successfully coded by demoapp:latest
```

The preceding command creates a Docker image using the Docker file in the current directory. The flag is used to specify a tag name for the new image so that it can be referenced later as demoapp:latest.

## Running docker image as a container

In the previous section, we created a Docker image that contains our Node.js project. Now we can run the image in a Docker container and test that our application is working correctly. Be sure to close all running instances of your application before running the following command:

```
PS D:\Demo> docker compose up --build
```

**Output:**

```
demoapp server started on port:3000
```

When you run a Docker image in a container, it creates a typical operating system process with a separate file system, network, and process tree from the host. Although we used the EXPOSE command in step 2 to show that the application in the container is listening on port 3000, this command does not make the container and port accessible from the host. It only ensures that another Docker container running on the same host can access the application running on the specified port.

To make container ports available to a host, you must publish it with the `--publish` or `-p` flag. This allows you to map a container and port to the corresponding host port.

For example, in the previous command, port 3000 of the host is connected to port 3000 of the container, so all requests to http://localhost:3000 are forwarded to the application listening on port 3000 of the Docker container.

Try it by opening http://localhost:3000 in your browser. You should observe the demo app working as usual.

# Kubernetes Introduction

Kubernetes is an open-source platform for managing Linux containers in private, public, and hybrid cloud environments. Many DevOps teams use Kubernetes to manage their microservices architecture, where each microservice is encapsulated in one or more containers. Kubernetes also supports the GitOps development model, where all changes to a Kubernetes cluster are fully automated and managed in source control.

Application developers, IT administrators, and DevOps engineers use Kubernetes to automatically deploy, scale, maintain, schedule, and manage multiple application containers on a node cluster. Containers run on a common operating system but are isolated from each other. Kubernetes allows you to create a set of hosts running Linux containers and have a large number of containers running on those hosts.

A Kubernetes environment is called a **cluster**. It contains one or more nodes.

A **node** is simply a machine that runs your containers. This can be physical hardware or a virtual machine. In addition to nodes, a cluster also has a **control plane**. The administrative level coordinates the work of the entire cluster. It schedules new containers to available nodes and provides an API server that you can communicate with. It is possible to run a cluster with multiple control plane instances to create a more flexible and highly available configuration.

# Key Components of Kubernetes

The following are the key components of Kubernetes:

- **kube-apiserver**

  This is the control plane component that runs the API server. This is the only way to communicate with a running Kubernetes cluster. You can issue commands to the API server using the Kubectl CLI or the HTTP client.

- **kube-controller-manager -**

  The controller manager starts and runs Kubernetes built-in controllers. A controller is an event loop that takes actions after changes to the cluster. They create, scale, and delete objects in response to events such as an API request or increased load.

- **kube-scheduler**

  The scheduler assigns new folders (containers) to cluster nodes. It determines which nodes meet Pod requirements and then chooses the optimal placement to maximize performance and reliability.

- **kubelet**

  A kubelet is a worker process that runs on each of your nodes. It keeps in touch with the Kubernetes control engine to receive its instructions. Kubelet is responsible for pulling containers and starting containers according to schedule requests.

- **kube-proxy**

  The proxy is another component found on individual nodes. This configures the host's network system so that traffic reaches your cluster services.

- **kubectl**

   This is most important part of a Kubernetes runtime environment. This CLI is required to interact with the cluster and its objects. After the cluster is configured, we can also install an official dashboard to manage Kubernetes from the GUI.

# Kubernetes deployment and services background

Kubernetes deployment and services are Kubernetes objects that are created when we deploy a container application to a Kubernetes cluster. The most common way to write files for Kubernetes deployments and services is in **YAML** format. This file contains all the settings of the container application. Kubernetes executes these yaml files and uses them to install the application on the Kubernetes.

A **Kubernetes deployment** defines directories and resources for a containerized application.

A **pod** is the smallest deployable Kubernetes unit that holds a containerized application in a Kubernetes cluster. It also specifies the Docker image that builds the container application.

A **Kubernetes service** describes how we want to expose a Kubernetes installation running in pods. We can decide whether to run the application only inside the Kubernetes cluster or outside the cluster. Kubernetes assigns an internal or external IP address to the pod. This depends on the Kubernetes service type described in the Service.yaml file.

# Deploying Node.js applications to a Kubernetes cluster

To deploy a Node.js application to Docker or Kubernetes, we must first create a container image. This is usually done by starting from an existing image and adding additional layers of functionality as needed. When building Node.js applications, the community provides several official Docker samples to get you started. These images contain Node.js binaries on top of an existing Linux distribution (usually Debian or Alpine). You can start with these official images and add your app as an additional layer.

**Choose your image**

There are three types of official Node.js images.

- **Complete Debian-based image** - Contains all the core components needed to build and test Node.js applications.
- **Thin Debian-based image** - contains only the minimum packages needed to run prebuilt Node.js applications.
- **Alpine-based images** - Ensures minimum container size.

**Configure the Docker file**

Starting with a base image, you use a Docker file to create a custom image containing the application.

The following is the simplest possible Docker file that copies your Node.js application (app.js) into the official Node.js container image.

```
FROM node: 18-alpine

Copy app.js.

EXPOSE 3000

CMD node app.js
```

**Create an image**

To create an image from a Dockerfile, place the file in the directory containing your application code and run the following command:

```
docker build -t myImage:new
```

This creates a Docker image called `myImage` with a new title based on the contents of the current directory.

**Compress the image to the registry**

For Kubernetes to use this image, you must publish it to the Docker Hub registry. You can then run and test your application on Docker or Kubernetes.

Run the following commands in the terminal:

```
PS D:\Demo>docker login
PS D:\Demo>docker push myImage
```

In the Kubernetes YAML file, we define a Docker Hub repository for our Docker image. Kubernetes takes a Docker image from this repository and creates a container application on the Kubernetes cluster.

The next step is to start the **Minikube** Kubernetes cluster.

### Starting the MiniKube Kubernetes Cluster

To start the **Minikube** Kubernetes Cluster we need to run the following commands:

```
PS D:\Demo>minikube config set driver docker
PS D:\Demo>minikube start
```

This will create and start a MiniKube cluster on local system.

### Kubernetes Deployment using YAML file

The usual way to deploy a Kubernetes application is through a deployment object which can be created by adding the following code to **deployment.yaml** file.

```yaml
apiVersion: apps/v1
kind: Deployment
metadata:
  name: simple-app-deployment
spec:
  replicas: 2
  selector:
    matchLabels:
      app: simple-app
  template:
    metadata:
```

```
        labels:
          app: simple-app
    spec:
      containers:
      - name: simple-app
        image: myImage
        resources:
          limits:
            memory: "256Mi"
            cpu: "500m"
        ports:
        - containerPort: 3000
```

The YAML file creates a Kubernetes deployment called **simple application deployment**:

- This will create 2 replicas or pods in the Kubernetes cluster. The application works both ways.
- This pulls the "`myImage`" image from the Docker Hub repository.
- This creates a container application called "**simple application**" in the Kubernetes cluster.
- It also sets resource limits for running directories. The container is running on port `3000`.

Once you have this YAML in place, you can run this command to create your Kubernetes cluster deployment:

```
kubectl apply -f deployment.yaml
```

To get Kubernetes Deployment, run the following command:

```
PS D:\Demo>kubectl get deployment
```

To get Kubernetes Services, run the following command:

```
PS D:\Demo>kubectl get service
```

To start application, run the following commands

```
PS D:\Demo>minikube service simple-app-service
```

This will start the Minikube tunnel and assign a unique external IP address to the pod. We can access our application using this external IP address.

**Note**: Some of the Kubernetes concepts are out of scope for this book.

# Conclusion

In this chapter, we have covered some of the key concepts related to the build and deployment of Node.js applications. CI/CD has become an important part of any DevOps team and most organizations are following the latest techniques to deploy their application and maintain infrastructure. As we are moving towards cloud deployment services most of the complexity inside CI/CD setup has been taken care of by the cloud providers like AWS, Azure, etc. We also covered briefly some of the basic concepts of Docker and Kubernetes which has become a popular way of deploying containerized applications.

In the final chapter, we will share more insight into advanced topics which was not covered due to the limited scope of this book.

# Further Readings

The following links can help understand more about build and deployments in depth.

- https://www.youtube.com/watch?v=yln_CffenYw
- https://www.youtube.com/watch?v=3BliDUq5vPc
- https://cloud.google.com/run/docs/quickstarts/build-and-deploy/deploy-nodejs-service
- https://blog.back4app.com/how-to-deploy-node-js-application/
- https://devtut.github.io/nodejs/deploying-node-js-applications-in-production.html
- https://matthewpalmer.net/kubernetes-app-developer/articles/kubernetes-deployment-tutorial-example-yaml.html

CHAPTER 15

# Future Scope

## Introduction

We will cover some of the topics that are out of the scope of this book and will help you understand how we can use these advanced Node.js features to build complex enterprise-level distributed applications. In this section, we are not going to cover topics in depth, but will give an overview of core concepts.

## Structure

The following are the topics to be covered in this chapter:

- Building highly distributed systems
- Event-based development
- Messaging systems like Kafka
- Multi-threaded system

## Distributed Systems

A distributed system is a set of computer programs that run using computing resources from several computing nodes available in clusters to achieve high performance. Decentralized systems aim to provide support and eliminate bottlenecks that are present in central points of failure in the system.

Distributed systems consist of multiple interconnected components deployed on separate nodes on different machines or servers and they mostly communicate with each other over a network. This approach enables the creation of highly scalable, fault-tolerant, and resilient applications that can handle large volumes of traffic.

Node.js has become a very popular server-side technology stack, which is an excellent tool for building distributed architectures. This has become possible due to its single-threaded architecture, event-loop, asynchronous event-driven programming model, and lightweight.

# Centralized systems vs Distributed systems

The following table states the major difference between centralized and distributed systems.

| Centralized systems | Decentralized systems |
| --- | --- |
| Low fault tolerance because the central server acts as a single point of failure. | High fault tolerance due to the absence of a single point of failure. |
| Low maintenance costs because the system runs on one main server. And the whole system is easier to control and manage with one main server. | High maintenance costs because each node in the system contains variable processing power and is spread across geographic areas. |
| Systems are only vertically scalable. Processing power can only be increased for the central server and only up to a certain limit. | Both horizontally and vertically scalable. Servers can be added/removed without affecting overall performance. |
| Less reliable than if the central server crashes and the entire system is not available to all clients. | More reliable as multiple servers are used and if one server goes down, the system as a whole can still survive. |
| Lower performance as a single-server model becomes a bottleneck when client requests increase. | Higher performance because processing power is distributed throughout the system. |
| The whole system is less complicated because the system can be managed by a central server. | The system is more complex because we have to worry about managing copies and maintaining consistency and security on the entire system. |

*Table 15.1*: *Difference between centralized and distributed*

# Key Features of Distributed Architecture

The following are the key reasons to use a distributed architecture with Node.js:

- **Resource Sharing**

    Distributed systems provide different ways of sharing resources like disk space, memory, and available network bandwidth to execute any no of tasks without having any performance issues.

- **Concurrent Users**

  In a distributed system, we use shared resources available on the server like disk, memory, networking, and so on, which enable the system to handle millions of concurrent users and clients.

- **Scalability**

  By breaking applications into smaller, more manageable components distributed across multiple servers, we can easily scale up or down based on the system's load. This means we can handle increased traffic and load without worrying about performance issues or downtime on the production environment, running multiple nodes inside clusters.

- **Fault tolerance**

  Distributed architectures are designed to be fault tolerant because components can be replaced or redirected in case of problems or system failures. This makes the application more reliable and reduces the risk of data loss or system downtime in the event of any failures.

- **Flexibility**

  With a distributed architecture, we can easily add or remove components as needed and change the behavior of your application without changing the entire system. This makes it easy to adapt to changing requirements or business needs.

- **Modularity**

  Node.js modular architecture design pattern helps to create a large-scale distributed system, with each module or package providing a specific set of functionality. This facilitates the creation of a distributed architecture where each component performs a specific task or service and can be easily replaced or updated.

## Advantages of distributed systems

The key benefits or advantages of distributed systems include:

- Flexibility and adaptability.
- Ability to handle applications and real-time data processing.
- Large ecosystem of third-party components and tools.
- Information contained in a distributed system is distributed to geographically dispersed users.
- Resource sharing. It is more cost-effective and flexible.

- Short response time and high performance.
- More reliable and less prone to component failure. It's scalable so you can expand your system to more remote locations and achieve exponential growth.

## Disadvantages of distributed systems

The following are some of the key disadvantages of distributed systems:

- Increased complexity and development time.

- Administrative costs and infrastructure requirements are high.

- Advanced knowledge of distributed systems and networks is required.

- Security issues as resources are shared between multiple systems and data can be easily accessed.

- Network congestion may cause data transmission to fail. This means that if the network is slow, users may have trouble accessing their data.

- Compared to single-user systems, the databases involved in distributed systems are much more complex and difficult to manage.

- If all nodes in a distributed system try to send data at the same time, the network will become overloaded.

# Event-based programming

Event-driven programming is a widely used design pattern in software development that allows organizations to build efficient and scalable web applications. Node.js's default event-driven architecture has made it an excellent platform for writing event-driven programming.

Node.js is a good platform for event-driven programming because of its non-blocking I/O model. This pattern allows Node.js to run multiple applications simultaneously without blocking the execution of other applications. This makes Node.js perfect for building real-time web applications that require fast processing and responsiveness. In Node.js, we use the `EventEmitter` class to handle events. This class allows developers to create custom programs and add event listeners to handle those events.

In event-driven programming, the program flow is determined by a set of events. `Events` are triggers that get executed by a program, for example, as user input or changes in data from an external source. When an event gets triggered, the program executes a set of instructions related to that event.

In traditional programming models, a program waits for one task to complete before moving on to the next, whereas event-driven programs can run multiple tasks in parallel, which makes them run faster and more efficiently.

Node.js is built on Google's V8 JavaScript engine and provides a non-blocking I/O model suitable for event-driven programming. In Node.js, all I/O operations such as file system access, network requests, and database queries, are synchronous and non-blocking. In other words, it does not block the main processing thread. Node.js uses an event-based architecture to handle asynchronous I/O operations. When you call a function that performs an I/O operation, a callback function is registered to be called when that function completes. While you wait for the I/O operation to complete, Node.js continues to perform other tasks, such as processing incoming requests or running other programs. When the I/O operation completes, Node.js starts a callback function, passing the required data as an argument. Node.js provides event-generation classes that can be used to generate and receive events. An event handler is an object that emits named events and can register callbacks for those events. When an event occurs, all registered callbacks are called.

## Building event-driven applications in Node.js

In Node.js, you can use the **EventEmitter** class to create custom events and add **event** listeners.

```
const EventEmitter = require('events');

class ClockTimer extends EventEmitter {
  constructor() {
    super();
    setInterval(() => {
      this.emit('tick');
    }, 1000);
  }
}

const clockTimer = new ClockTimer();
```

```
clockTimer.on('tick', () => {
  console.log('Clock timer ticked!');
});
```

This example uses the **EventEmitter** class to emit a custom event for a clock timer. We create a **clockTimer** object and then attach the event listener '**tick**'. When an event is fired from inside of the **setInterval()** method, a message is written to the console after the event has been listened to by the **clockTimer** object.

The following example shows how to use event-driven programming to build efficient and scalable applications in the real world.

```
// Import the 'events' module
const events = require('events');


console.log("Start");


// Create an EventEmitter object
const eventEmitter = new events.EventEmitter();


// Handler used to process fired the event
const connectHandler = function connected() {
    console.log('Connection established.');

    // Fire the corresponding event
    eventEmitter.emit('data_received');
}


// Binds the event with handler
eventEmitter.on('connection', connectHandler);


// Listen to the events for the data received
eventEmitter.on(
```

```
        'data_received',
        function () {
            console.log('Data Transfer Successful.');
        });


    // Fire the connection event
    eventEmitter.emit('connection');


    console.log("Finish");
```

Here we have created an **eventEmitter** object and used it to hook our event listener and later in the code we have trigged event using **emit()**.

# Messaging systems like Kafka

Kafka is a messaging system that is used extensively in distributed computing while providing a platform and set of tools for supporting data exchange capabilities.

A publish/subscribe system consists of two components. The first one is used for sending some kind of data or information and the second one is used to receive this information. In other words, one component publishes data, and the other subscribes to the publisher to receive the published data.

**publish/subscribe model**

The publisher (Pub/Sub) model is a messaging model where event producers (publishers) send events without targeting specific consumers (**subscribers**). Instead, events are sent to an event channel (sometimes called a topic or queue) and consumers subscribe to the channel to receive the events. In a Node.js application, you can implement the Pub/Sub pattern using the **EventEmitter** class. Here is a simple example:

```
    const EventEmitter = require('events');
    const pubsub = new EventEmitter();


    // Publisher for event
    setInterval(() => {
```

```
    pubsub.emit('message', 'Hello, subscribers!');
}, 5000);


// Subscriber 1 for message
pubsub.on('message', (message) => {
  console.log('Subscriber 1 received:', message);
});


// Subscriber 2 for message
pubsub.on('message', (message) => {
  console.log('Subscriber 2 received:', message);
});
```

In this example, we create a single `EventEmitter` instance (`pubsub`) which can be used as an event channel. Then we set up a publisher that sends a message every five seconds. At the end of this process, two or more subscribers are registered to (`pubsub`) listen to the message event and log the received message to the console.

# Key concepts of Kafka

The following are the key concepts that are important for understanding Kafka in depth:

### Producer

The first part of a publish/subscribe system is the publisher, a **producer** in Kafka. A producer is defined as a data source that produces or sends messages to the Kafka messaging system. This data can be of any nature, like GPS signals from a car or requests from a front-end server.

### Subscriber

The second part of the publish/subscribe system is the subscribers, which are called **consumers** in Kafka. Clients can subscribe to, listen to, and consume messages from the Kafka messaging system without the knowledge of the producer. Clients can subscribe to multiple data streams regardless of the type of data they consume. This means you can make a single request and pull data from as many sources as you want. Kafka enables easy access to the data you need while maintaining control over processing operations.

## Message template for publish and subscribe

Apache Kafka is a publish and subscribe communication system used to simply pass messages between a sender and one or more receivers using a single destination (Topics) pattern. Each topic can have multiple subscribers, and each subscriber receives all messages posted to the topic. Topics enable immediate, pull-based delivery of messages to subscribers, which is one reason why a publish-subscribe messaging system like Apache Kafka allows you to process large volumes of data in real-time.

## Live broadcast of the event

Event streaming implements the message publish and subscribe model with some additional features. Apache Kafka is an event-streaming platform, which means they not only publish and subscribe to events but are also used for storing and processing them in the same sequence as the event occurs. For example, when using order processing, the customer may have added or removed items from the cart or made payments. Each of these will be a triggering event that will get published to the Kafka topic so that all the consumers can process them.

## Kafka clients and servers

A distributed Kafka system consists of one or more servers (called **Kafka brokers**) that can span multiple data centers, allowing you to build applications that can communicate with Kafka brokers to read, write, and process events. Kafka servers and clients use a custom binary format over TCP, a well-known communication standard that connects the server and client and allows them to exchange messages with each other.

## Kafka Consumer Groups

A consumer group is a group of consumers who work together to read messages on a particular topic. If we limit to only one consumer, our application may not be able to receive all messages from the subject (or producer). By grouping multiple consumers into a single consumer group,  Kafka allows multiple consumers to read from multiple topics, increasing communication capabilities inside our distributed system. In a consumer group, multiple consumers read the same topic, but each consumer reads from exclusive sections.

## Kafka clusters and Kafka brokers

Kafka broker arranges business between producers and consumers. Brokers handle all client requests to write and read transactions.

A Kafka cluster is simply a collection of one or more Kafka brokers.

### Kafka topics and Kafka partitions

Inside Kafka, the basic unit for organizing all the events occurring in a distributed system is called a **topic**. A Kafka topic is the name of a user-defined class or stream to which data is stored and read. For example, an e-commerce website might have a topic called **orders-processing** that receives a message whenever a user places an order.

Kafka topics are divided into different partitions, where we divide a topic into multiple logs that separate Kafka brokers can use at the same time. This results in a highly scalable distributed system because it allows client applications to publish/subscribe to multiple brokers simultaneously. As multiple brokers can be placed in different locations within a given cluster, it provides high data availability, as partitions are replicated across multiple brokers. For example, if one Kafka broker crashes in your cluster, Kafka can safely switch to partition replicas with the other brokers.

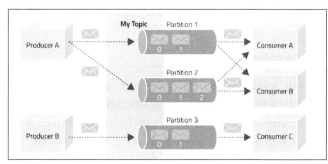

**Figure 15.1**: *Topics and Partitions in Kafka Messaging System*

### Kafka topic replication

We know that partitions can run on separate Kafka brokers, which is the main way Kafka protects against any kind of data loss in case of a failure or system crash. This is achieved by specifying a subject replication factor, which determines the number of copies of data from multiple brokers.

For example, a replication factor of three suggests to the Kafka store that there is a need to store three copies of the data for each partition of the other available brokers.

### Masters and followers

To sync data among different replications in a cluster, Kafka follows a master-follower system. In this way, one broker can be appointed as head of a subject topic and other brokers as followers of this topic, and only the head topic can be used to process these client requests.

**Apache ZooKeeper**

ZooKeeper is a centralized management service that allows you to coordinate and manage distributed systems. Zookeeper coordinates various distributed tasks, including polling, managing topics, maintaining metadata, monitoring the status of Kafka Brokers, etc.

**Note**: Zookeeper will be deprecated as of Apache Kafka version 3.0.0

**Kafka Connect**

Kafka Connect is an Apache Kafka data integration framework that helps to get data into your Kafka cluster from some external source, such as a message queue or relational database. It can also help to extract data from a cluster or sync to an external source. This is achieved through **connectors**, which are reusable components that we use to connect to common repositories.

The following are two types of connectors in Kafka:

- Source connectors are connectors that receive data from the data store
- Sink connectors are connectors that push data from Kafka topics to the data store.

**Kafka Streams**

Kafka Streams is a Java API for building streaming applications that can process and transform data in Kafka topics. In short, Kafka Streams allow us to read real-time data from a topic, process it, run transformation logic, and write the resulting data to another topic or other storage systems.

## Running Kafka locally

Before we create a Kafka-based application in Nodejs, we need to set up the following components on our local system:

- Java
- Kafka binary

  Download the latest version from https://kafka.apache.org/downloads

  Extract the downloaded file to C:\kafka_2.13-3.6.0

Now run the following command inside the bash.

```
c:/kafka_2.13-3.6.0> ./zookeeper-server-start.sh
```

**Output:**

```
$ ./bin/windows/kafka-server-start.bat ./config/server.properties
[2023-12-23 01:27:21,512] INFO Registered kafka:type=kafka.Log4jController MBean
 (kafka.utils.Log4jControllerRegistration$)
[2023-12-23 01:27:21,788] INFO Setting -D jdk.tls.rejectClientInitiatedRenegotia
tion=true to disable client-initiated TLS renegotiation (org.apache.zookeeper.co
mmon.X509Util)
[2023-12-23 01:27:21,877] INFO starting (kafka.server.KafkaServer)
[2023-12-23 01:27:21,877] INFO Connecting to zookeeper on localhost:2181 (kafka.
server.KafkaServer)
[2023-12-23 01:27:21,892] INFO [ZooKeeperClient Kafka server] Initializing a new
 session to localhost:2181. (kafka.zookeeper.ZooKeeperClient)
[2023-12-23 01:27:21,896] INFO Client environment:zookeeper.version=3.8.2-139d61
9b58292d7734b4fc83a0f44be4e7b0c986, built on 2023-07-05 19:24 UTC (org.apache.zo
okeeper.ZooKeeper)
[2023-12-23 01:27:21,896] INFO Client environment:host.name=host.docker.internal
 (org.apache.zookeeper.ZooKeeper)
[2023-12-23 01:27:21,896] INFO Client environment:java.version=18.0.2.1 (org.apa
che.zookeeper.ZooKeeper)
[2023-12-23 01:27:21,896] INFO Client environment:java.vendor=Oracle Corporation
 (org.apache.zookeeper.ZooKeeper)
[2023-12-23 01:27:21,896] INFO Client environment:java.home=C:\Program Files\Jav
a\jdk-18.0.2.1 (org.apache.zookeeper.ZooKeeper)
```

*Figure 15.2: Running Kafka Zookeeper*

Open another bash and run the following command:

```
c:/kafka_2.13-3.6.0>./bin/windows/kafka-server-start.bat
./config/server.properties
```

```
$ ./bin/windows/zookeeper-server-start.bat ./config/zookeeper.properties
[2023-12-23 01:26:19,834] INFO Reading configuration from: ./config/zookeeper.pr
operties (org.apache.zookeeper.server.quorum.QuorumPeerConfig)
[2023-12-23 01:26:19,842] INFO clientPortAddress is 0.0.0.0:2181 (org.apache.zoo
keeper.server.quorum.QuorumPeerConfig)
[2023-12-23 01:26:19,842] INFO secureClientPort is not set (org.apache.zookeeper
.server.quorum.QuorumPeerConfig)
[2023-12-23 01:26:19,842] INFO observerMasterPort is not set (org.apache.zookeep
er.server.quorum.QuorumPeerConfig)
[2023-12-23 01:26:19,842] INFO metricsProvider.className is org.apache.zookeeper
.metrics.impl.DefaultMetricsProvider (org.apache.zookeeper.server.quorum.QuorumP
eerConfig)
[2023-12-23 01:26:19,844] INFO autopurge.snapRetainCount set to 3 (org.apache.zo
okeeper.server.DatadirCleanupManager)
[2023-12-23 01:26:19,844] INFO autopurge.purgeInterval set to 0 (org.apache.zook
eeper.server.DatadirCleanupManager)
[2023-12-23 01:26:19,844] INFO Purge task is not scheduled. (org.apache.zookeepe
r.server.DatadirCleanupManager)
[2023-12-23 01:26:19,845] WARN Either no config or no quorum defined in config,
running in standalone mode (org.apache.zookeeper.server.quorum.QuorumPeerMain)
[2023-12-23 01:26:19,846] INFO Log4j 1.2 jmx support not found; jmx disabled. (o
```

*Figure 15.3: Running Kafka server*

Let's create one simple Node.js application that uses Kafka as a messaging system.

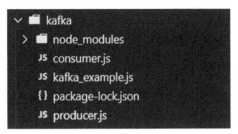

**Figure 15.4**: *Application structure for Kafka example*

Add the following code in **Producer.js.**

```
// import the `Kafka` from kafkajs library
const { Kafka } = require("kafkajs")

// the client ID for who's producing the messages
const clientId = "my-app"

// list of brokers in the cluster
const brokers = ["localhost:9092"]

// topic to which we want to write messages
const topic = "message-log"

// initialize a new kafka client
const kafka = new Kafka({ clientId, brokers })
const producer = kafka.producer()

// we define an async function that writes a new message each second
const produce = async () => {
    await producer.connect()
    let i = 0

    // after the produce has connected, we start an interval timer
    setInterval(async () => {
```

```
        try {
            // send a message to the configured topic with
            // the key and value formed from the current value of
    `i`
            await producer.send({
                topic,
                messages: [
                    {
                        key: String(i),
                        value: "this is message " + i,
                    },
                ],
            })

            // if the message is written successfully, log it and
    increment `i`
            console.log("writes: ", i)
            i++
        } catch (err) {
            console.error("could not write message " + err)
        }
    }, 1000)
}


module.exports = produce
```

Let's create another file for writing code for the consumer.

```
    // import the kafka instance
    const { Kafka } = require("kafkajs")


    // create a new consumer from the kafka client,
    const clientId = "my-app"
```

```
// list of brokers in the cluster
const brokers = ["localhost:9092"]
const topic = "message-log"

const kafka = new Kafka({ clientId, brokers });
const consumer = kafka.consumer({ groupId: clientId })

const consume = async () => {
    await consumer.connect()
    await consumer.subscribe({ topic })
    await consumer.run({
        // this function is called every time the consumer gets a
new message
        eachMessage: ({ message }) => {
            // here, logging message
            console.log(`received message: ${message.value}`)
        },
    })
}

module.exports = consume
```

We need to write a node application that will be used to run the Kafka service.

```
const produce = require("./producer")
const consume = require("./consumer")

// call the `produce` function and log an error if it occurs
produce().catch((err) => {
    console.error("error in producer: ", err)
})

// start the consumer, and log any errors
```

```
consume().catch((err) => {
    console.error("error in consumer: ", err)
})
```

**Output:**

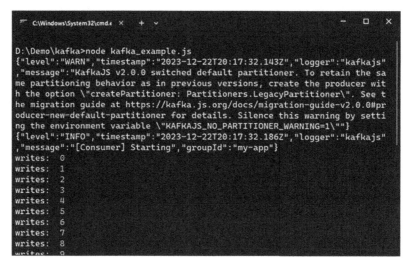

*Figure 15.5: Running Kafka example shows messages received*

# Multi-threaded system

Multithreading is a program execution environment that allows more than one thread to be created inside a process. They are executed independently and parallelly using shared resources of the system like CPU, memory, and disks.

For example, if we run the set of commands in an easy single-threaded method, the execution will wait for the previous operation to complete execution. Whereas in a multithreaded program, commands can run simultaneously in different threads.

Node.js is single-threaded by design and, in most of the cases, it performs all the operations using one thread. But in the case of performing I/O extensive operations like accessing data from a database or reading document operations, Node.js delegates them to a separate pool of threads controlled through a C library known as libuv.

# Advantages of Multithreading

The following are the key benefits of using multithreading:

- **Better performance:**

  Multithreading helps keep the application responsive and we don't have problems when running CPU-intensive tasks or any long-running I/O operations.

- **Better use of resources:**

  Multithreading allows Node.js to utilize multiple CPU cores, improving resource usage and application scalability.

# Running parallel child processes in Node.js

We can spin up a new thread with the use of Node's `child_process` module. This thread can handle all the operations and in fact, can talk through a messaging system and run tasks independently, performing all the operations in isolation.

A `child_process` can be created by using the following command:

- `spawn()`
- `exec()`
- `execFile()`
- `fork()`

# Define Worker Threads

Worker threads can run CPU-intensive operations without blocking off the event loop from getting executed.

`worker_threads` have been introduced in Node.js 10.5.0.

Before this version, we could not get entry to the module except if you run the Node.js software with the use of the `--experimental-employee` flag.

## Use of worker threads

The following are the key areas where we can use concepts of work thread:

- **CPU-intensive tasks:**

These threads can offload some of the CPU-intensive tasks, such as image processing and video encoding, to separate threads to avoid blocking the main thread.

- **Network I/O:**

  The worker threads can handle time-consuming network I/O operations such as making HTTP requests or sending emails and the main thread continues to perform other operations while the thread is waiting for the I/O to get completed by the worker thread.

- **File read and write handling:**

  Worker threads can handle many file I/O operations in parallel, such as reading or writing large files which can avoid blocking the main thread and improve the performance of the overall system.

- **Improve scalability:**

  Worker threads can run database queries in parallel, enabling the system to handle multiple queries simultaneously and improve scalability.

## Child process example

Let's create a simple application that will show how to use a child process to invoke some set of commands.

Create a file named **child_process.js** and add the following code.

```
const exec = require('child_process').exec;
exec('test.bat', (err, stdout, stderr) => {
    if (err) {
        console.error(err);
        return;
    }
    console.log(stdout);
});
```

Now, the preceding code requires a **test.bat** file which will be called when executing the child process. This batch command will simply create a new child directly under the given folder.

```
dir

mkdir child
```

After running the application, we will get the following output:

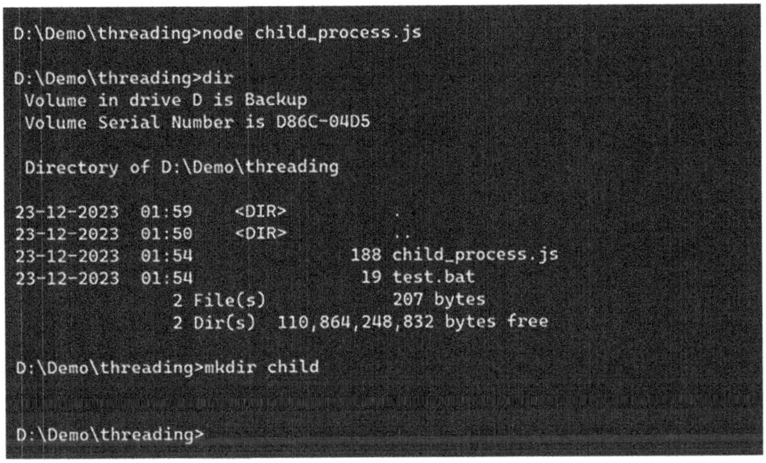

**Figure 15.6**: *Output of creating a child process in Node.js*

# Conclusion

In this chapter, we have discussed some of the core concepts of distributed systems and why they have become increasingly popular these days due to their high availability, scalability, and fault tolerance. Node.js is an excellent platform for event-driven programming because it has an event-based architecture that enables fast and responsive processing. Kafka has become one of the popular tools for developing distributed systems on the Node.js platform that can scale easily. Multi-threading is a great way of improving the performance of the system and in Node.js `work_threads` provide support and useful modules required to do CPU-intensive tasks.

# Further Readings

The following links can help us understand more about some of the concepts that we have discussed in this chapter.

- https://www.ibm.com/docs/en/txseries/8.2?topic=overview-what-is-distributed-computing

- https://www.techtarget.com/whatis/definition/distributed-computing
- https://www.youtube.com/watch?v=X_VHWQa1k0k
- https://www.youtube.com/watch?v=6-1N8wIZ1ic
- https://moduscreate.com/blog/understanding-microservices-with-an-event-driven-approach/
- https://www.youtube.com/watch?v=gMtchRodC2I
- https://www.codingninjas.com/studio/library/multithreading-in-nodejs

# Index

Made in the USA
Las Vegas, NV
24 October 2024

10418913R10240